CUNT

A DECLARATION OF
INDEPENDENCE

CUNT

20TH ANNIVERSARY EDITION

INGA MUSCIO

SEAL PRESS

Seal Press
Hachette Book Group
1290 Avenue of the Americas, New York, NY 10104
www.sealpress.com

Printed in the United States of America
Third Edition: March 2018

Published by Seal Press, an imprint of Perseus Books, LLC, a subsidiary of Hachette Book Group, Inc. The Seal Press name and logo is a trademark of Hachette Book Group, Inc.

The Hachette Speakers Bureau provides a wide range of authors for speaking events. To find out more, go to www.hachettespeakersbureau.com or call (866) 376-6591.

The publisher is not responsible for websites (or their content) that are not owned by the publisher.

Print book interior design by Amy Quinn

Library of Congress Cataloging-in-Publication Data

Names: Muscio, Inga, author.
Title: Cunt : a declaration of independence / Inga Muscio.
Description: 20th anniversary edition. | Berkeley, California : Seal Press, [2018]
Identifiers: LCCN 2017045194 | ISBN 9781580056649 (pbk.)
Subjects: LCSH: Women. | Women—Social conditions. | Women—Psychology. | Women—Identity. | Human body—Social aspects. | Sexism in language. | Feminism.
Classification: LCC HQ1233 .M87 2018 | DDC 305.4—dc23
LC record available at https://lccn.loc.gov/2017045194

ISBNs: 978-1-58005-664-9 (paperback); 978-0-78675-051-1 (ebook)

LSC-C

10 9 8 7 6 5 4 3

In loving dedication:
To everyone with Cuntlove in their hearts,
especially my Sacred Mother.
I thank you for giving me life.

Contents

Author's Note

Unless otherwise stated, throughout this book the words *gentle-man*, *man*, and the like are used to refer to the tightly knit male social power structure as it is recognized in American patriarchal society.

Let it be known that the author is fully cognizant of the fact that many men in this world strive for women's rightful place in society. Without the work, study, love, and support of certain members of the male sector of humanity, this book would not have been as thoroughly articulated as it is. The author is grateful and indebted to many members of this sector of humanity, both living and dead.

The author would also like to acknowledge that masculine and feminine nouns and pronouns impose unrealistic limitations on lived human experience. The author looks forward to the time when our vocabulary reflects the reality and complexity of our multigendered human nature.

All that said, the author continues to be free to talk some serious shit.

Preface

Cunt is arguably the most powerful negative word in the American English language. *Cunt* is the ultimate one-syllable covert verbal weapon any streetwise six-year-old or passing motorist can use against a woman. *Cunt* refers almost exclusively to women and expresses the utmost rancor. There's a general feeling of accord on this.

Except for some friends who know all about this book, no one calls me a *cunt* to communicate what a cool and sublime human being they think I am. Up until a certain time in my life, I never employed *cunt* to express respect or admiration.

I qualify these statements because my relationship with *cunt* is no longer what it once was.

One day I came home from third grade and asked my pops, "What's a wetback?"

With resignation and a sigh, Dad elucidated a brief history of *wetback*. He concluded, "Don't you *ever* say it."

A list of words I was similarly not to utter was forthcoming: *nigger, beaner, kike, wop, jap, injun, spic*. The only formal cuss word included on his roster was *cunt*.

Coming, as I did, from a family where us kids were allowed to strew profanities like birdseed at a wedding, I was mighty affected by all this. Why, in my father's way of thinking, could I call someone an asshole, but not a wetback kike cunt?

The foreshadowings of a mystery.

In my childhood home, the 1965 *Random House Dictionary* was as much a part of dinnertime as laughter, arguments, 'n wanton table manners. Throughout dinner, my siblings and I were required to spell and define new vocabulary words. It was a custom I enjoyed very much.

I was raised to appreciate the power of words.

Little did I know that when I grew up, out of the billion and one words in the 1965 *Random House Dictionary* and beyond, there would exist no word that I could use to adequately describe myself.

This wouldn't be much of a problem except that there are millions of me's: articulate, strong, talented, raging, brilliant, grooving, sexy, expressive, dancing, singing, laughing women in America, of all shapes, hues, ethnicities, sizes, sexual orientations, and dispositions.

We are everywhere.

But what are we?

The only dimly representational identifying term that truly, authentically recognizes the actual realities of women in this world is *feminism*. This is a relatively youthful word. Our actual realities, on the other hand, are rooted deep. We are born with them in our hearts.

Inherited them from our mothers.

Grandmothers.

Under the influence of this dilemma, I've asked myself whether there might be a word as old, as universal, and as deeply rooted as women's actual realities in patriarchal society. Hidden somewhere in the English language, could there be a word with power steeped in our history, a word that truly conveys the rage and hope of *all women*?

And, lo and behold, I return to the one formal cuss word on Pop's roster:

cunt.

This book is about my reconciliation with
the word
and
the anatomical jewel.

In Part I of *Cunt*, "The Word," I assert that the context in which *cunt* is presently perceived does not serve women and should therefore be thoroughly reexamined.

English is considered the "universal language" because it is the language of the victors of history's present telling. Seizing control of this language and manipulating it to serve your community is a very powerful thing to do, and—on the basis of a variety of specific elements, such as ethnicity, musical tastes, credit limits, and/or sexuality—it is done a lot in America. Creating a general, woman-centered version of the English language, however, is just insanely difficult.

Womankind is varied and vast.

But we all have cunts, and it does not matter if they are biological, surgical, or metaphorical. A cunt's a cunt.

Though one word maketh not a woman-centered language, *cunt* is certainly a mighty potent and versatile contribution. Not to mention how *deliciously satisfying* it is to *totally snag* a reviled word and elevate it to a status that all women should rightfully experience in this society.

When viewed as a positive force in the language of women—as well as a reference to the power of the anatomical jewel that unites us all—the negative power of *cunt* falls in upon itself, and we are suddenly equipped with a word that describes all women, regardless of race, age, class, religion, or the degree of lesbianism we enjoy.

Part II, "The Anatomical Jewel," examines why having a cunt in this society might just be worse than being called one. Our cunts bleed and have weird, unpredictable orgasms. The birthing process is painful and messy. Lordisa knows what our cunts are up to. Generally speaking, we don't understand them, we don't like them, and we often think they're ugly.

A more sublime way of looking at this is that our cunts are the symbolic and physical zenith of our existence.

When our cunts bleed, *we* are *bleeding people*. Clairvoyant dreams visit our sleepytime heads. Sometimes, the swaggering braggadocio of human males causes our wombs to clench up in spasms of pain. When cunts have stupendous orgasms, we may reel for days and have a fetching smile for every person we meet when we're walkin' down the street. When cunts get filled up with sperm, women sometimes get pregnant and experience either the trauma of aborting or the courageous and under-appreciated tribulation of devoting *the rest of our lives* to another human being. When men fuck our cunts against our will, we often feel like a diarrhea shit has been offed upon the very essence of our soul, and we may live *the rest of our days* cleaning it off in whatever way we see fit.

An aisle in all American grocery stores is devoted to various commercial products, dreamed up by corporations owned and operated by men, that are designed to "care for" and deodorize cunts. An entire branch of Western medicine, male style, exists because of the infernal, confounding magic of cunts. Doctors who treat cunts have special names.

Famous cunts in history have caused empires to rise and fall.

Sex industries throughout the world enjoy exorbitant profit margins because of the wonderful things cunts do and represent.

When women endure cultural customs such as clitoridectomies, chastity belts, Mississippi appendectomies (i.e., forced sterilization), infibulation, forced prostitution, slavery, and rape, cunts are where? Why, in the spotlight, of course.

Yes, though they often play supporting roles to cocks, cunts deserve star billing in the marquee of every woman's life.

Cunts are very important.

Unfortunately, cunts are important to all the wrong people for all the wrong reasons.

Cunts are not important to women because they are the very fount of our power, genius, and beauty. Rather, cunts are important to men because they generate profits and episodes of ejaculation and represent the precise point of vulnerability for keeping women divided and, thus, conquered.

History, the media, economic structures, and justice systems have led women to the understanding that delighting in a love affair with our cunts will get us no further than Sitting Bull had he opted to have a passionate love affair with the Seventh Cavalry.

Which, of course, he did not.

Why should Sitting Bull love the Seventh Cavalry? The Seventh Cavalry consistently represented the undoing of his people.

Why should women love our cunts? They, too, consistently represent the undoing of our people.

The main contention here, of course, is that the Seventh Cavalry did not reside between Sitting Bull's legs.

"The Anatomical Jewel" makes up the bulk of *Cunt*. The fact that women learn to dislike an actual, undeniable, unavoidable physical region of ourselves results in a crappy Sisyphean situation, warranting an intense focus of attention.

Part III is called "Reconciliation." One definition of *reconciliation* is the reestablishment of a close relationship that has experienced estrangement somewhere along the line.

My cunt is *mine*.

To reestablish a close relationship with my cunt, I must take responsibility not only for what it is to me today but also for everything it has become as a result of the seemingly endless throng of spin doctors, past and present. My cunt serves me in ways *cavernously* unrelated to generating profits, promoting episodes of ejaculation in males, and representing the precise point of vulnerability for keeping women divided and, thus, conquered. It is therefore my responsibility to ensure this reality resides at the forefront of humanity's consciousness when history is rewritten once again.

We women have a lot of responsibilities.

Here are a few:

Seizing a vocabulary for ourselves.

Teaching ourselves to actively perceive cunts—ours and others'—in a manner that generates understanding and empathy.

Taking this knowledge out into the community.

Learning self-protection.

Seeking out and supporting cuntlovin' artists, businesses, media, and role models.

Using our power as consumers.

Keeping our money in a community of cuntlovin' women.

We arrive at reconciliation by confronting learned, internalized misogyny and reeducating ourselves on our terms. Three of the most important aspects of reconciliation involve fighting with our minds, art, and money to create a cultural consciousness that supports and respects all women. The power and potential of these weapons—minds, art, and money—are exalted in Part III.

Closing Regards

One of *Cunt*'s aspirations is to contribute to a language and philosophy specifically designed to empower and unite *all women*.

I do not, however, expect my personal experiences necessarily to pluck on the heartstrings of said *all women*.

I am white, so many complexities of individual and institutional racism are not present in this book like they would be if I were, say, a Filipina American writer whose ancestors founded a ranch outside Houston before the Treaty of Guadalupe Hidalgo was signed in 1848.

I am a lesbian who wouldn't oppose a tumble in the hay with my housemate's boyfriend's twenty-year-old brother who lives in Peru and is *achingly* beautiful, so likewise with rigid strictures of hetero- and homosexuality.

I am an American citizen from a mid-middle-class family that was supported solely by the sweat of my mother's brow. As such, I have never been without shoes, food, education, shelter, and other fine trappings of subsistence.

When I was three, an accident with a street-cleaner bristle blinded me in my right eye. I've lived through the deaths of my father and youngest brother. I started writing as a child to survive a spiritually blighted landscape. I obsessively devoted my life to writing so I wouldn't go insane after my brother died. I'm a vegetarian, but I like watching people eat spareribs.

All this greatly influences my perspective.

As does a prayer my mother has hanging in her kitchen, now, then, and in the hour of her death: "You are a child of the universe, no less than the trees and the stars. You have a right to be here, and whether or not it is clear to you, no doubt the universe is unfolding as it should."

From the poetry of Sappho to the zines of Riot Grrrls, personal experience has proven to be a very effective way for women to communicate. Sharing individual knowledge contributes to the whole and has been a foundation of women's power, in cultures spanning the globe, since time out of mind.

Here in America, at the dawning of the postpatriarchal age, a growing understanding of our differences and commonalities continues to emerge full force. Because we now have more means to communicate than ever before, histories based on personal experience are poised to unite *all women*.

Women are blue-black as the ocean's deepest knowledge, creamy-white 'n lacy blue-veined, freshly ground cinnamon brown. Women are Christian motorcycle dykes, militantly hetero Muslim theological scholars, Jewish Chinese bisexual macrobiotic ballerinas, and Chippewa shawomen who fuck not just lovers but Time and Silence too.

Women are drug addicts, antiabortion activists, and volunteers for Meals on Wheels. Women have AIDS, big fancy houses, post-traumatic stress disorder, and cockroach-infested hovels. Women are rock stars, Whores, mothers, lawyers, taxidermists, welders, supermodels, scientists, belly dancers, cops, filmmakers, athletes, and nurses.

Not many things unite *all women*. I have found *cunt*, the word and the anatomical jewel, to be a venerable ally in my war against my own oppression. Besides global subjugation, our cunts are the only common denominator I can think of that *all women* irrefutably share.

We are divided from the word.

We are divided from the anatomical jewel.

I seek reconciliation.

Introduction to the 20th Anniversary Edition

Dear You,

Happy 20th Anniversary!

I'm excited to tell you a bunch of things, but first things first, I wanna tell you about this one time *Cunt* made me cry.

It was after a lecture in San Antonio, Texas.

Five, maybe eight young ladies came up to the book-signing table with a communal battered copy. I like a good battered copy. The more battered, the better. Coffee rings, tear stains, weed burns, blueberry yogurt dribbles.

All, always, beautiful to me.

But this copy of *Cunt* was pummeled to absolute heck 'n back, and the young women were *so very keen* about it, almost as if they wrote it themselves.

I was highly intrigued.

They explained to me there were around twelve or so in their group. Each friend chose a different colored ink to make color-coded notations throughout the book. Utilizing the blank pages at the back, they elucidated points important to them.

Everyone knew whose ink was whose.

It was glorious.

They made an Endless Soup Pot out of my book.

Over the years, I've worked on saving my tears for later.

People come up to me at readings and throw down the emotional gauntlet a lot, and who wants to see a blubbering author signing their book?

No one, that's who.

But now, with these ladies standing before me, showcasing their masterpiece, yeah, through the tears, I begged them to let me borrow their copy to peruse overnight.

They were . . . hesitant.

Yeah, that's right.

I, the one who wrote the sucker, am sobbing before them, beseeching, and these folks still weren't overly enthused about letting their *Cunt* out of their possession.

I love, cherish, worship this moment.

This was the absolute highest, most crowning honor I've achieved as an author.

No one can ever take that away from me.

I sometimes revisit that memory if I feel down.

Eventually, they agreed to meet me the next morning for coffee, but I goddamn best have their book or my ass = grass.

I stayed up late, poring over it, riveted, and, bet yer bottom dollar, I was at that coffee shop on the dot.

Y'all are probably in your thirties now, sparkling out there in the world.

Thank you for shining your lights in my life.

They shine still.

This is a special book.

I don't say that because I'm the author, even though it's also true that every book I've written is special to me. *Cunt* is *objectively special*.

It felt special when I was writing it, which generally happens to writers when they're writing books.

It felt incredibly special the first time I saw it *as a book* instead of as a mess of paper that other people (Faith Conlon, Holly Morris, Jennie Goode, Ingrid Emerick) helped to make, but that's probably because it was *so fucken pretty* (Ingrid Emerick, again) and, this can't be stressed enough: A BOOK.

A product that would sit on shelves in public places for borrowing or for purchase. *Librarians* all over the place would hold it in their hands, and I made it.

Librarians touching my words!

Lordie, that was special.

Again, though, not objective at all, and not why this sweet little daisy-kissed book is such a wee treasure bouncing around the world.

The first thing that happened after *Cunt* came out was a cavalcade of emails from bookstore employees arrived. What fun they had on their PA systems, or yelling across the store to each other, often needlessly, along the theme of: "Do we have any *Cunts* in the house?"

Then came the customer experiences: demanding *Cunt* from unenthusiastic bookstores and disobliging miscommunications with less fun-filled employees.

"Tent?"

"No, '*Cunt*,' '*Cunt: A Declaration of Independence.*'"

"Ohhhh! You mean Kant?"

"No, I mean *Cunt*. As in, what a little cunt you are being for pretending I am saying Kant and Tent when you can very well hear me say *Cunt*."

The first reports of what became an iconic transformation soon followed:

Our fearless reader makes sure the clerk bags their *Cunt* then slips carefully away with it. After reading a few pages, trepidation is replaced with exaltation and sheer joy at brandishing it in public, accompanied by a mad desire to work *cunt* into every conversation conceivably possible—much to the annoyance/intrigue of many a parent/child/partner/housemate, bless all yer souls.

That transformation—which, itself, makes it a bit difficult to bridge the experiential gulf between new and veteran readers—is where we start to leave behind the general novelty of a book with a nasty-worded title and head into bona fide special-assed-shit territory. Whereas the actual text itself is liberating, the physical presence of *Cunt* in one's possession is equally emboldening, like an amulet handed down through the years, worn close to the heart.

Story after story inundated me, and my all-time favorite came in the form of a decade-old email I simply cannot find. It was from a sixteen-year-old kid who snuck into his sister's room to snoop through her diary. Instead, he came across *Cunt*, and decided it would be filled with delicious smut. He

spent a day or so reading it, riveted by mysterious inner workings of the female body. The email was to thank me because he
felt he had a huge dating edge over other kids his age.

If you are this person, I owe you at least two cumulative
hours of laughter.

That's another thing.

In my wildest fantasies, I did not anticipate the chick
magnet aspect of this book. I learned this from young men,
who unceremoniously informed me that prominently carrying around a copy of *Cunt* inspired the young ladies to make
conversation.

I will get a huge kick in the pants out of this until my dying
day.

And when Sergeant Jennifer Scalia was called as a witness
in the court-martial of a guard at Abu Ghraib prison, she
showed up carrying a copy of *Cunt*, I guess to read while waiting
to testify. A *Baltimore Sun* photographer snapped the moment
Sergeant Scalia entered the courtroom, *Cunt* in hand, for all
the world to see.

Hot off the next day's press, the *Baltimore Sun* issued an
apology, which was arguably more entertaining than Sergeant
Scalia herself:

A photograph published yesterday with an article about the
court-martial of a guard at Abu Ghraib prison showed a
book cover that contained an obscenity. The obscenity went

unnoticed during editing and should not have been published. Publication of the photo violates the *Sun*'s guide-
lines. The *Sun* apologizes for the oversight.

Another day, another hearty chuckle from *Cunt*.

I can't tell you how much laughter this book has brought
into my life.

A lot.

Then there was the Cunt Company in Iraq. A soldier read my
book and asked me to send him some stickers. I said, "Sure,
no problem, dude, I'll pop a couple in the mail tomorrow."
"No," he said, "you don't understand. I want stickers for everyone in my company."

So I sent him a stack and he sent me photos of *Cunt* stickers
on helmets, guns, trucks, everywhere.

The Cunt Company in the US Army.

You can't make this shit up.

Of course, no 20th Anniversary Edition introduction would
be complete without remembering the Teamsters Incident.

I'm at the American Booksellers Association convention
in Los Angeles. This is the big one: celebrities and politicians
hawk their ghostwritten wares here.

I walk into the massive, sprawling, acres of convention
center and am stricken with anxiety.

"Just find the person who gives you a badge," I guide myself, filled with loathing of the creepy dog-butt-sniffing hierarchy at these things, where your badge color denotes your contextual importance and people immediately treat you accordingly.

I find the badge person, who directs me to my publisher's booth.

"Point B to Point C," I say to myself, as I tuck the badge under my clothing and make my way to the booth. "Point Shit-stain B to Point Suckass C."

I hate these convention things.

Finally, my nice publishers show me where I need to be.

My job is to stand at a table among a row of tables extending in either direction as far as the eye can see, signing books. On my left is Billy Dee Williams. Obviously, with that caliber of human being standing next to me, I can't remember who was on my right.

But the thrilling Billy Dee Williams realization comes later. For the time being, while waiting to sign books, I don't have anything to do or anywhere to be. I'd been informed of a green room, but, believe me, no one with social anxiety has any business in a green room.

People will talk to you in there. They'll ask you questions about your book that you don't want to answer in the first place, but they're only asking so they can tell you about their book. You're supposed to compete with them, in a really nice, jovial way, so that attention turns back to *your* book, and they then politely jostle for the attention to get back to *their* book, and it goes on and on like this, until someone else urbanely butts in, wanting their book to have attention too.

Instead, I go behind the massive floor-to-ceiling curtain separating the signing area from the book staging area and just stand around like a fool for a few minutes.

Looking like a fool is still preferable to being in a green room.

I sit down on a pallet of *Cunt*s and witness Inner Workings. (Never underestimate the joy of witnessing Inner Workings.) Teamsters are busting ass, forklifting pallets of the correct books into place directly behind the proper curtain slit for the exact right time slot.

No small feat, with hundreds of signings scheduled every half hour.

A gigantic sweat-stained man walks up to me and asks why I'm sitting on the books.

"I'm signing my book in a while, so I'm just, uh, here, I guess. Happy to stay out of your way."

The gigantic man cranes his massive neck, like a polar bear investigating the credentials of a wayward penguin, consulting his clipboard.

"You the *Cunt* lady?"

"Uhh, yeah . . . I s'pose I am. The *Cunt* lady. As it were. Uhm."

His eyes light up, he busts into a jaw-dropping grin, turns away from me, cups his hands to his mouth, and hollers, "SHE'S HERE!"

All activity stops, every forklift comes to a halt.

Imagine a loud, involved video game crashing, unspeakably.

A band of men—and I do mean cis-gendered men in every sense of the word—stream out of each crevice of book-box towers, moving toward me.

What.

The.

Flying.

Fuck.

They crowd around, pelting me with good, interesting, imploring questions.

They want to know about feminism, they want to understand, they want *information*.

I fall in love.

This particular gang of teamsters are avid readers and make sure they get the ABA gig every year. They stalk the book boxes and plan out who they want books from, much like actual attendees, inversely.

Cunt was one of the books they were collectively excited about that day.

I never imagined such an honor.

They grilled me, as I signed *Cunt*s for them, their daughters, mothers, sisters, partners.

Twenty-plus teamsters crowded around, filling my day with an inexplicable joy in which I learned, yet again, to never, ever judge books by their covers.

It's rather surprising how many times I've learned that lesson.

There's evidently no end of preconceived notions to stumble on.

In gratitude for this experience, and so many others, I'd be honored to send a lovingly signed copy of *Cunt 20* to anyone who furnishes me with proof of their affiliation with the US Army or Teamsters Union.

Thank you.

I've experienced this book from so many points of view that it's hard to keep track of what's unequivocally *mine*, though for all intents and purposes it is and will always be my book.

Cunt kindles a fire that consumes the reader's heart.

I did not do that.

No one can do that.

Artists serve as mediums between the mundane and the divine. That's the highest objective of any artist. All artists know about the divine. We tangle with it in our daily lives, not unlike archbishops, scientists, imams, mothers, rabbis, and electrical engineers.

Artists can *contrive* to make something special—various formulas are designed to pull at heartstrings, make people bop around, want to buy more, that sort of thing, but no matter how much money, time, social media manipulation, marketing, or inspiration is thrown at it, Fortuna forever rules opening day.

The economics of the vast casino known as Hollywood poses a material manifestation of Her power and capricious sway.

Also, Wall Street.

I didn't actually contrive to do much of anything with this book.

In a general sense, I set out to write something I wished I had when I realized I was gonna be a woman in a society that, at best, is hell-bent on disrespecting my sort.

Vengeance wended its way in there, for my heart was filled with rage at two anonymous men who assaulted my mother when she was a child, subsequently affecting the span of my upbringing.

I wanted *something* to *be* in the world, and *Cunt* came out of those strong feelings, but it is an entity quite separate from me. I've always known that, have always felt humble and small in its presence.

When I signed on to being a writer, I operated under the concept that writing, alone, was my job. This proved to be false. I came to understand there are other jobs after the writing is done—speaking in public, promotion, selling T-shirts, a lot of travel, answering emails, sending people stickers; hell, the job description involves very little actual writing, when you come down to it. There's a profusion of other jobs at hand.

One of the most important is to respect and protect *Cunt* in any way I can.

Cunt is what it is.

I have no other power here.

For this reason, I don't see that I have any right to make changes to the existing text beyond a few corrections and timely tweaks.

Let's also be clear about a few things.

I am a fuck-up.

I say the wrong thing at the wrong time, embarrassing people I treasure, such as my sister and mom. I am blunt in a non-endearing manner. The only reason my writing is readable is because of editors, and even then, lotsa folks wish I'd please stop existing.

Furthermore, I am a dork and a geek, and not in the cool or financially productive ways of dork/geekdom. I sleep with a plastic bitey in my mouth because I suffer from something called "grinding trauma." Another affliction, central audio processing disorder, means I appear to be a person who can hear, whereas I am, in fact, not a person who can hear.

Does drool gather in the corner of my mouth so I have to suck it in periodically?

Why, yes, yes, it does.

Couple all of these physical realities with the fact that I comprehend celebrity culture as an ego-infested clapboard house of horrors—a perspective gleaned in my early twenties, through interviewing celebrities; I was in no way prepared for my first wildly successful reading tour across the USA.

I remain delighted that *Cunt* resonates with readers.

That means I did a good job mediuming, and, as mentioned earlier, I can't think of anything further a writer might want to ask of this world.

Besides financial compensation for their difficult work, of course.

I didn't understand that people would consider *me* in the way that celebrities are considered.

Ignorant and absolutely ill-prepared, that was me.

We're gonna take a dark turn here, so get ready.

At a reading in Austin, Texas—is Texas the center of the *Cunt* Universe? *Maybe.* Certainly something to consider—two things happened, one happy, one sad.

Let's go with the sad one first 'cause it ties in with our dark turn.

I walk into the bookstore, up to the front counter, and politely ask the woman at the register where the reading is. She's rude and surly. With an angry little onion in her mouth, she says, "You're early, but it's back there," generically waving her hand to rid me from her presence.

A while later, tasked with bringing the author a bottle of water, this same employee realizes that I'm *the esteemed and terribly important guest* rather than a low-life, runna-the-mill skuzzball customer. She apologizes to me for her earlier behavior, which, all said, makes the situation more hideous.

I don't recall exactly how I responded, but, rest assured, it wasn't anything brilliant or teachable. I mostly just accepted her apology because I was gearing up to do a reading and it wasn't a good time to put thought into the issue.

Nevertheless, I cannot adequately express how deeply this woman's behavior crushed my soul, so I will therefore not endeavor to do so.

I had the opportunity to think about it later, however.

Quite often, in fact.

I'd love to say nothing like that ever happened again, but I'd be lying.

I'd also like to say that I never glossed over this shit behavior again, but I have. Many times.

You see, I've never figured out how to honestly respond to this strain of lie. You may think it doesn't matter, but when this sort of interaction happens consistently over the course of many years, it piles up and, yeah, it ends up mattering.

When you're considered important, whatever the context and however meaningful/less that importance might be, people tend to be on their *best false behavior* around you. You may choose to surround yourself with people who consider you terribly important, in which event, you will grow to believe that everyone is nice, when not everyone is nice.

So that's a lie, and many important people of various stripes choose to live like that, and although it might seem like a good idea, it's just not.

Living a lie, no matter its nature, leads to a severe disconnect that gets worse—and, not unlike a drug addiction, more difficult to control—over time.

The results of this disconnect are on display in the many performance-based celebrities who end up with severe addictions, mental health problems, and suicidal desires/ accomplishments.

Others, who luxuriate in various degrees of privacy—the artists and writers, the academics and scientists, the entrepreneurs and tech/gaming wizards—comfortably ensconce themselves in elaborate structures built by their fans and maintained by enormous egos, none of which safeguards them from the aforementioned perils.

So, please take note:

This book is special and I, the author, am not.

No one is. Stop thinking other people are more special than you are. It's disempowering for you and debilitating for the object of your adoration.

If you're a celebrity, also stop doing this. You know what a piece of shit/glorious dream-kitten you are, same as everybody.

Your ego will not save you and you are not more important than anyone else.

Please entertain these distinctions for a moment, because herein lies a serious assault on your power as a human being. Though I love myself dearly and am thankful I wrote this book, it is nothing without you. There is no power in attributing *Cunt*'s specialness to me.

You picked out this book, for whatever reason.

You were drawn to it, in whatever manner.

You read it.

You made sense of it in your heart.

For my part, I thank you for taking the time.

I wrote it for you.

You are the shining light in this world.

Thank you for being courageous in cowardly times.

Thank you for thinking. Thinking is not easy and *everything* is positioned against you doing that.

Thank you for paying attention to your mind, your heart, your love.

These parts of yourself will serve you faithfully through difficult days.

You, dear reader, are best served recognizing that no one is allowed into your heart and mind without your explicit permission, and that is a gift you give to any artist.

If we meet at a reading, tell me something good. Tell me what you had for dinner. Tell me the funny thing your kid said this morning. Tell me how you fight each and every day.

Treat me like the fuck-up I am and you are, as well.

Assume I think you're important, because you are and I do.

The other thing that happened at the very same reading in Austin reaffirmed my faith in humanity.

After the soul-crushing interaction with the bookstore employee, I do my work and read from *Cunt*. Then I sit at the ubiquitous table signing books for folks. Up next, an elderly white man, who looks exactly like a wealthy rancher, with a stack of fifteen *Cunt*s. He tells me he's a wealthy rancher and his favorite—he made no bones about this—granddaughter kept badgering him to read this dang bad-word book. He saw I was gonna be in town, so decided to come hear what I had to say.

You know, to shut her up.

Instead, he was gonna call her—she's going to college back East—when he got home and tell her that he's sold.

The books are for his wife, children, and the rest of his grandchildren. He has their names neatly written down on a slip of paper that obviously comes from a small notepad he assuredly keeps on his person at all times. He holds my gaze steady and asks mundane dad questions, such as how I support myself and what my family thinks of this book, and then he tells me the book is Good.

Instinctively, I know compliments from this man are rare currency, tersely delivered, from the bottom of his heart.

That's another memory I hold dear, and though I'll sign 'em lovingly, y'all wealthy Texas ranchers gotta buy your own books, you betcha.

I hope you receive this book in the spirit in which it was written.

I hope it brings your fight into focus.

I hope it lends you freedom and joy.

And an endless stream of cuntlove.

With gracious thanks,

Inga

PART I

THE WORD

On the choice occasions popes and politicians directly refer to female genitalia, the term *vagina* is discreetly engaged.

If you will be so kind, say *vagina* out loud a few times. Strip away the meaning and listen solely to the phonetic sound. It resonates from the roof of your mouth.

A vagina could be an economy car:

"That's right, Wanda! Come within five hundred dollars of the actual sticker price, and you'll win this! A brand-new *Chrysler Vagina!*"

Or a rodent:

"Next on *Prairie Safari,* you'll see a wily little silver-tailed vagina outwit a voracious pair of ospreys."

Say *cunt* out loud, again stripping away the meaning. The word resonates from the depths of your gut. It *sounds* like something you definitely don't want to tangle with in a drunken brawl in a dark alley.

A cunt could be a serious weather condition:

"Next on *Nightline,* an exclusive report on the devastation in Kansas when last night's thunder cunt, with winds exceeding 122 miles an hour, ripped through the state."

Or a monster truck:

"The City Arena is proud to present the Coors Crush 'Em Demolition Round-Up competition, where Randy Sam's *Beast of Burden* will challenge Mike Price's undefeated *Raging Cunt* in the 666-barrel jump."

Moving from phonetics to etymology, *vagina* originates from a word meaning "sheath for a sword."

Ain't got no vagina.

Cuntist Mystique

I came across the power of *cunt* quite accidentally. After writing an article for a newspaper, I typed in "word count," but left out the O. My editor laughingly pointed out the mistake. I looked at the two words together and decided "Word Cunt" seemed like a nice title for a woman writer. As a kind of intraoffice byline, I started typing "Word Cunt" instead of "word count" on all my articles.

The handful of people who saw hard copies of my work reacted strongly and asked why I chose to put these two words on my articles. After explaining my reasoning to editorial assistants, production magis, proofreaders, and receptionists, I started wondering about the actual, decontextualized power of *cunt*.

I looked up *cunt* in Barbara G. Walker's twenty-five-year research opus, *The Woman's Encyclopedia of Myths and Secrets*, and found it was indeed a title, back in the day. *Cunt* is related to words from India, China, Ireland, Rome, and Egypt. Such words were either titles of respect for women, priestesses, and witches or derivatives of the names of various goddesses:

In ancient writings, the word for "cunt" was synonymous with "woman," though not in the insulting modern sense. An Egyptologist was shocked to find the maxims of Ptah-Hotep "used for 'woman' a term that was more than blunt," though its indelicacy was not in the eye of the ancient beholder, only in that of the modern scholar. (Walker 1983, 197)

The words *bitch* and *whore* have also shared a similar fate in our language. This seemed rather fishy to me. Three words that convey negative meanings about women, specifically, all happen to once have had totally positive associations with women, specifically.

Of the three, *cunt* garners the most powerful negative reaction.

How come?

This was obviously a loaded question to be asking myself, 'cause the answer evolved into quite the life-consuming project.

According to every woman-centered historical reference I have read—from M. Esther Harding to bell hooks—the containment of woman's sexuality was a huge priority in emerging patrifocal religious and economic systems.

Cunts were anathema to forefather types. Literally and metaphorically, the word and anatomical jewel presided at the very root of many earlier religions, impeding phallic power worship. In Western civilization, forefather types practiced savior-centered religions, such as Catholicism. Springing forth from a very real, very fiscal fear of women and our power, and eventually evolving into sexual retardation and womb envy, a philosophy and social system based on destruction was called to thriving life. One of the more well-documented instances of this destruction-oriented consciousness is the Inquisition. It lasted for more than *five hundred years.* That is how long it took the Inquisition to rend the collective spirit of non-savior-centered religious worshippers.

The Inquisition justified the—usually sadistic—murder, enslavement, or rape of every woman, child, and man who practiced any form of spiritual belief that did not glorify savior-centered phallic power worship.

Since the beginning of time, most cultures honored forces that had tangible effects on human lives, such as the moon, earth, sun, water, birth, death, and life. A spirituality that was undetectable to any of the human senses was considered incomprehensible.

One imagines victims of the Inquisition were not hard to come by. Women who owned anything more than the clothes on their backs and a few pots to piss in were religiously targeted by the Inquisition because all of women's resources and possessions became property of the famously cuntfearing Catholic Church. Out of this, the practice of sending "missionaries" into societies bereft of savior-centered spiritualities evolved.

Negative reactions to *cunt* emanate from a learned fear of ancient yet contemporary, inherent yet lost, reviled yet redemptive cuntpower.

Eradicating a tried-and-true, stentorian-assed word from a language is like rendering null the Goddess Herself.

It's impossible.

Ancient, woman-centered words and beliefs never, like, *fall off the planet.* Having long done taken on a life of their own, they—like womankind—evolve, and survive.

Chameleon style.

For women, this has involved making many, many concessions, such as allowing our selves, goddesses, priestesses, and words to be defined and presented by men.

Many words found in woman-centered religions, such as *cunt, bitch, whore, dog, ass, puta, skag,* and *hag,* along with the names of just about all goddesses—over time—collected bad connotations. As matrifocal lifestyles became less and less acceptable, *cunt* survived, *necessarily* carrying a negative meaning on into the next millennium.

Words outlive people, institutions, civilizations. Words spur images, associations, memories, inspirations, and synapse pulsations. Words send off physical resonations of thought into the nethersphere. Words hurt, soothe, inspire, demean, demand, incite, pacify, teach, romance, pervert, unite, divide.

Words be powerful.

Grown-ups and children are not readily encouraged to unearth the power of words. Adults are repeatedly assured a picture is worth a thousand of them, and the playground response to almost any verbal taunt is "Sticks and stones may break my bones, but words will never hurt me."

I don't beg so much as command to differ.

For young girls in this society, coming into the power we are born with is no easy task. As children, our power is not cultivated in us as it is in boys. Still, cultivating power is—above and beyond all social conditioning—a very surmountable *task* to which womankind collectively rises higher each day.

But we need a language.

A means of communication demands and precedes change.

I posit that we're free to seize a word that was kidnapped and co-opted in a pain-filled, distant past, with a ransom that cost our grandmothers' freedom, children, traditions, pride, and land. I figure we've paid the ransom, but now, everybody long done forgot *cunt* was ours in the first place.

I have lived the past couple years of my life writing a book called *Cunt*. When people ask me what I do, sometimes I bypass the whole conversation and say I'm a taxidermist. A book called *Cunt* always leads to an intense grilling. Ain't never encountered ambivalence. At this juncture, I am still absolutely unable to gauge reactions to this word.

Living with the title of this book as such a huge fixture in my day-to-day life has been a very weird anthropological study unto itself. *Cunt* is a bad, bad word, but *damn* if it don't *intrigue* people when it's the title of a book instead of a mean-spirited expletive.

Because everybody already knows that the diabolization of *cunt* is an absolute reality of our language, nobody has to waste time and energy defending its honor.

A cunt by any other name is still a cunt.

Cunt is a highly satisfying word to utter on a regular basis.

Every girl and lady who is strong and fighting and powerful, who thrives in this world in a way that serves her, is a rockin', cuntlovin' babe doing her part to goad the postpatriarchal age into fruition.

Cunt is the crusty, disgusting bottle in the city dump pile, bejeweled underneath and with a beautiful genie inside.

Here is a nice story about the transformation of destructive, negative crapola into constructive, positive brilliantiana.

Once upon a time, civil rights activist Dick Gregory went into a restaurant and ordered some chicken. Three or four men who wore pointy white hoods as their nighttime fashion statement presently came into the restaurant and said (I'm paraphrasing here), "Yo, boy. Anything y'do tah dat chicken, we're gone do tah yoo."

Mr. Gregory looked at the chicken on the plate before him and was silent.

The men repeated, "Anything y'do tah dat chicken, boy, we're gone do tah yoo."

Everybody in the restaurant stopped what they were doing and stared.

Mr. Gregory sighed, picked up the chicken, and gave it a big ol', sweet ol' kiss.

Perhaps, as some "historians" may have it, I fabricated the historic considerations in reassessing the way we presently perceive *cunt*.

Even if *cunt* were simply four spontaneous letters someone strung together one day 'cause his wife didn't have dinner on the table when he got home from a hard day's labor offing witches or indigenous peoples, it is still *our word*. Demographically, the women who have *no chance* of negatively being called "cunts" throughout life can be found in totally cloistered nunneries and maybe Amish communities.

Based on the criteria that *cunt* can be neither co-opted nor spin-doctored into having a negative meaning, venerable history or not, it's ours to do with what we want. And thanks to the versatility and user-friendliness of the English language, *cunt* can be used as an all-new, woman-centered, cuntlovin' noun, adjective, or verb.

I, personally, am in love with the idea.

PART II

THE ANATOMICAL JEWEL

If it were my job to mathematically figure out which women despise more—being called a cunt or having one—I'd be hating life.

I'm glad that is not my job.

Instead, my job at present is to discuss some of the different ways 'n means women learn to hate our cunts, which still isn't the most savory task on earth, but it is attainable.

Women comprise over 50 percent of this country. Women comprise just over 50 percent of this planet. There's plenty of power in numbers. If we don't have power, it can't have anything to do with mass.

I conclude it must have to do with some stuff inside ourselves.

To know oneself *truly* is to love oneself. Because women do not learn the veritable nature of ourselves in this culture, the likelihood that we love ourselves and/or one another is highly suspect.

All cunts belong to *all women*.

The responsibility sits between our legs.

Blood and Cunts

One fine spring day, after the lunchtime recess in sixth grade, Miss Cothran announced that all the boys were to join Mr. Rogers out on the playground for a game of softball, while all us girls were mandatorily invited to accompany her to the cafeteria.

My friends 'n me knew what was up. We had heard about the infamous Period Movie around fourth grade. Most of the boys were no less familiar with this legendary film and teased us relentlessly as they filed out to the softball diamond.

In the cafeteria, the girls from Mrs. Wolff's class, Mr. Rogers's class, and my class assembled into tittering rows. The school nurse stood in the front of the room, between the pull-out movie screen and a table displaying all of the various disposable bleeding paraphernalia we would one day come to know so well. She explained the ways to affix pads to our panties and dabbled a little in tampondom; then the Film Projector Monitor was called to do her duty, and the Period Movie started.

To date, it is the most intellectually impaired film I've ever seen, taking into account the *combined* fatuity of *Basic Instinct* and *Ace Ventura: Pet Detective*.

A cartoon of the female form demonstrated how this dot in your head travels down to your cunt and makes you bleed. The doctorly-sounding male narrator insisted that we not take baths or exercise during this "special time" but should be sure to keep *spotlessly clean* with lots and lots of soap and showers because menstruating girls tend to stink up the room if they're not completely at one with personal hygiene. He also informed us that any pain or discomfort we might feel resided "in our heads" and had been collectively imagined by womankind for thousands of years.

Were we told anything about how our uteruses are almost exactly like the moon, shedding their linings, growing new ones, and shedding all over again? Did the Period Movie teach us *thing one* about how miraculously cool and sublime the human body's reproductive system is when you're a girl?

Fuck no.

All I truly gleaned from this experience was that my cunt was the yucksville reason I had to sit in that stupid cafeteria watching some hack nurse show me how to safety-pin a three-mile-wide wad of cotton to a pair of brief underpanties even my grandma wouldn't be caught dead in, while the other half of the sixth-grade population was out in the sunshine playing softball. This was the first formal instruction in estrangement from my cunt—of a lifetime's barrage—that I consciously recall.

With all the prepubescent hoopla surrounding periods, I was inclined toward totally vivid nightmarish visions of complete humiliation that would usher in my initiation to womanhood. A recurring one was related to the shower scene Carrie endured—where she was pelted with tampons—in the Hollywood/Stephen King rendition of menstruation commencement. I was *wholly unprepared* for the simplicity and intuition I encountered at the inauguration of my blood.

In seventh grade, I was walking home from school with Teresa and Joyce. We were halfway down Tunnel Street and suddenly I *knew* I was bleeding. It was the first time I remember *knowing* something in this manner. I told Teresa and Joyce, "Hey, I just started my period," and that was that. I went home, grabbed a pad out of my mom's store, and bled on it.

Tampons didn't come along until my fourth period, when Amy Ajello instructed me in great detail over my teen talk phone line. It was tricky holding the phone to my ear and inserting a tampon for the first time, but, thank god, I managed, 'cause pads creeped me out the door. Whenever I wore one, I imagined Jimmy Vallejo and Andrew Vasquez pointing at the gigantic bulge moshing up my ass as I walked down the hall. In my vision, they howled, à la Beavis and Butt Head, and everyone else, of course, would hear about it and I'd be the laughingstock of the whole middle school.

Shame kept a close watch on me and all my girlfriends.

It was shameful to bleed, to be seen bleeding, for blood-soaking paraphernalia to be visible on or about one's person at any time whatsoever, to speak of bleeding, to look like we were bleeding, to be excused from PE because of the crippling cramps that sometimes accompany bleeding, to display frailty, vulnerability, or mood swings because we were going to be bleeding soon, and to express any emotion other than contempt and disdain in reference to our blood.

No one, least of all my peers—who, verily, whispered about this proscriptive subject in hushy undertones, behind closed doors, in only the most trusted of boyless locales—thought bleeding a pleasant reality.

Girls are told bleeding is a *bad thing,* an *embarrassing thing,* a *secret thing* that we should hide and remain discreet about come hell or high water.

Boys are told to go outside and play sports while the girls learn about some creepy, cootie-laden mystery that makes blood ooze out from our you-know-whats.

Given my swimmingly fetching cultural milieu, getting used to this bleeding business took quite a while. In the meantime, I fervently asked people why the hell this happened to us girls. Various sources consistently informed me that it was (big sigh) "just part of being a woman" (big sigh) or, the good ol' standby, the curse we inherited from Eve.

My period was not only a "curse," but for the first years of bleeding, I was completely incapacitated with mind-numbing spasms of pain. For at least one day out of every month, I didn't go to school or work. I lay in bed and cried, unable to do anything about the agony of my uterus. Frequently, because of this "imagined" pain, I fainted and puked.

I find it fascinating that men's description of the pain en-kindled by a knee to the groin sounds awfully similar to what I have experienced for up to thirty-six unflagging hours. And yet, imagine the hue and cry if men were informed that the horrifying symptom of pain accompanying a swift kick in the nuts was purely psychosomatic.

A coupla years after my period started, the newspapers across our fair nation announced that women *weren't* imagining those intense pains. *Scientific studies* proved that the pain *is real!* As you might surmise, this was but a *load* off my mind.

After all those days I vomited because the midsection of my body was clenched in a fist of throbbing excruciation; when I sat in the bathtub crying for five hours straight; when I couldn't get out of bed or leave the house for fear of fainting in public; suddenly, because a group of men took the time to study a group of women and found there was indeed a ra-tional reason for these symptoms wracking our bodies once a month, I was allotted the pale comfort of knowing this pain *actually* existed!

Oh, joy.

Cynic that I am in such arenas of contemplation, I won-der if perhaps this generous allotment wasn't bestowed upon womankind because pharmaceutical companies came to the magnanimous conclusion that sales for pain relievers would skyrocket if only they invested in a little "research" to counter the "in her mind" myth and recondition the general public into believing there was a veritable malady at hand.

In the spring of 1995, I had the momentous honor of interviewing Barbara G. Walker, an American author and feminist, at her home in New Jersey. Among many other things, she told me about menarche parties women in her community throw for the newly menstruating. Ms. Walker described a menarche she attended a few months prior to our interview. The honoree wore a red dress. Her mother made a beautiful red cake for her. A bunch of women, young and old, brought her red gifts wrapped in red paper. The older women talked about the symbolism of the moon and the miraculous joys of both bleeding and not bleeding anymore, while the younger girls who hadn't yet started to bleed duly expressed reverence for the honoree and enthusiasm about starting their periods.

I mean, wouldn't that be wonderful?

Wouldn't you feel like a total princess if your mom or whoever did that for you? Wouldn't that put a whole new slant on bleeding from the get-go?

I was deeply moved by Ms. Walker's account, but in all honesty I must acknowledge my bittersweet envy. My mom's a dang smart lady, and I admire her above and beyond all women on the planet, but it was a bummer to realize that if she hadn't been so busy dealing with the social constraints of single motherhood during the early '80s, sans the aid of a supportive community of women, she might have had the inspiration to hostess a menarche for my sister and me. Whereupon, I sincerely doubt I would've spent almost a decade of my life teaching myself to love the blood that coursed out my stunning cunt every month.

Throwing menarche parties for our younger sisters, nieces, and daughters is a very simple and profound way of effecting positive change for the next generation.

Get off your ass and do it.

If Pippi Longstocking were the nation's covergirl, rest assured that women would have a superlative role model in the fine science of accepting ourselves. Ms. Longstocking is extremely outspoken in response to negative social beliefs:

The children came to a perfume shop. In the show window was a large jar of freckle salve, and beside the jar was a sign which read: DO YOU SUFFER FROM FRECKLES?

"What does the sign say?" asked Pippi. She couldn't read very well because she didn't want to go to school as other children did.

"It says, 'Do you suffer from freckles?'" said Annika.

"Does it indeed?" said Pippi thoughtfully. "Well, a civil question deserves a civil answer. Let's go in."

She opened the door and entered the shop, closely followed by Tommy and Annika. An elderly lady stood back of the counter. Pippi went right up to her.

"No!" she said decidedly.

"What is it you want?" asked the lady.

"No," said Pippi once more.

"I don't understand what you mean," said the lady.

"No, I don't suffer from freckles," said Pippi.

Then the lady understood but she took one look at Pippi and burst out, "But, my dear child, your whole face is covered with freckles!"

"I know it," said Pippi, "but I don't suffer from them. I love them. Good morning." (Lindgren 1977, 18–19)

Unfortunately, Pippi Longstocking is *not* the nation's covergirl.

All the way through my teens and into my twenties, I loathed my period. *Menstruation* was synonymous with unmitigated physical pain on a monthly basis.

But then I got to thinkin'.

Maybe because I was in college, and what are you supposed to do in college if not think? Maybe because I noticed a marked difference in the way women reacted toward menstruation at this point in human development. Maybe because, for the first time in my life, I found myself surrounded by women who were greatly intrigued by the workings of our bodies. Maybe because by the time I went to college I'd taken enough psychotropic plant forms to feel more or less At One with the Universe instead of lost at sea in the swimmingly fetching cultural milieu I'd previously more or less accepted as reality.

During this period of thinking, I read books and watched the moon.

All women throughout time have had the *opportunity* to see the moon. From Africa and Asia to the Americas and Europe, plenty of these ladies started noticing that the moon grows, recedes, and grows again, over and over every twenty-eight days. Those not detached from their menstrual cycle couldn't help but trip out on how their own blood rhythm also occurred over the span of approximately twenty-eight days.

This is how the moon links one up with a form of history none of the textbooks can possibly touch upon: a *psychic* history with all the women who've ever bled on this planet.

By reading some books, investing in a lunar calendar, and poking my head out the window every night or so, I figured out how to tell time by the moon. I learned her phases and moods. The springtime full moon has a much different luminescence than the autumntime full moon. When I went to a party on a dark moon, I generally had a shitty time. When I went to a party during the moon's waxing phase or, better, when it was full, I had a whopping good time.

And on and on.

Soon after me and the moon got to be buddies, the strangest thing happened. The simple act of *hanging* with the moon invoked beliefs my brain had never computed before. Suddenly, all the period propaganda shoved down my throat since that fateful day in sixth grade was far away and beyond ridiculous.

Lo and behold, my period stopped hurting!

I designated the first day of my blood a Special Time when I consciously guarded my quiet. I soaked in mineral salted baths, read *Pippi Longstocking*, mended clothes (before this, shortening a skirt involved the use of duct tape and an iron), and cooked Creole Tomato Soup.

I quit taking ibuprofen. My period mellowed out even more. For the first time in my life, I actually *enjoyed* bleeding. I gauged myself with the movements and rhythms of the moon. I still got cramps, but I didn't faint or puke at all.

Hip, hip!

One month I had pretty bad pains and took some ibuprofen. The following month, the pain was even worse. Then I did an experiment. Some months I took pain relievers and some months I didn't. Every time, the month *after* I took pain relievers, I'd have, as Holiday Golightly would say, the Mean Reds.

Though the medication brought *immediate* relief, the following period was excruciating. Taking menstrual-pain drugs became a vicious cycle. I never realized it before, and it was so obvious once I saw it, but I needed more and more ibuprofen to keep the pain at bay each month.

This little experiment resulted in an *absolute mistrust* of everything I had ever learned about being a woman in this culture. I began the arduous task of questioning, reevaluating, researching, and rewriting the entire information-cataloging system in my brain.

For two years, I did not watch television, read newspapers or any magazines that did not reflect a standard of womanhood with which I identified. Dr. Leo Daugherty, one of my esteemed instructors at the Evergreen State College, told me that for one whole year he read books only by women writers, and I did that too.

All this activity started with my period, but it soon encompassed my entire life and history as well as my way of perceiving the lives and histories of every woman with whom I came into contact.

The way I had learned to deal with my bleeding ways was a reflection of what our society teaches us about everything cunt-lovin' and female and rhythmic and sexual. These are things that must be somehow "controlled" with shame, embarrassment, taboo, violence, or drugs. In order to serve the destructive tendencies of our society, everything that is cuntlovin' must be sequestered away far in deep recesses of the collective unconscious *somehow*.

Therefore, like our cunts, our blood is weird, messy, and ugly. The negativity surrounding menstruation is an illusion that falls, falls, falls away the instant perspective shifts.

And all this mental activity started with me and the moon.

The moon has consistently proven herself to be every woman's ally since the beginning of time. The moon renders fearful illusions of social conditioning petty riffraff that gets in the way of a cuntlovin' lady's life. The moon fucken rules.

Once you decide your body is your fine-tuned hot rod to tool you around this earth as you desire, buy a lunar calendar

(I highly recommend the one published by Luna Press). Put it where you'll see it every morning. Slap it up by the coffee maker, on the bathroom mirror, or above your bed. Wherever. Look at it every day. Notice where the moon is on the calendar. As often as possible, notice the moon in the sky. That's all you have to do, nothing fancy, just notice the moon. The clincher here is *consistency*. Watch the moon grow and recede every month. Be able to eventually wake up in the morning and know where the moon will be that evening without looking.

This is aligning yourself with the moon. Because, like I said, the moon has been teaching us ladies about our insides since we developed the eyeballs able to see that high, there's no wrong way to do this. The moon will teach you just as it taught your distant ancestors.

When you get your period, make a (red) mark on your moon calendar. What did the moon look like when you got your period? What did it look like last month at that time? Sooner or later, you'll get a rhythm going with the moon. You'll have your period every new moon or every waxing moon, or maybe one month you will get your period on the full moon, the next month on the waning moon, next on the new moon, and next on the waxing moon. It varies just fantastically. There is no way of knowing what your cycle is until you lunarly track it. Even then, it is likely to traverse the moon's phases throughout the year, but if you keep a good record and watch what goes on between your cunt and the moon, you'll be able to predict, *to the day,* when you start your period, *even if you are "irregular."* Again,

I can't stress enough: this takes time. You may not have a full grasp of your cycle for six months or even longer.

Patience is this: a virtue.

As you begin to groove with your fine cunt workings and the moon, you'll be able to perform all kinds of neat-o miracles. You can figure out if you're in for a hellish period. Nasties like yeast infections can be easily nipped in the bud because you're so *utterly hip* with yourself. What were once faintly clairvoyant premenstrual dreams take on more lucid clarity and depth. Sex becomes more intense and ecstatic. Menstrual cramps diminish. You can determine when you will and won't get in the family way—if you investigate the matter fully.

Our society creates a hospitable climate for cuntpower to be transfigured into profits amassed by large corporations. Pharmaceutical and feminine hygiene companies, plastic surgeons and weight-loss centers are designated to care for our bodies in our stead. We learn to rely on various "experts" and authority figures who patronizingly inform us how we should respond to our bodies. We are not offered the opportunity to consider how we'd like to respond to bleeding, nor are we presented with how women menstruated in the past or in other cultures.

Becoming responsible is about quitting the "expert" addiction, feeling and listening to what is going on inside of us, and responding in ways that feel good and right to us. Learning to be responsible for your body *takes time*. It's taken you *all your life* to learn how to alienate yourself to the point of total irresponsibility.

If it took society, say, twenty-five years to teach you that you have no control, it'll take you less than a tenth of that time to learn yourself otherwise. In the long run, that's not much time at all, but still, it does indeed amount to roughly two point five years.

It is of utmost importance to be patient with yourself, your ignorance, and your curiosity. Any stockbroker in her right mind will tell you: the return on an investment is wholly dependent upon the investment itself. By the time we're twelve or so, society has convinced the vast majority of us that it is in our best interest to remain incontestably oblivious to our bodies, outside the realm of tormenting ourselves into reflecting a certain standard of physical beauty. Therefore, it is entirely reasonable that we never pause to invest in ourselves on terms that we ourselves define. Our subjugation continues because women are estranged from our actual realities.

Taking responsibility for one's bleeding ways is part of the reality-based revolution founded between the soft, luscious thighs of every woman on the planet.

A more material aspect of this revolution is downsizing the percentage of our funding we use to support corporations that exist for no other purpose than to constrain women in the throes of body alienation and to perpetuate our deleterious relationships with our cunts.

Here is my story about that.

I went to Anystore USA to buy a box of tampons. I had but eleven dollars to my name. I went down the aisle where I would find "feminine hygiene" products, bitterly playing that term through my mind.

Why are words like *hygiene* and *sanitary*—which imply that a woman's cunt is unclean—acceptable in our society? Why are these people trying to sell me feminine deodorant spray? That's like hawking floral air freshener to a lady who lives in a rose garden.

Also, excuse me, but what's so clean about dicks?

One never hears of sanitary jock straps, deodorant condoms, perfumed Hershey-Squirt protection pads, or hygienic ball wipes, whereas I've heard tell of need for such products.

So anyway, with thoughts such as these playing through my mind, you can imagine my dismay on tampon-buying excursions. If I happen to be in a good mood, it's simply annoying. If I happen to be in a bad mood, I am a green monster who lives in a trash can with a grand piano. On this occasion, I was in a bad mood.

I grumbled down the aisle, openly sneering at all the products on the shelves. New Freedom this and Light Days that.

Comfort, security.

Plastic applicators.

Discreet disposal pouches printed with flowers that do not exist.

I positively *fumed* as I scanned the prices. Five, six, seven bucks for *a box of cotton.* Sixty, seventy bucks a year.

Why the *flying fuck* should a woman have to *pay* some huge corporation over and over because the lining of her uterus naturally, *biologically* sheds every month?

Among my small circle of friends, I tally seven hundred dollars spent on tampons and pads a year. I estimate the women in my apartment building spend thirteen thousand dollars a year to swell the already enormous profit margins of "feminine hygiene" companies.

Reluctantly, I made my selection: a box of Tampax Slender Regulars for $7.19. I stormed my way to the checkout line. In front of me was a young man who said hello.

I replied, "Do you realize that I will have barely three dollars in the whole wide world after I purchase this box of tampons because my period is coming and I find it unsavory to bleed in all my clothes and on every seat I occupy for the next few days?"

He told me that he'd considered this very conundrum. His girlfriend had bitched about the same thing at length.

We fell into a checkout-line conversation on the matter, comparing men's hygienic expenses to those of women and, also, how the moon is totally disregarded in our culture in relation to womb-type activities.

The couple behind us—a well-to-do-looking pair in their lawn-bowling sixties—kept clearing their throats, saying ehh-hemmm and harrummphh. The woman, especially, gave me extremely disdainful looks for speaking so tactlessly and loudly in the Anystore USA checkout line.

A few days later, I related this experience to my friend Ashley Goldenrod, who, at the time, had just organized a small women's health collective in Olympia, Washington.

She said, "Oh, Inga! I've been using sea sponges! Have you heard about them?"

I said no.

Ashley told me all about them. She bought three sea sponges for $1.59 apiece. Besides their obvious economic virtues, she said, you use them over and over, so they're more ecologically desirable; when your sponge gets soaked with blood, no matter where you are, you just haul it on out, wash it real good with hot water and mild soap, then pop it on back in; you never have to trouble yourself with remembering to bring a tampon reserve; they're totally comfortable and fun to play with in the bathtub. Also, you can squeeze the blood out into a jar, fill it with water, and feed it to your houseplants, who, Ashley assured me, "absolutely adore the stuff."

I asked her about toxic shock syndrome and whether sea sponges harbor yucky things that can make a girl sick.

Ashley said that it is very, very important to keep your sponge *super-duper clean,* washing it thoroughly every time you use and reuse it.

Trusting my friend as I do, I bought a couple of sea sponges at the local health food co-op and gave them a whirl. The only problem I've had is that when a sea sponge is full, it is *full.* If you laugh or yell when the sponge has absorbed its maximum capacity, your nice white panties will get a big red how-do-you-do on them.

Other than that, sea sponges are the coolest. I've developed an endearing friendship with my sponges. They are miraculous little animals that once lived in the ocean, which is also ruled by the moon. And they don't carry that impersonal, flushable, bleached personality tampons possess.

Sea sponges can be found at almost all Anystore USA–type stores, usually in the make-up or bath-time section. If you're lucky enough to have a health food co-op in your town, they're sure to have them. At under two dollars apiece, they pay for themselves after one month.

Keep them clean. Boil a new sponge before you use it for the first time. Store them in a little cotton bag. Wash them and let them dry completely before putting them away for the month, but *always* wash them again before using. I've heard that you can use more than one at a time if you bleed a lot, but I've never tried this. I wouldn't recommend using the same sea sponge for more than a few months because the natural fibers wear out after a while and it gets kinda disintegratey.

A friend of mine who uses sea sponges once told me about an experience in a public restroom. She was at a busy nightclub, waiting in line with eight or so other women to use the toilet. There were four stalls and at least that many women at the sinks, primping and washing their hands. Suddenly, all normal bathroom conversation came to a crashing halt as a voice from behind one of the stall doors pealed out, "I'm coming out with my sea sponge, so if you're gonna gross out, shut your eyes." A woman then emerged from her stall, sea sponge in hand. With all eyes upon her, she washed it carefully at the sink, went back into the stall, and finished up her business. One woman actually did close her eyes, but everyone else stood transfixed, witnessing the woman's ritual with her sea sponge. When the woman came out again, she fielded quite a number of questions about where to get sea sponges and how to use them. The whole room of women came together for a few moments, laughing and talking about our blood.

I enjoy imagining how the culture of restrooms would be different if our periods weren't all hush, flush, 'n rush.

The Keeper is another fabulous gizmo for catching blood flow. It is a natural rubber cup with a stem that has a small hole in the end. The cup fits over your cervix, and when it's full, little drips of blood flow through the stem, letting you know it's time to tend to your Keeper.

I have never tried the Keeper because I don't like things covering my cervix, but I still average around two emails a month from ladies extolling the Keeper's virtue. It is, I've been informed by sources all over the globe, reusable, incredibly comfortable, and convenient.

Using sea sponges and the Keeper are very good ways for women to cut down on contributions to large corporations that don't readily promote the idea that cunts are sacredholy and responsible for the entrance of every human being walking this earth.

But some ladies just don't like internal blood-soaking devices at all. Some ladies like to bleed *onto* something.

Even though me and my period have come to terms quite nicely over the years, I still can't put anything up my cunt on the first day of my period. My uterus rebels if a stray pubic hair finds its way up my canal on that ultrasensitive first day.

So I asked my grandmother, "What did ladies bleed on before Kotex dreamed up those thick-as-white-wall-tire pads and elastic security belts?"

She blinked her desert tortoise eyeballs before replying, "Child, where do you think the phrase 'on the rag' comes from?"

So smitten was I with not spending my money on tampons, I started safety-pinning rags to a pair of boys' underwear. (Why are BVDs so comfy, while Maidenform makes all these panties that cost too much and skooch up one's ass?)

I cut up a towel for my rags: a few are around four inches long and six inches wide, and the rest are five inches long and two inches wide. I wrap the wider-width rags around my underwear, placing as many of the thinner ones between the wide rag and the underwear panel as I'll be needing.

It takes some practice to figure out how to get the rags situated just so. I can't really offer any suggestions, because it depends on how much you bleed, how you walk, sit, and stand, what kind of fabric you choose, how you decide to affix the rags to the undies, et cetera and et cetera.

Many health food stores sell ready-made flannel rags with Velcro fasteners.

If you sew, design your own rags.

If you don't sew, contact Lunapads, GladRags, or any of the other wonderful companies that do the sewin' for you. Heck, these organizations are *so dang cool,* get in contact with them regardless. They feature cuntlovin' bleeding products, reading materials, panties, and many other revolutionary products.

And then, of course, there's the trusty Blood Towel.

I've had the same Blood Towel for seven years. It is blue. Terra-cotta shadows stain it everywhere.

Linus from *Peanuts*?

Me and my Blood Towel.

When I'm on my period, I sleep with my Blood Towel between my legs. We all know you're not supposed to wear tampons or sea sponges to bed, and rags and pads always seem to mosh up the ol' ass. Maybe a Blood Towel isn't the most alluring thing to wear to bed, but it sure is comfortable and keeps the sheets clean.

In the morning I walk around the house with my Blood Towel wrapped around my waist. It catches the flow when I sit down. I use it to wipe the insides of my legs. Otherwise, the blood splatters on my feet, the floor. I step in it and get it everywhere.

Sometimes I don't clean it up right away.

Messy, messy. Fingerpaints in kindergarten messy.

I like to do this for a very good reason:

Because I can!

Isn't it amazing.

By the simple act of not wearing panties, I can stand in the middle of my kitchen and *change the way it looks.* Without moving a muscle, a pool of blood appears between my feet.

Like magic.

Bleeding on sea sponges, the Keeper, rags, and Blood Towels may *seem* undesirable when compared to commonly accepted standards for absorbing blood flow. But these "inconveniences" are founded solely upon our indoctrination in this society. Spending time with your blood is a constructive action. Bleeding every month is a part of life that we are taught to ignore. When we choose, literally, to *see* it, we open up to our actual reality as cuntlovin' women.

Rinsing out a sea sponge or the Keeper in the bathroom of a fancy restaurant or washing bloody rags by hand may not be as "convenient" as flushing all one's cunt ambrosia away into the city sewer system, but it reconnects a cuntlovin' woman with her body and, indirectly, with the bodies of every cuntlovin' woman, living and dead, who has ever known the sensation of blood flowing out of her cunt.

You have a ritual for bleeding on throwaway cotton. *You and only you* know your bleeding technique. Sure, it takes time to learn another one, but the nice thing is:

Human beings are the most highly adaptable mammals on the planet. You'll figure out a system.

If, for example, you were to decide that using rags and sponges was impossible except when you are home at night, that'd still cut your dependency on large corporations' products anywhere from 20 to 50 percent.

In some situations, I use tampons (preferably the unbleached kind found in food co-ops and healthy rainbow sister stores). But instead of being *solely reliant* on tampons, instead of coughing up the money every single period, it takes me three to five months to empty a box.

When I *unconsciously* relegated the right to be in charge of how I bleed to various commercial and corporate entities that have no interest in me as a living being, much less as a woman, the distribution of my power did not serve me. Feminine hygiene corporations fund the lives of a small percentage of men who *remain* in power because they are so good at convincing us ladies that the most *natural and convenient* thing for us to do is to give them ours.

Speaking of men.

As individual husbands, fathers, brothers, sons, and lovers, rather than as the most affluent team of business associates on the planet—men are involved with this bleeding situation in a deeply subconscious way.

Men do *themselves* a *great service* learning about women and the moon. Unless they're incarcerated, it is just about impossible to avoid interacting with us.

Bleeding ladies are taught to be, at best, intolerant of a month-to-month physiological occurrence that clocks the time of our bodies. We therefore act mighty peculiar. Disliking something unavoidable takes its toll after a while. Some people call this PMS.

If, at every stage of life, society commanded men to despise their hard-ons, how pleasant would they be when this bodily function that they are incapable of desisting occurred?

Society fails to acknowledge that our bleeding cycle affects men's lives tremendously. This is further compounded by the fact that women who live or work in close proximity to one another tend to merge bleeding cycles. Chances are, every woman in a given household or workplace is bleeding at the same time. Sometimes men are surrounded on all sides by cranky, bleeding cunts.

To the incognizant, we seem entirely unpredictable. We may bite a man's head right off for the smallest vagrancy.

They know this.

There is no way for them not to know this.

But chances are, they don't understand, and act like jerks 'cause their courage is tested. When most men who don't understand women see how really scary we are, courage usually segues to fear. This results in anger, frustration, violence, and the perpetuation of general disrespect of women. Bottom line: men are afraid of our blood.

How's this for some serious chickenshittedness:

Keep away from women in their courses,
and do not

approach them until
they are clean.
But when they have
purified themselves,
You may approach them
in any manner, time, or place,
Ordained for you, by God.
(Koran, Sura II, 222)

The ancient world's most dreaded poison was "moon-dew"
collected by Thessalian witches, said to be a girl's first menstrual blood shed during an eclipse of the moon. Pliny said
a menstruous woman's touch could blast the fruits of the
field, sour wine, cloud mirrors, rust iron, and blunt the
edges of knives. If a menstruous woman so much as laid a
finger on a beehive, the bees would fly away and never return. If a man lay with a menstruous woman during an
eclipse, he would soon fall sick and die. (Walker 1983, 643)

Can't say that I blame men for fearing our bloody cunts.
We be powerful people when we bleed.
    When women bleed, all of the frustration and anger we've
stored in our bodies for the month is physically manifested in
a sudden and swift change in hormone levels, resulting in an
openness and vulnerability that cannot be described. Menstruation is a monthly purging and cleansing. We hear, taste,
and smell things that are usually indiscernible. Whether we
consciously recognize it or not, we feel threatened when our
heightened senses are assaulted.

I assert that menstruating women intuitively want to be *left alone* or with other bleeding women, as many of our great-great grandmothers firmly believed.

A number of societies certainly have the right idea prohibiting highly sensitive menstruating women from entering churches where a son-sacrificing, war-mongering, sadistic god is worshipped. Unfortunately, this prohibition is enforced because of the belief that menstruating women are "unclean" and not because we'd rather spend the sabbath quietly paying homage to ourselves and the moon.

A few friends and I spoil each other silly if we're hanging out on the first day of someone's period. We fry up sweet 'n sour tofu, give massages, play Toni Childs and Sade, or bring each other chocolate-covered strawberries. Mostly, we sit quietly and stare out the window and demand absolutely nothing of each other.

The social requirement that we fulfill the responsibilities of our nonmenstruating selves at all times throughout our cycle is the source of our alleged PMS.

We're taught to distrust everything about our very compelling blood mystery. Yet the clickety-clack, passive-aggressive business world of men and machines is the absolute antithesis of everything our senses crave on the first few days of our blood. In our souls, we still know this. In our DNA, we want to be quiet with ourselves. In this society, where a day to ourselves might very well mean no one to care for the children and no food on the table, bleeding women are naturally irritable.

The evils of our blood recede when—however fleetingly—we're free from the demands of this unfeeling world. When we sit reverent and peaceful. When those around us respect our silence. This is when the negative becomes positive.

Every woman has a different way of honoring her blood.

Every so often, Bambi, my housemate, has a ritual of painting fantastic gold leaf menstrual homages, framed in total baroque. Bambi's not a painter, she's a musician. Her period tells her when it's time for another painting. "I seem to make one every eighteen months or so," says Bambi. She has no idea why she started painting with her menstrual blood in gold.

Some women cook fabulous dinners for themselves; some save up money to take in a weekend by the sea.

When you open yourself up to learn how to honor yourself, the *how* part just falls into place via your imagination, passion, and lifestyle.

It takes a lot of time, focus, and energy to realize the enormity of being the ocean with your very own tide every month. However, by honoring the demands of bleeding, our blood gives something in return. The crazed bitch from irritation hell recedes. In her place arises a side of ourselves with whom we may not—at first—be comfortable. She is a vulnerable, highly perceptive genius who can ponder a given issue and take her world by storm. When we're quiet and bleeding, we stumble upon the solutions to dilemmas that've been bugging us all month. Inspiration hits and moments of epiphany rumba 'cross de tundra of our senses. In this mode of existence one does not feel antipathy toward a bodily ritual that so profoundly and routinely reinforces our cuntpower.

Reproductive Control for Cunts

Just because I don't envision myself in a romantic, sexual relationship with a man anymore doesn't mean I never have.

The first time I got pregnant, I was nineteen and living in the agricultural community on the California coast where I'd lived all my life. A mere two weeks separated me from my move away from home to Seattle. Making such a major move with a tiny human growing inside my body seemed a pretty contradictory way of setting off on my own.

The thoroughly unsavory "option" of hanging around town for nine months and then giving my child to an adoption agency didn't hold my attention for more than two puffs off the continuous cigarette I'd had in my mouth since I got back my test results.

So I went to Planned Parenthood for a clinical abortion. In the waiting room, there always seemed to be fifteen or twenty other women, no matter how many left with the nurse.

Evidently, it was "abortion day."

We were shuffled through the clinic like beef cows. All of the women had the same horror-stricken, empty look on their faces. It was one of those situations where one can assume one

holds the same expression as everyone else without looking in the mirror. I sat there for an hour and a half, nervously leafing through *People* magazine in a desperate attempt to give a rat's ass about the lives of Daryl Hannah and Whitney Houston.

When they called my name, I probably would have shit my pants if there had been any digestion going on in my intestines, which there wasn't. It's hard to eat when you're pregnant with a child you do not want.

My boyfriend accompanied me into the exam room. I was told to strip and lay on the table, feet in the stirrups. I still remember the ugly swirl designs and water marks on the ceiling. After a while, the nurse came in and explained what would be happening.

She referred to the machine used for clinical abortions as a "suction device," which is a more professional way of saying "vacuum cleaner." In theory, if not design, this machine is quite like the Hoover Upright, the DustBuster, or the Shop-Vac in your closet at home.

The nurse didn't mention how useful vacuum cleaners are for cleaning up messes. In our society, a pile of kitty litter on the floor is treated much the same as an undesired embryo. The main difference, though hardly recognizable to Western science, is that kitty litter is sucked from cold linoleum and an embryo is sucked from a warm-blooded living being's womb.

Instead, because I was crying like *La Llorona,* she said, "Are you sure this is what you want?"

What other goddamn choice did I have?

I muttered, "Just do it, please."

With the ugliest needle I'd ever seen, she shot something into my cervix. I don't think my cervix was residing under the belief that it would someday have a large needle plunged into it, and so protested accordingly. The pain was overwhelming; my head swam into the netherworld between intense clarity and murky subconscious.

Then I heard a quiet motor whirring.

The lady told me to recite my ABCs.

"A, B, C, D, E . . ." Something entered my cunt, deeper, deeper, deeper than I imagined anything could possibly go.

"F, G, H, I, O, W . . ." The walls of my uterus were being sucked, felt like they were gonna cave in. I screamed, "O, P, X, X, D, VOWELS, WHAT ARE THE VOWELS? R? K? A! A's A VOWEL!" And then my organs were surely being mowed down by a tiny battalion of Lawn-Boys.

"S, did I say S?" My boyfriend was crying, too, didn't tell me whether I said S or not.

There was a white-wall-tire pad between my legs then, and blood gushed out of me. The motor had stopped whirring. I was delirious. I asked, "What do you do with all the fetuses? Where do they go? Do you bury them?" The lady ignored me, which was fine, I had to puke. She led me into a bathroom and I vomited biley green foam. Then I went to a recovery room, lay down, and cried.

There was another nurse woman in there. She patted my hand, reassured me, "I know just how you feel."

"You've had an abortion before too?"

"No, but I know how you feel."

I told her to get the fuck away from me.

For two weeks, there was a gaping wound in the center of my body. I could hardly walk for five days.

Then, stupid me, a couple of years later, I got pregnant again. I still lived in Seattle but was just about to move to Olympia, to begin school at Evergreen.

I couldn't really envision myself having an academic edge with a bun in the oven, so I faced the reality of going to that machine once again. This time I was more terrified than before. I knew all too well what that rectangular box and its quiet motor had planned for my reproductive system.

Have you any idea how it feels to willingly and voluntarily submit to excruciating torture because you dumbly forgot to insert your diaphragm which gave you ugly yeast infections and hurt you to fuck unless you lay flat on your back anyway? I was to withstand this torture because I was a *bad girl*. I didn't do good. I fucked up.

I had the same choice as before, that glowing, outstanding choice for which we ladies fight tooth and nail: the choice to get my insides ruthlessly sucked by some inhuman shitpile, not invented by my foremothers but by someone who would never, ever in a million years have that tube jammed up his dickhole and turned on full blast, slurping everything in its path.

Abortion number 2 took place in a clinic that was under so much political pressure, I wasn't even allowed to recuperate. Twenty minutes after the vacuum cleaner was out of my body, I was dressed and walking home.

Felt like a piece of shit.

On one of Olympia's main thoroughfares is an abortion clinic. I passed it every day on my way to and from school. Almost always, there were old women, young girls, and duck hunters standing on the corner outside the clinic, holding signs in their hands showing you pictures of dead fetuses with some words underneath to the effect that this may have been the next president of the United States of America.

Whenever I saw those people out there, especially the young girls, I'd see myself yanking the bus cord—in all probability, snapping it in two—vaulting off the bus, crossing the street, and morphing into a walking killing machine, kicking in faces, stomping on hands. There were times when I gripped my own wrist so I wouldn't yank that cord.

At this point in my life, I'd begun to study different kinds of medicines and healing methods. One thing I learned in college was that knowledge helps me transcend anger. Upon examining my desire to physically assault individuals whose convictions were in direct opposition to mine, I delved into histories and applications of medicines far and wide. At the same time, I was hanging around with a group of women who were asking a lot of compelling questions about our reproductive systems. We found many of the readily available answers to be thoroughly unsatisfactory and started discovering our own.

In this research, we found one constant: healing starts from within. It appeared to be some kind of law. No, more than a law. Is breathing a law? Is waking up every morning a law? If so, maybe the notion of healing coming from within is a law as well.

I had never been comfortable with the idea that healing comes from the physician or his bag of tricks, because I learned years before, when I had my own health challenge with polio, that healing has only one source. The doctor can aid the body by removing foreign particles, injecting chemicals, setting and realigning bones, but that does not mean the body will heal. In fact, I am certain, there has never been a doctor anywhere, at any time, in any country, at any period in history who ever healed anything. Each person's healer is within. The doctor is at best one who has recognized an individual talent, developed it and is privileged enough to be able to serve the community by doing what he does best and loves doing. (Morgan 1991, 91)

This concept is completely alien, even deviant, in our culture.

In this society, we look to the outside for just about everything: love, entertainment, well-being, self-worth, and health. We stare into the TV set instead of speaking of our own dreams, wait for a vacation instead of appreciating each day, watch the clock rather than listen to our hearts. Every livelong day we are bombarded with realities from the outside world, seemingly nonstop. Phones, car alarms, pills, coffee, beepers, ads, radios, elevator music, fax machines, gunshots, bright lights, fast cars, airplanes overhead, computer screens, sirens, alcohol, newspapers. One hardly has the opportunity to look inside for love and peace and other nice things like that.

Western medicine, that smelly deaf dog who farts across the house and who we just don't have the heart to put out of its misery, is based on a law opposed to the one the rest of the universe seems to go by, namely: Healing Has Nothing to Do with You, Just Follow the Directions on the Label.

In America, we don't (nor are we encouraged to) look inside ourselves for healing, finding truths or answers. If you want to know something, you find out what the Person in Charge of This Area says. The weather is not to be discerned by looking at the sky, the mountains in the distance, or by listening to the song of the wind. You will find it in the Report of the Meteorologist. And likewise, if you are pregnant and don't want to be, you don't look to yourself and the immediate, personal resources in your immediate, personal world; you pay a visit to the Abortionist, who will subsequently predict the climate in your body for two weeks, guaranteed.

And so, la dee dah, once, twice, three times a cuntlovin' lady, I got pregnant again. It was the same boyfriend as the other two times only now we were breaking up. It was the fuckedest one of all because I didn't want to be with this man and I shouldn't have fucked him, but it was his birthday and he was obviously fun to romp with and blah dee blah blah blah. No force on earth could make me feel like I wanted this child. Furthermore, I promptly decided there was to be no grotesque waltz with that abhorrent machine.

So, I started talking to my friends about abortion alternatives. I lived in a small town with a high population of like-minded cuntlovin' women, so that was one thing in my favor right there. Against me was the fact that I was eight weeks along, which is too advanced for an organically induced miscarriage. According to naturopathic physician Loraine Harkin, six weeks of pregnancy is the outside limit for herbal abortions. Because they are effective about 60 percent of the time, she said it was important to schedule a surgical abortion as a backup plan. I made an appointment at the women's clinic (the one with the protesters, who'd since moved on to haunt other neighborhoods) in case my way didn't work out.

My dear friend Judy, the masseuse and scientist, was my biggest resource. She and Ashley found some herbal tea recipes a Boston anarchist-feminist group printed. (I tried to contact this group, but they have evidently disbanded.)

Judy came to my house almost every night and massaged my uterus; you are not supposed to massage pregnant women who want to keep their babies. She also did reflexology by rubbing either side of my Achilles tendon on both feet.

A naturopath in Olympia was one of my sources of inspiration for learning about healing from within. She taught me this thing called "imaging." It may sound terribly New Age, but through imaging, I got rid of this weird bump I'd had on my labia *all my life*. Because imaging goes on in your own head, I can't tell you how to do it specifically. The basic idea is: *every* night, when you are falling asleep, graphically imagine the part of your body that's giving you problems *changing*. For the bump on my labia, I imagined all this beautiful soft flesh growing over and absorbing the bump. When I was pregnant, I *vividly, consistently* (I do believe these are the operative words when imaging) imagined the walls of my uterus gently shedding.

Eight days passed from when I started inducing miscarriage to the morning my embryo plopped onto the bathroom floor.

Judy's daily massages and my continuous imaging of the lining of my uterus shedding away at every moment of my days, I feel, were *the most crucial* elements of my success story. I was absolutely focused on miscarrying and I *felt* Judy's gentle, yet firm massages prodding things along quite nicely.

It was an incantation.

Me and my women friends did magic.

Esther's love made magic. She supported me and stayed with me every day. Bridget's thoughtfulness made magic. She brought me flowers. Possibly most magical was the fact that, after the first coupla days, I possessed not one filament of self-doubt. With that corps of supportive women surrounding me and with my mind made up, I was pretty much invincible.

I stress this because in America we tend to hold that popping medicine in our mouths and swallowing is the extent of our involvement in the healing process. We believe that if we get better, it's because the *medicine* worked magic, not the *person*. Many women I know have tried to induce miscarriage and failed because they took certain herbal potions and went about their lives as if everything were normal, waiting for the herbs to work their wonders. To successfully induce miscarriage, one must devote One's Entire Life to the attainment of this goal. *I place an enormous amount of emphasis on this point.* When I induced miscarriage, I breathed, ate, shat, and slept thinking of nothing else but the lining of my uterus shedding.

The herbal teas and other oral and topical applications I prescribed to myself were *little helpers.* They served to further direct *my own focus* and *aid* me in achieving my goal. Herbs are *particularly* good little helpers because plants easily and synergistically jibe with one's own magic and are quite willing to work with you if you respect them.

The herbs I chose were blue cohosh root and pennyroyal leaves. The information I am providing is to illustrate how I, *one specific individual,* induced a miscarriage. Hundreds of emmenagogues and abortifacients grow on the planet. The two I decided to use were chosen after a lot of discussion and reading.

After a week of nonstop imaging, massages, tea drinking, talking, and concentrating, I was brushing my teeth at the sink and felt a very peculiar mmmmbloommmp-like feeling. I looked at the bathroom floor and there, between my feet, was some blood and a little round thing. It was clear but felt like one of them unshiny superballs. It was the neatest thing I ever did see.

An orb of life and energy, in my hand.

And Jesus H., wasn't I the happiest clam? It hardly hurt at all, just some mild contractions. I bled very little, felt fine in two days. I wore black for a week and had a little funeral in my head.

Organically inducing a miscarriage was definitely one of the top ten learning experiences in my life thus far.

You know, it's like when Germany invaded Poland. I once read how in the ghettos of Warsaw, the people fighting the Nazis were real amazed at first that a Nazi soldier would die if you shot him. They *suspected* that Nazis could die but *felt* like they were somehow superhuman.

That's how I felt after I miscarried a child without paying a visit to the beef cow clinic and that sickening vacuum cleaner. I felt the way I imagine any oppressed individual feels when they see that they have power and nobody—not men and not their machines—can take that away.

Terminating a pregnancy in any manner is a harrowing, traumatic experience. At the time, my emotions were an odd juxtaposition of untold grief and profound exhilaration. When the sadness settled quietly into my heart, I felt *so happy* to be a woman. I looked at all my women friends with such an intense, burning rush of joy. My cuntlovin' friends and I did something *amazing* to *affect my destiny* in the most conducive possible way.

I learned that the fight for human rights does not take place on some bureaucratic battleground with a bevy of lawyers running from congressional suite to congressional suite, sapping resources into laws. The war for peace and love and other nice things like that is not waged in protests on the street. These forms of fighting are a reaction to oppression, giving destructive power that much more energy. The real fight for human rights is inside each and every individual on this earth.

While traversing along this particular train of thought, I realize I just might sound like a woman who has never experienced the unspeakable horror of back-alley abortions, and

I am. I also realize that it might seem as if I'm ungrateful to all the cuntlovin' women who fought their hearts raw for legal abortions, which I am not. The fact that there now exists a generation of women who can actually consider clinical abortion to be an oppressive diversion from our own power is *based wholly upon* the foundation that our mothers and sisters built for us. I sincerely thank the individuals who fought so hard that I may have the luxury of the belief I now hold. Evolutionarily speaking, it is quite natural for this fight to progress into a new arena, for the fight is not over, it has not ended. The squabble between pro-lifers and pro-choicers serves only to keep our eyes off the target, and nothing more.

Without the women in my life, both living and dead, I would have been roadkill simply ages ago. All women benefit from concentrating our energy on the power within our own circle of friends, creating informal health collectives where we discuss things like our bodies and our selves.

Abortion clinics, in their present incarnation, will be completely unnecessary when we believe in our own power and the power of our immediate communities. The abortion issue can become a personal, intimate thing among cuntlovin' women friends.

Can you say Amen.

Nobody here is saying abortion is a form of birth control.

It isn't.

Having an abortion totally sucks. Practicing a birth control lifestyle is a fabulous all-expenses-paid, carte blanche vacation in Tahiti compared to terminating a pregnancy.

Birth control is preventive medicine (referring, of course, to the nurturing, woman-centered definitions of "medicine"). It is actively sustaining a lifestyle that grosses and nets the fewest possibilities of conceiving a child. Having an abortion, on the other hand, is terminating the progress of something that is already quite under way.

However, since the morning-after pill was cleared by the US Food and Drug Administration, abortion and birth control have kinda merged a bit.

The morning-after pill was not available to me the three times I was pregnant. If it had been, I do not know if I would have taken it, because I am deathly fearful of pills and am unclear on the long-term side effects we're talkin' here. There is definitely an allure to a pill one can take "just to be safe." Absolute knowledge of conception is a nonissue. Take the pill, have your period, and if it's a little heavy and clotty, figure ya mighta been, but then again maybe not.

Kinda preventive, kinda Terminator style.

Yeah, the morning-after pill runs 'long a misty boundary.

One thing I'm pretty certain about, though. Featuring this pill as a fabulous star in one's birth control lifestyle would rend untold—quite possibly irreparable—damage to the lining of one's uterus. Because it's now accessible, I am concerned that women could start relying on it too heavily.

My opinion of the morning-after pill also runs along a misty boundary. It's damn important for a lot of reasons. But to the day I keel over, I'll be a diehard, furrow-browed skeptic whenever male-run industries are involved with us womenfolk's business.

That said, I know of three birth control lifestyles that are 100 percent safe and infallible.

The first—abstinence—is no fun and extremely unhealthy, so forget that one.

Masturbation *is* fun. Lordisa, is masturbation fun. It's also liberating, empowering, and a superlative form of safe sex. You cannot get pregnant or become HIV positive even if you are in a circle jerk with everyone and her sister. Besides all of these outstanding qualities, masturbation is an *absolutely peerless* cure for the hiccups.

Masturbation is a high art. I have a cuntlovin' friend who masturbates without touching herself. She ornately concentrates on an erotic adventure until she comes her brains out. She's rolled her eyes and moaned on public transportation and in long lines at the grocery store. Comin' her brains out. Another friend of mine goes the manual route but has specialized her timing and precision in elevators.

For those of us less mentally talented and/or dexterous, there are vibrators, dildos, Ben Wa balls, butt plugs, and massage wands shaped like everything from dill pickles to elephants with trunks raised clit high. Also, of course, the five holy and munificent fingers on each hand.

Sex exclusively with girls is also fun. Unless pregnancy is on the agenda, or something immaculate occurs, lesbians do not usually conceive. Women do not have sperm. Thus, women cannot accidentally get each other pregnant. HIV, though, is another scenario. Women are able to pass HIV to each other. The research done thus far on the possibility of transferring HIV woman to woman is inconclusive, but the risk should be taken seriously. Trust no one but yourself, and always practice the safest possible sex.

In conclusion, the only 100 percent safe and infallible birth control lifestyles worth considering are masturbation and/or sex exclusively with women. When neither of these life-styles coincides with a cuntlovin' woman's reality, the prevention of unplanned pregnancy is often an issue.

There are ways for cuntlovin' women to deal with this issue without the pill, barriers against the cervix, hormone implants, or whatever other "choices" male-centered medicine's birth control industry has palmed off on us.

What, exactly, is the life cycle of a *woman's* body *doing* under the jurisdiction of a medical science established, defined, and implemented by people who *do not have cunts*?

It's like suddenly, one day in the Middle Ages, people figured men should be in charge of women's bodies because they were in charge of pretty much everything else.

In context, at the time, perhaps it made sense.

It does not make sense anymore.

Maybe we lost contact with our archives somewhere along

the way. Maybe we kinda went ahead and played along like we were dumb. Maybe we got beaten and raped and tortured and enslaved into submission.

That is the past.

It's something to reckon with but also: it's gone.

Face it, forget it.

Focus on the present: the age of communication.

We gots us the Internet.

You can email government officials in Pakistan and plead mercy for the fifteen-year-old girl sentenced to death for killing the man who raped her. You can find the chemical compound for Depo-Provera and see how that chemical compound affects the human body. You can hop on Diamanda Galás's website and find out what in good Lordisa's name she's up to now. You can download all the recipes for chocolate chip cookies on the planet earth and follow a different one each month when you and your friends are PMSing.

And that's just the Internet.

Living as we do in an age of communication, it is pretty much acceptable to go, "Hey, Gramma, what'd you use for birth control, how did you bleed, what was sex like back then, how many lovers did you have, how many abortions, when, where, how, why?"

Bam, connection with history.

Our communication environment fosters vast, far-reaching, and intricate networks of women who utilize fanzines, small presses, schools, record companies, magazines, television shows, and movies. Women from all socioeconomic strata communicate in mediums that in the past were either not accessible or not invented.

It is *perfectly socially acceptable* for you to write down every thought you've ever had about *anything*—from your gorgeous prize wisteria, to the insane relationship you have with your hair, to your all-consuming love for the clitoris—then slap the words together with some cool pictures, make five hundred copies, staple each, and sell them to every woman you do and don't know for a buck a pop.

Bam, everybody profits.

All these situations are now in context and they now make sense.

We are able to share knowledge, history, experiences, recipes, and remedies like our motherkin could not. As more and more women communicate, a new language and sense of community evolves. Equipped with language, a means of communication, and the desire to talk to one another, our voices, histories, and dreams whirling-dervish into regenerative cuntpower.

The story of you gives the life of me personal power in my body, my eating and health habits, and my political, spiritual, emotional, and ethnic beliefs.

Without you, I am ignorant, oppressed, alone.

Without you, I am powerless.

As we all know, up to this point American women have tended to rely upon methods of birth control founded upon a body of knowledge created by men.

This holds true, even after it's religiously proven to us like water torture on our foreheads from the cradle to the grave: men have a vested *financial* interest in controlling our lives, histories, and bodies. Men dearly love, cherish, and respect women until death do us part as long as we're:

consumer	counselor
wife	nag
teacher	nurse
helper	threeholestopenetrate
bitch	cook
lover	mother
accountant	daughter
housekeeper	prey
orphan	Whore.
punching bag	

Tangle, tangle, tangle, mother, grandmother, sister.

We been told for centuries, he's father, lover, husband, brother, son and really, truly does have our best interests in mind.

Pa-shaw.

"Our best interests" are naturally, unquestionably predefined by a social power structure that, at the turn of the twentieth century, witnessed an ad for Lysol with a recipe for douching to keep wives from experiencing "embarrassing odors" during intimate moments with their husbands.

Nowadays, most women who think about this kind of stuff—and have the opportunity—matronize the offices of women healthcare providers. Women go to male gynecologists—I can only imagine—because it's a family tradition or there's no better option. For me, personally, anyone who didn't have a cunt and tried to look at my cunt in an exam room would get a silly slap upside the head with a cold speculum.

I know women *do* choose to go to male doctors because I see the names of these doctors in the yellow pages: Richard, Ted, Michael, James, Peter. I can only assume this means there is a demand for male gynecologists.

I don't know any women who go to male doctors, though.

A lot of women have decided that the whole way we interpret healing in our culture is based entirely on a male construct. These women go to women naturopaths who rely on healing straight from Big Mom's Bosom.

Her thuja oil, for instance—with the expertise of a healthcare provider—can cure chlamydia. Her red raspberry leaf tea tones and strengthens the uterus. Her acidophilus bacteria in yogurt cures yeast infections by restoring the natural acidity of your cunt.

And then there is you.

You who are a child of the universe. Whether or not it is clear to you, you came from Big Mom's Bosom too. Birth control and health care are very much integral aspects of your spirituality, self-esteem, and power. Not only do you have vast wonders of communication at your beck and call but also Big Mom provided you with a mind and a will—the most omnipotent panaceas on the planet—to wield.

The naturopath I mentioned earlier asks new patients to document everything they eat for a week and fully detail personal and family medical histories. On the first visit, she conducts an interview to get the psychological and emotional context before doing *any* physical examination. She procures a whole picture of what's going on before ever touching someone's body. You know: holistic medicine.

This lady taught me a lot.

We learn to respect everything our doctor tells us. Doctor knows best. Perhaps. But the doctor learned about healing in a destructive school of thought. The doctor learned to isolate and napalm physical ailments. Vicariously, through the doctor, we too learn to deal with our bodies and health destructively.

We kill headaches with aspirin, which also weakens immunity to headaches.

Meditation and yoga soothe the stress that causes headaches, while a plethora of herbal teas calm the spirit.

We kill infection with antibiotics, which also weaken immunity to infection.

Keeping cuts clean and drinking lots of fresh water to flush out the system make topical infection a nonissue. Internal infection and viruses are nipped with garlic, witch hazel, cayenne pepper, echinacea, goldenseal, chaparral. These and many other plant substances feed the immune system, which fights its own battles.

Accessing Big Mom's resources, while passionately communicating and accepting your power to heal yourself, is constructive-assed, cuntlovin' medicine.

There are two basic, commonly accepted models of birth control. Both are, to greater or lesser degrees, based on the destructive model of "health care":

1. Chemical manipulation of the hormones
2. Barriers placed between the os (opening of the cervix) and sperm

I will suggest a third method of birth control, based on a philosophy intrinsic to a cuntlovin' woman's life.

Chemicals, i.e., Napalming

Three unplanned pregnancies be damned, I'm gonna go for broke here and assert I'd be hard pressed to come up with more systematic and refined forms of chemically induced oppression than synthetic hormonal birth control products. Birth control pills, Depo-Provera, and Norplant all function in pretty much the same way—they control a woman's reproductive cycle by manipulating hormones.

Depo-Provera and Norplant were introduced on the market in the 1990s. It has come to light in recent years that the side effects of hormonal implants are far-reaching and extremely detrimental. Unfortunately, decades will pass before the pernicious effects of these "new developments" are firmly established.

Because the pill is the oldest of the three, more is known about its insidious effects on a woman's body. The pill diminishes sexual desire; causes undue weight gain through laboratory-generated manipulation of the hormones;

obstructs the natural menstrual cycle and flow; represses ovulation; causes heart problems, irritability, and migraines; has been linked, unlinked, relinked to cancer; and synthetically dictates one's entire physical agenda. The pill creates a constant state of false pregnancy. Women on the pill do not have a natural menstrual cycle. Bleeding occurs when placebo pills instigate a false period.

The reproductive cycles of women on the pill are choreographed and maintained by Ortho-Novum factories.

Depo-Provera and Norplant are simply newer products of an industry that profits from control over women's lives. Any "developments" in the birth control industry will always reflect a cavalier attitude toward our bodies.

A lovely woman named Marcy Bloom, the director of Aradia Women's Health Center in Seattle, Washington, once smoothly countered my rant against the pill. Ms. Bloom's is a very thoughtful and judicious perspective on the issue:

What you say about the pill is true. However, it is the most successful method of birth control as well—that's the Catch-22. For some women, the pill is the only method that works, or the only one they're willing to use because either they don't want to touch their bodies, or their lover is very resistant to using condoms. Sometimes the pill is the only psychosocial method a woman is willing to use, because all other methods require a woman to touch herself.

First off, let's get the Condom Matter behind us.

A gentleman who doesn't have the physical and/or emotional sensitivity to use condoms *couldn't possibly* possess the self-confidence required to procure the satisfying sounds of pleasure from the depth of a woman's being, via the endlessness of her cunt.

At least not with his dick.

Insecurity about a physical lack of sensitivity in their bodies overrides their lover's mental and physical health. Cro-Magnon sociopsychological beliefs (i.e., "Women are the ones who get pregnant—they should deal with birth control.") also contribute to this ignorance.

This says nothing about what kind of dumbass would completely disregard the threat and reality of HIV.

Men who refuse to use condoms do not deserve to be fucked by anyone but other men who refuse to use condoms.

Taking *any* hormonal birth control product because we don't want to touch our bodies beats all our much-needed revolutionary, resurrectionary cuntlovin' synapses into hibernation 'n submission. This makes it difficult for a woman to just plain and simple love being a woman. By encouraging a physical aversion to our own bodies, the pill only adds to the unspeakably large number of ladies inclined toward cunthatred presently existing within the body of womankind.

Loving, knowing, and respecting our bodies is a powerful and invincible act of rebellion in this society. This fundamental, entirely crucial act is not possible while we buy in to destructive philosophies at the root of hormonal birth control products.

I've had countless discussions with birth control advocates who regard synthetic hormones as a right that allows us freedom.

What is the frame of reference we draw upon to reach this conclusion? Are we not basing this on the experiences of our ancestors who were dicked around, relatively speaking, no more and no less than we are to this day but who had access to quite a bit less information?

The only reason hormonal birth control products are considered a "right" is because women haven't yet decided to construct an entirely woman-based frame of reference with all of the information our ancestors could not communicate to each other through the Internet, zines, books, periodicals, shows, conventions, sporting events, festivals, and fax machines.

The main freedom involved in using hormonal birth control is freedom from thinking about—and ultimately facing—our reproductive power. This "freedom" essentially results in an ignorance of our bodies that costs us, individually and collectively, dear, dear, dearly. We cannot love ourselves if we do not know ourselves.

There is bliss, but no freedom, in ignorance.

We have the means to educate ourselves and rely wholly upon rights and freedoms that totally jibe with the rhythm of womankind in every way. If you are on hormonal birth control products, you *cannot* educate yourself about your body because *your body is not under your own Goddess-given jurisdiction.*

I return to the same argument I offered about using sea sponges, rags, the Keeper, and Blood Towels. We've learned to place patriarchal rhetoric at the nexus of our thoughts. We're all reared in a society where the real, honest-to-Goddess power of women intimidates just about everybody. Especially people who, historically and futuristically, have not a hope in hell of seeing blood course out from 'tween their legs or of giving birth to members of the human race.

What it boils down to is this: if it didn't *originate* with women or the Goddess, if it does not *spiritually, emotionally, physically, psychologically, and financially benefit* women, it does not serve women.

So fucken chuck it.

Barriers (Isolation)

Women-initiated barrier methods—such as the diaphragm, cervical cap, and various spermicide-soaked sponges—do not eclipse a woman's cycle. A woman using barrier methods ovulates and bleeds. Barrier methods require physical contact with one's cunt, and that's *always* a good thing.

I, personally, have not had good experiences with barrier methods when I've been sexually active with men, which is neither here nor there.

Barrier methods have been used for thousands of years. Lemon halves and sponges or mosses soaked in spermicidal herbs were used by some of our greatest grandmas.

Mass-produced cervical caps were around in the 1930s, and home-jobbies were used in many ancient cultures.

The sole reason I am negatively disposed toward the use of barrier methods is that the industry that creates them is not run by women.

If it were run by women, the following story just could not, ever, happen.

Once upon a time, there was something called the IUD. This stands for intrauterine device. The IUD was implanted in women's uteruses and inhibited the natural growth and shedding of the uterine lining. It made the uterus an inhospitable place for an egg. These IUDs caused uterine cancer, infertility, and—when they didn't cause death—tore the insides of many women's bodies asunder.

After wreaking havoc on hundreds of thousands of American women's uteruses and lives, an IUD called the Dalkon Shield was finally taken off the market in 1976. This was not an act of graciousness on the part of A. H. Robins (the corporation responsible for the Dalkon Shield). It was removed from the American market because six hundred lawsuits were pending against the company. These six hundred were but a spit in the ocean compared to the 306,931 lawsuits filed by 1986. And these three hundred thousand—plus lawsuits represented a mere 8 percent of women potentially harmed by the device (Bloss, Cornell, Moon, and Tomsich 1997).

Meanwhile, what do you do with 697,000 surplus IUDs? The instruments of terror were sold to USAID (United States Agency for International Development). These 697,000 IUDs were then "distributed"—willingly or not, I couldn't venture to say—to women in impoverished nations, who, unlike American women, did not have the relative luxury of a legal system (Raymond 1993, 15).

Condoms are a barrier method of birth control I advocate for three reasons: they were designed by and for men, they work, and they are proven to reduce the risk of acquiring HIV.

I've never heard of condoms that make men's dicks shrivel off their bodies. I assert that this is a calibrated reflection of who produces what for whom.

If a collective of women designed a method of barrier birth control, produced it in a women-run company, and ran advertisements depicting positive images of cuntlovin' women from all ethnicities and walks of life in women-owned mediums, I would jauntily support it.

At present, however, there is no such method of birth control, and I do not trust the birth control industry. I do not believe the needs of women are taken into consideration at all. I do not like knowing a multi-billion-dollar corporation that inherently cannot regard our bodies as holy-rhythmic gets all its money from us.

The birth control industry is a Big Business. We are mere consumers in this context. Our bank accounts are much, much, much more important than our bodies. If birth control is indeed "the womenfolk's responsibility," let's seize our responsibility with vigor, shall we.

Cuntlovin' Ovulation Alert

In no way do I claim to be a health practitioner.

I am a woman and a writer who has thought about and experimented with the workings of her cunt with passion and vigor.

When you start teaching yourself about your cunt, you get a rhythm going. It is your rhythm and only you understand it 100 percent. When you breathe deeply and stay with this rhythm in your body, you will notice it encompasses every aspect of your life.

What I am about to discuss is not "the rhythm method." The objective here is not to understand the rhythm of your ovulatory cycle. The objective is to tap into the rhythm of your ovulatory cycle as a means of perceiving a broader rhythm inside yourself that shows you how powerful you are every day of your life.

Long before physicians started "curing" people with charming procedures like putting leeches all over their bodies, birth control was a normal part of life. There are as many forms of birth control as there are cultures in the world. It wasn't until popes and missionaries preached the sinfulness of sex outside of reproductive purposes for a couple hundred years that people started distrusting their medicinal regimes. Lots of people still practice their own kind of reproductive medicine, only now it's invalidated and called "voodoo," "black magic," or "folk medicine."

The big problem today with forms of birth control founded in the people, the plants, and the moon is that no one trusts them. They all completely depend on the individual woman and her community to be effective.

Few in our society have trusted the individual woman and her community to take absolute control. En masse, women haven't trusted ourselves or subsequently been trusted for over two thousand years.

The nice thing, though, is everything's changing. It's not *impossible* for small groups of women all over the nation to learn about our cunts and trust each other together. In the mite of a moment, we can get online. We can post what we know and find what we're looking for. We can sit in a café with our three best friends and discuss our erotic fantasies. We can purchase books that tell us all about our cervix.

Assuredly, the best place to start learning and trusting is the place from which you entered into this world.

Your Cervix: Axis and Ally

Everything your uterus produces—blood, eggs, babies, and a variety of miraculous secretions—eventually passes through your cervix before leaving your body.

Your cervix is the doorway of humanity. Have you ever seen it? If you haven't, you dang well should. Viewing your cervix will not be a disappointing experience, I promise on a stack of holy *Beloved*s by Toni Morrison.

Go to your local women's health clinic with probably a five- or ten-dollar bill. Ask for a small, medium, or large plastic speculum, and hand the nice health clinic lady the five or ten dollars. Along with the speculum, ask her to give you an instruction sheet. If you live in one of the more woman-negative states like Utah, Florida, Texas, or Mississippi, you may need to purchase a plastic speculum through the mail.

Read the instructions that come with your speculum. If you're lucky enough to have a supportive women's clinic in your community, ask any questions you may have before leaving. If you buy a speculum through the mail, either call the company you ordered it from, or call the woman-positive health clinic nearest you by referring to the appendix in *A New View of a Woman's Body*, a book I vehemently urge you to purchase.

With your speculum, you can further investigate and learn of your wondrous cunt. Besides the speculum, you will need a flashlight, possibly some lube, a hand-held mirror, and maybe some gentle patience. Practice opening and closing the spec a few times before inserting. Keep in mind that speculums were not designed for self-exams. It can be frustrating trying to get that thing to work right the first one or nine times, but try to relax. Tight cunt muscles don't facilitate this maneuver.

To insert a speculum: lie down with some pillows under the small of your back. Spread them legs. Hold your cunt lips apart with two fingers of one hand. Insert the speculum sideways, longest handle facing your body. If things are parched down there, employ the lube, but use it sparingly. One of the main objectives here is to be able to see your juices in their natural element. Ya won't be able to distinguish the lube from the juice if you lay it on too thick. Once you get the speculum in about halfway, turn it so it lies flat. Don't open it up when it's sideways. Gently insert it on in to the hilt and open it up. Wheee! There's a little lock mechanism on these things; click it into place when you get it opened as wide as you can.

Mind, this is not *the most comfortable* sensation in the world, but it shouldn't hurt at all (unless you have an infection or open sores or something) so long as you don't pinch any o' that tender skin as you open the speculum. However, if you're not used to having things in your cunt, especially hard, plastic things, you may experience more discomfort at first. Keep trying. Remember to relax.

Once the speculum is in, opened, and locked, grab that flashlight and mirror. If you can't see your cervix, either you have a long cunt canal or a shy cervix. For the former scenario, try the exam again just before, right after, or on the lightest day of your period. This is when your cervix is most visible. For the latter, bear down like you do when taking a shit. That cervix will overcome its stage fright in a matter of seconds. If lots of flesh is bulging around the speculum, you probably need a larger size.

Take a good long gander. Note the shape, color, and texture of your cervix. It changes appearance according to where you are in your cycle. If your cervix looks kinda bluish or is indeed bright blue, it's time for a pregnancy test. If you're ovulating, you may see mucus, your cervix will be pulled higher up, it may be softer and larger than usual, and the os may be open slightly. The os looks like a Q-tip wouldn't pass through it, but it is altogether capable of dilating to accommodate the head and shoulders of a new human being.

Cuntjuices: Know Your Ambrosia

Look, touch, smell, and taste your cuntjuices. *Never* gross out on tasting yourself. You are an acquired taste. Acquire it. You swallow your spit without a qualm millions of times each week. It's filthy in comparison to your delectable cuntjuices.

This is another very good way of getting a rhythm going. You taste different when you're about to bleed than when you're ovulating, and it's completely up to you to make distinctions.

A woman's body releases an egg once a month. This egg sits around in your uterus, waiting for some sperm to show up. It is not stupid. After twelve to twenty-four hours, it figures no sperm's gonna take it on a hot date and it makes an exit without further ado.

Sperm can live in your body anywhere from seventy-two hours to five days. What this means is, if some sperm finds its way into your uterus up to *one working week* before your body releases its egg, you *can, feasibly,* get pregnant.

When an egg is present, you are ovulating. Generally, not always, but *generally,* a woman ovulates halfway through her menstrual cycle. Therefore, if you had your period when the moon was new, then there's a good chance you'll ovulate when the moon is full.

Another indication that you're ovulating is a slight twinge of pain in your lower abdomen. It doesn't feel like a menstrual cramp; it's more of a tight, pinched-nerve-type pain. If you masturbate, you can sometimes feel it after you come.

Also, I should probably add that when you are ovulating, you will often become insanely horny. You may feel the urge to couple with the kitchen-table leg, though I wouldn't necessarily take this as an ovulatory symptom.

The *most* reliable way to tell when you are ovulating is by intimately familiarizing yourself with the posh setting of your cunt by interpreting messages from your cervix.

Stick your finger—middle finger's best—up your cunt, swipe it around and around your cervix, being careful not to neglect the underside, where secretions like to settle. If you are ovulating you will find a nice blob of snot on your finger. There's no seemly way to describe this. It's snot, quite unmistakably, plain and simple, snot. It has no odor or color, it's just clear snot, and as such tastes a little salty. This snot's function is to create a warm, cushiony thoroughfare for sperm to travel to your egg.

The unique characteristics of ovulation snots are created by a rise in the hormone estrogen. Before you ovulate, the discharge on your finger is milky and creamy. Right after you ovulate, when you stick your finger up your cunt, you'll find sticky, tacky, maybe curdy, white stuff. If the sticky white stuff is there, with either a little snot mixed in or no snot at all, figure you just ovulated. Estrogen decreases at the approach of your period and progesterone rises, making your cunt dry up a tad.

As you get used to checking your cuntstuff, you'll be able to recognize what's what.

Now, if you're gonna be making expeditions in your cunt with your fingers, *keep those fingernails clipped and wash your hands*! If anybody else is of the mind to explore your cuntal regions with their digits, make goddamn sure they keep their nails clipped and hands clean too. Many minor infections are attributed to the hairline lesions caused by fingernail scratches. If you're prone to these minor infections, examine your lover's fingernails and hand-washing habits.

I've made it my business to peruse my cuntjuices once or twice every week when I'm not bleeding. The best time to do this is while taking a shower, when my hands are already quite clean and I'm already quite naked. I've incorporated this investigation into my shower ritual, so on any given week, I know exactly where I am in my cycle. When you make knowing your cunt's cycle an important part of your *normal* bathroom regime, it becomes rote.

After a few months of familiarizing yourself with your snots and milky or curdy or tacky white stuffs, ask yourself this question: "How can I get with child if I know exactly when I am fertile and, therefore, take precautionary measures?" Precautionary methods may involve the use of condoms, engaging in sexual activities that do not involve dick 'n cunt intercourse, or investigating erotic fantasies based on titillation and masturbation.

Cuntlovin' Ovulation Alert is of obvious benefit to women who *want* to get pregnant. It's also a divine service for women who aren't at all preoccupied with the possibility of conception. Your cunt's rhythm affects perspective, mood, and creative and erotic expression. What is day-to-day life but perspective, mood, and creative and erotic expression? Knowing and grooving with your cunt is *such* a huge assistance in these matters.

Cuntlovin' Ovulation Alert furthermore helps you:

1. Plan and navigate your way through any given week.
2. Anticipate and deflect negative interactions with people you care about.
3. Love yourself, which in turn effects positive changes for future generations of women. Counting you, that's one more cuntlovin' woman in the world who is contributing to an environment of cuntlove.

Cuntlovin' Ovulation Alert dictates compassion and respect for all women.

Once you get to the point where you anticipate what juices your cervix is letting loose, emotional and psychological rhythms inside you become more lucid.

After that, there's no stopping you.

You rule.

We are at the juncture of examining the repercussions of truly, candidly understanding our cunts.

Let's say now you've made some serious decisions about your body. Let's say you've developed a keen interest in reigning at the helm of your body's rhythm. Optimally, let's say you're open to falling in love with yourself in a way you only remotely considered in the past.

According to my little theory, a highly developed sense of compassion for your physical self has a rippling effect in the subconscious. It leads to the development of a psychic sense of compassion for everyone with a cunt. Once you understand your personal rhythm, you intuitively connect yourself with all the people who share a similar rhythm.

These people are womankind.

Which leads us to honoring the single most excoriated group of women in the world.

Not virgins.

Not mothers.

One more guess.

Whores

I am thankful to have been blessed with a fairly well-developed sense of entitlement during the composition of every chapter in *Cunt*.

Except this one.

This one's been difficult.

I've never *been* a Whore.

I've read about and thought about and talked to Whores. As a woman living in this society, I'm *consistently reminded* I am a *potential* Whore whenever a man is not escorting me, which is rather most of the time. None of this, however, is the same as consciously *experiencing* Whoredom firsthand. If I were a *truly* resourceful and courageous individual, I would've learned how to be a Whore for subsistence while I wrote this book. Alas, I am an impractical chickenshit in this regard.

Whores are a very important part of *Cunt*. Every time I've tried to explain why, though, I've met this insecurity inside myself. It is a very cranky insecurity that says stuff like, "You don't know what it's like to *be* a Whore, you dang fool. Can't base no chapter on sneaky suspicions."

But Whoredom is a massive part of our history and power as women. When fully instructed in the art of sacred sexual power, Whores are the people who can teach us all the stuff we grow up not learning about sexuality, our bodies, and our innate sexual power. Our cultural ignorance and intolerance of Whores keep Whores from realizing the full potential of Whoredom. It likewise robs women and men of Teachers who can help us understand women's sexual power.

Whores were a central part of religion, spirituality, and everyday life in times when the Goddess—a *truly* sexual being—was overtly worshipped. It took a lot of work, study, devotion, and commitment to become one of the Goddess's sexual priestesses. People were free to visit the temples of Whores, and did so to learn, to love, to open up physically, to heal.

I ruminated over this chapter for a long time and prayed the Goddess would help me. Like always, She came through. This time She manifested Herself in a woman named Carol Queen, a writer, sex activist, and Whore.

You won't find Carol Queen in the acknowledgments section because I know people don't always read the praises in books, and I want everyone to know:

Carol Queen fucking *rules.*

Woman, you saved my ass and

I thank you

from the bottom of my heart.

Ms. Queen's book, *Real Live Nude Girl,* published in 1997 by Cleis Press, casts resplendent light on the history of sacred Whoredom. Carol Queen reveals that the depravity surrounding Whoredom is not based on the fact that Whoredom exists, but rather it is based on the *perception* of Whoredom's existence.

> My "ardent worshippers" and I have no temple today in which to perform a dance that sometimes seems more profane than sacred. In a culture that does not worship the Goddess any longer, these are degenerate times indeed, but not because a once-holy act is still being negotiated in hotel suites, in massage parlors, on city streets. In fact, if prostitution is ever eradicated, it will be a signal that Christianity's murder of Eros is complete, the Goddess's rule completely overturned. Perhaps most prostitutes today are unaware that their profession has a sacred history, and doubtless most clients would define what they do with us as something other than worship. But I believe that an echo of the old relationship, when he was the seeker and she was the Source, [is] still present when money changes hands today. (Queen 1997, 190)

It would be *so wonderful* to visit a Sacred Whore temple. Kick down some cash to mix with and undulate in the ol' Goddess's love juices for a while.

Damn, I'm so seethingly jealous of those olden time people.

I daresay the loss of our sacred sexual temples grieves the heart of Carol Queen threefold.

Whoredom has existed, in various guises, for thousands and thousands of years. A main artery of the Goddess's life force, it is too powerful to annihilate.

Whoredom has been successfully vilified.

Whoredom is presently accepted as a very, very bad thing, while its history debases this idea beyond all reckoning.

Sound like any old word that is the title to a book you've been reading lately?

In our present mode of collective consciousness, a Whore is simply a person who exchanges sex for financial resources.

I accept this to be true, but only if it's recognized as one *part* of a much broader cultural-financial order that women participate in for survival. There is no difference between a woman who marries a very powerful man because it is the only way she is guaranteed a "place" in society and a streetwalker who's never known the illusion of a "guarantee."

Some women opt to be Whores because procuring semen from men's bodies is a bona fide way to make a living in a society where we are viewed as highly expendable citizens.

Ms. Streetwalker exchanges womanly wiles for subsistence.

Some women—such as the late Princess Diana, who once referred to herself as the highest-paid prostitute in the world— don't actually *opt* to be Whores but realize nonetheless that that is exactly what they are.

Ms. Powerwife exchanges womanly wiles for a fancy house in the hills.

In this way of thinking, the issue is *class* rather than Whoredom.

Hugh Grant and Eddie Murphy could lecture on this subject.

Sacred Whore temples flourished in ancient India, the Middle East, Africa, Europe, the Americas, and Asia. The word *whore* was a title, used in much the way our word *reverend* is employed today. *Whore* is associated with many words, including husband, hussy, *puta* (Spanish for "whore"—in Vedic literature, *puta* means "pure" or "holy"), *ghazye* (Egyptian), *devadasi* (Sanskrit), *horae* (Greek), and *hor* (Hebrew). Whore-priestesses were revered because they taught "a combination of mother-love, tenderness, comfort, mystical enlightenment and sex." (Walker 1983, 820)

Mary Magdalene was a Whore, and Jesus dug her because she taught him the most sacred thing a man can ever hope to learn in his lifetime: how to fuck. Stud that he was, Jesus knew to humble himself to this woman.

I imagine the sex was spectacular.

Let's interpret the notion of Jesus visiting a Whore in a cuntlovin' way. Let's pretend Jesus and his Apostle frat brothers didn't visit Mary Magdalene after a hard night tossing off forty-ouncers and tipping cows in the holy land.

From all the things I've heard about Jesus, he sounds like a pretty decent sort. He looks nice in most of his pictures. You can *tell* Adolf Hitler and George Washington were dickheads just by looking at them. Looking at Jesus, he seems cool. By and large, Jesus evidently had a lot of love and compassion swimming around his heart. He had a pretty huge impact in certain parts of the world, yet left it when he was only thirty-two. You gotta figure Jesus didn't waste a lot of time dinking around. Even if he *did* dink around, he doesn't seem like the kind of guy who'd take an impersonal toss in the hay for a budgeted degree of arousal.

I seriously doubt Jesus perceived Mary Magdalene as anything less than an esteemed Teacher. In Jesus's time, Whores were still prophets of sexual power. They taught people how the physical body is a conduit of energy. If Jesus was able to manifest the love in his heart in all the physical actions the bible alleges, Mary Magdalene was certainly one of the people in his life responsible for helping him figure out how to do it.

Though Whores were integral and respected in many times and places, the fear and/or awe of female sexuality certainly rivals Whoredom in age.

I don't know if that big dyke Lilith was a Whore or not, but she was certainly too sexually aggro for Adam's and God's liking:

> Hebraic tradition said Adam married Lilith because he grew
> tired of coupling with beasts, a common custom of Middle-
> Eastern herdsmen, though the Old Testament declared it

a sin (Deuteronomy 27:21). Adam tried to force Lilith to lie beneath him in the "missionary position" favored by male-dominant societies. Moslems were so insistent on the male-superior sexual position that they said, "Accursed be the man who maketh women heaven and himself earth." Catholic authorities said any sexual position other than the male-superior one is sinful. But Lilith was neither a Moslem nor a Catholic. She sneered at Adam's sexual crudity, cursed him, and flew away to make her home by the Red Sea.

God sent angels to fetch Lilith back, but she cursed them too, ignored God's command, and spent her time coupling with "demons" (whose lovemaking evidently pleased her better) and giving birth to a hundred children every day. So God had to produce Eve as Lilith's more docile replacement. . . . The story of Lilith disappeared from the canonical Bible, but her daughters the *lilim* haunted men for over a thousand years. Well into the Middle Ages, the Jews were still manufacturing amulets to keep away the *lilim,* who were lustful she-demons given to copulating with men in their dreams, causing nocturnal emissions. Naturally, the *lilim* squatted on top of their victims in the position favored by ancient matriarchs. (Walker 1983, 541–542)

The *lilim* that haunted men in their dreams were manifestations of a growing terror of female sexuality. In our society, this fear has gone past fruition and is presently rotting.

I feel pretty cheated about Whores for a number of reasons:

1. Whores generally subsist within men's domain, under conditions men have formulated for the past odd thousand years, and are largely inaccessible to women.
2. Most Whores are completely unaware of how important they are to society, and subsequently do not have the opportunity to learn how to be all-compassionate, all-loving, all-giving, and all-receiving incarnations of the Goddess.
3. I've never been with a Whore because any Whore who knows she's one of the Goddess's priestesses would cost my entire disposable income for six months.

I do, however, have a frame of reference because I know what it is like to be in the arms of the Goddess.

One time I got blessed by this Goddess incarnation named Ammachi. She's not a Whore, but she's by far the closest personification of an olden time sacred temple priestess I've ever personally encountered.

Ammachi is a woman from India who comes to America and has these ashram things. The first time I went to her ashram thing, I had no idea what it was about. I saw a bunch of mostly white people dressed in white clothes who bugged me with their "Oh, I am so very holy and drink herbal tea constantly" vibration.

But the music was amazing.

Ammachi sat in the front of the room on a bunch of pillows. Musicians, attendants, children, and flowers surrounded her. Thousands of flowers, like when Princess Diana died. She sat there with her eyes closed and chanted. Probably, she was meditating. Wearing a flowing white sari, she was covered with chiffon, silk, everything soft and whispery. I figured she understood the concept of an ashram far better than I, so I did the same as her. Closed my eyes, sat and listened.

This lasted a long time, but like in a dream, I don't know how many minutes and hours passed.

Then there were the rustling sounds of people standing up. I opened my eyes. Everyone was forming a double-file line that led to Ammachi.

My friends told me she was gonna bless people, so we queued up. The line was very, very long, snaking throughout the entire large building we were in. If it had been a line at the post office that I *absolutely had to stand in* for some reason or another, I woulda sold my soul to the person in front to give me cuts. But this line was different. The music and nice quiet felt good. Being blessed by an incarnation of the Goddess is also much more alluring than overnighting IRS forms.

Before I knew it, I was next.

An attendant led me to her and kinda helped me kneel down right. Ammachi seized me gently—if you can imagine that—and pulled me into her lap. She cradled me, murmuring sweet chanting sounds into my ear. Her body engulfed mine and I relaxed—almost melted—into her. My face buried in her shoulder and neck, I breathed in her smell.

This is when I really, truly started to freak on the wonder of Ammachi. After holding hundreds of people in this manner, you would think she'd start to kinda stink. I was nowhere near the beginning of the line. The sun set and went down, down, down to Australia while I stood in that line. A lot of people were in her arms before me, but the woman smelled like flowers. Not perfumey at all. Like if you covered every inch of your bedroom floor with freshly cut bouquets of jasmine, gardenia, roses, hyacinths, carnations, sweet peas, and freesia is what she smelled like. And this smell wasn't coming from the flowers around her; it exuded from her skin, the fabrics of her sari and veils. It filled my whole body, permeated my pores. Her smell made me so giddy the attendant had to help me stand back up again. She stared deeply into my eyes and pressed flower petals and chocolate kisses into my hand.

I stumbled away like a drunk.

Like I just had one 'dem orgasms to raise the dead.

Lordisa.

For a whole week afterward, my entire apartment smelled like Ammachi. Everywhere I went, I smelled her smell. Walking down the street with one of my friends, the smell of Ammachi would assail me. I'd go, "*Damn*, do you smell that?" And my friend'd go, "Car exhaust? What?"

As Ammachi's smell faded from my life, I started thinking about what happened when she blessed me.

It was the first time in my life I felt *loved*. Physically, emotionally, psychically, spiritually, *deeply loved* from the epidermis
of my skin that featured a couple of ugly zits to the core of my
heart that is still traumatized by the death of my brother, abortions, mean-spirited lovergirls, and other nasty hurts. It is a
consciousness-broadening freak-out to feel love in this way.

"What," I wondered, "is the difference between Ammachi
and a Whore?" Ammachi gave me unconditional love, no questions asked. She healed me and helped me understand more
about love. I was one of many people cradled in her embrace
that day. Ammachi needs money to keep spreading her love,
and I bought plenty of Ammachi paraphernalia to support her.

She doesn't offer erotic love to people, but any cuntlovin'
Whore will tell ya, eroticism is just one *part* of love.

After Ammachi blessed me, after her flower smell took
over my life for a week, after I sat down and thought about it
long and hard, I realized her gift. She clues people in on what
love really, really is. That way, it's easier to know what love
really, really isn't. She helps people identify love so we can call
it into our lives. In the grand panorama of my life, I was in
Ammachi's world, in Ammachi's arms, for mere moments.
Those moments changed me forever.

This is some serious-assed power founded in cuntlove.

The nemesis of this power is sexual cuntfear. One of the many,
many, many casualties of our culture's negative sexual fear was
executed in 2002.

Aileen Wuornos was an ex-Whore put to death in Florida. She murdered seven men. She is the only "serial killer" ever to plead self-defense.

Not long after Ms. Wuornos walked through the prison doors, I attended Diamanda Galás's performance of a vocal composition entitled *Schrei X.* Ms. Galás's three-and-a-half-octave range left me reeling in pain. Her haunting, stunning presence shattered all my fear.

I interviewed her the next day and asked, "What inspired *Schrei X?*"

Well, one thing was Aileen Wuornos. It's a long story. There's a documentary out called *The Selling of a Serial Killer* about Aileen Wuornos. It's a very, very interesting movie. She's a real hero of mine because without taking a predatory stance, you're fucked. In her case, literally.

If you're a prostitute and somebody rapes you, it's just fucken a shitty feeling. Aileen would go through the sex part and then the John would want to do something else, like fuck her up the ass and put alcohol up her ass. She got to where she went over the edge and said, "No more." She reached Critical Mass, said *No,* and started killing people who were abusing her. And because she was seen as being predatory, she got the death penalty. She's not seen as somebody who has the law on her side for the job that she was doing. A job that is, very effectively, if not legalized, condoned, as long as she pays out the cops. She didn't *have* any protection and it got to where she had to protect herself. So she protected herself and went to prison. As a woman, she's obviously powerless, but she's *really* powerless. A lesbian prostitute is seen as totally powerless trash.

The silence at the end of *Schrei X* is the silence that her dumbfuck lawyers sang to her because she was found guilty. Guilty, guilty, guilty.

Because Ms. Wuornos was perceived as being "totally powerless trash," because Ms. Wuornos lived in an exceptionally cuntfearing society, and because Ms. Wuornos's case yielded quite a bit of media interest, her "lawyer" seemed to have come to the conclusion that he could make a pretty penny selling her "story." *Especially* once his client was put to death. After watching *Aileen Wuornos: The Selling of a Serial Killer,* one is rather confronted with the idea that the people who one would traditionally expect to support Ms. Wuornos—namely, her attorneys—were plainly itching for her to be executed as a ferocious serial killer.

Which she is not.

Aileen Wuornos was an economically challenged woman who defended herself and who needed a decent, intelligent lawyer to get her the fuck out of jail.

But that's not what happened at all.

If I may be so bold, I would like to dedicate a portion of Kinnie Starr's song "Buttons" to every Whore who suffers under the influence of our sexually retarded, destructive culture:

and we could call it out when it doesn't suit us both
'cause
there's a magnitude of choices and a really big boat
and that big boat floats on a restless ocean
singing about the chances of protective devotion

for the girlfriend who stands on a street waiting on
a trick
some man demands that she lift her skirt quick
she's got a mother, a daughter and a lover
you tell me why she shouldn't have safe cover

'cause if the laws made sense
she would have a legal fence
to keep her clientele clean
and she could still pay the rent
she's got a mother, a daughter and a lover
you tell me why she shouldn't have safe cover

A few years ago a friend of mine was twenty-five cents short for bus fare. None of us had change either. She turned to a gentleman at the bus stop and asked if he could spare a quarter. He responded, "*What? What you* askin' me for a quarter for? Girl, you got a *goldmine* between your legs."

This sentence rang in my ears for years.

Cuntlovingly decontextualized, "a goldmine between your legs" is a wonderful sentiment. Like what you find at the end of the rainbow. The idea of women having a goldmine between our legs was so appealing to me, I wrote a little blues song about it:

you gotts a goldmine between your legs,
a goldmine between your legs,
no need to be poor in the u.s.a.
you gotts a goldmine between your legs.
honey why you givin' it away?
we all know them boys'll pay
equal pay for equal labor,
not only love but charge your neighbor.
no need to be poor in the u.s.a.
you gotts a goldmine between your legs.
my momma's broke and all alone
even though she made me a home.
if only she'd charged dear old dad
momma'd be drivin' a shiny jag.
no need to be poor in the u.s.a.
you gotts a goldmine between your legs
does hubby make more money, honey?
wouldn't it be really funny
if he didn't get no fine puss-say
unless he lined your coffers, hey hey.
you gotts a goldmine between your legs,
goldmine between your legs,
no need to be poor in the u.s.a.
you gotts a goldmine between your legs.

All ladies have the power to cash in on the goldmine between our legs. Not necessarily with the objective of financial security or spiritual fulfillment but for the most important reasons of all: future generations and our cuntlovin' selves.

On a less metaphorical level, nothing but good and fabulousness would come from erecting temples in honor of women's sexuality, filled with women and women-trained male Whores who offered us lessons in how to love and be loved.

Whores were in business back before the Red Sea ever thought about parting. Whores have no labor unions, no health insurance, no retirement fund, no unemployment insurance, and no legal rights. Because a chain is only as strong as its weakest link, the nonexistent rights and freedoms of women who understand the power of cunts conceivably more than any other group of women in our society bespeaks the constitution of the chain we ladies are dealing with here.

Is it a mere coincidence that women so specifically, physically associated with cunts have no rights in this culture?

Get out.

Without honoring Whores, we cannot truly understand and transcend the dynamics of violence, destruction, and ignorance fostered in our cuntfearing society. The fact that some women are considered "bad" is a puritanically based value judgment that reinforces a fatal division between women. Many women allow our lives and sexual expression to be dictated by the threat of being perceived as "Whores." Because of thinking like this, our society is brimming with women who have a hard time understanding, for instance, that Whores *can be and are* sexually assaulted.

"How," one might ask, "can a woman who accepts money for sex *be* raped?" Or perhaps, "What does a woman who puts herself in that position *expect*?"

The fact that either question is considered *at all plausible* reflects the self-defeating ignorance we ourselves perpetuate.

The measure of respect Whores receive is in direct proportion to the measure of respect all women receive. Until there is an established, respected place for Whores in this society, no woman will have an established, respected foundation of power.

There is no circumventing this.

Until there is a shift in consciousness about the potential of Whores, we will continue to live in a society that offers no formally acknowledged Teachers to awaken us to our power as sexual beings.

Ain't no getting 'round this one either.

The fact that Whores are no longer exalted and respected is very much a reflection of our culture's collective sexual retardation and fear of women's innate sexual power.

The aptly named Carol Queen is my personal prophet on Whoredom's future in our society.

To guide another person to orgasm, to hold and caress, to provide companionship and initiation to new forms of sex, to embody the Divine and embrace the seeker—these are healing and holy acts. Every prostitute can do these things, whether or not s/he understands their spiritual potential.

For us to see ourselves as sacred whores, for our clients to acknowledge the many facets of desire they bring to us, can be a powerful shift in consciousness. We show the face of the Goddess in a culture that has tried for millennia to break and denigrate Her, just as some today claim *we* are broken and denigrated. They are not correct, and the Goddess will not be broken. In our collective extraordinary experience we prostitutes have healed even those who do not honor us. Were the attack on us over, we could begin to heal the whole world.

After seven thousand years of oppression, I declare this the time to bring back our temple. (Queen 1997, 204–205)

Whoredom is a constant.

Perception fluctuates evermore.

I don't know about you, but I like the idea of respecting things that have been around a lot longer than me. I drive old cars and live in old houses. I gravitate toward old souls and listen to what old folks say. My favorite games—chess and backgammon—are old, old, old.

So you see, if I were to find Whoredom and the Perception Surrounding Whoredom at a garage sale, I'd definitely buy the Whoredom.

Even if it was dented up, needed a new paint job, and cost a coupla bucks more.

Orgasms from Cunts

Thanks to the perception surrounding Whoredom in our culture, no one teaches us how to fuck. We grow up and either figure it out for ourselves or settle into some habitual bog of sexual expression. Whatever.

Sexual expression must be made manifest in the physical world, *somehow*. Because it cannot be completely repressed, people sometimes hide stuff and get into weird things like eating shit. Sexual expression is a current of kinetic energy running through our bodies. It whirligigs up our cunts, charges through our entire being, and slam dances on out into the world back through our cunts.

Comin' our brains out.

Sometimes we holler 'n shake the windows in their panes.

Our cunts are powerhouses.

Cuntlovin' women who make the conscious decision to oversee the smooth operation of our powerhouses know all this.

One of my prized possessions is my 1965 *Random House Dictionary*. It lived in my parents' house before I. Though technically it belonged to everyone, I took it with me when I moved away. No one complained. Ever since I could read, that dictionary and I were inseparable.

When I was ten, I invited a boy I liked very much over to our house. We hung out in my room, mooning over each other and listening to records, until my father opened the door. He told the boy to go home and steered me by the elbow into the kitchen. There, at the table sat my mother and my dear friend, the *Random House Dictionary*. I sensed I was in deep shit but didn't know why. Mom had a serious look on her face and Dad seemed kinda pissed.

He said, "Look up the word 'reputation' and read it aloud."

My father, the devout atheist with the photographic memory who knew the *Encyclopaedia Britannica* by heart, had us quote from the dictionary in much the same manner as children in other families were required to quote from the Holy Book.

I read the definition for *reputation*:

rep·u·ta·tion (rep ye ta shen), n. 1. the estimation in which a person or thing is held, esp. by the community or the public generally: *a man of good reputation*. 2. favorable repute; good name: *to ruin one's reputation by misconduct*. 3. a favorable and publicly recognized name or standing for merit, achievement, etc.: *to build up a reputation*. 4. the estimation or name of being, having, having done, etc., something specified: *He has the reputation of being a shrewd businessman*.

I was thoroughly mystified, but after reading the definition of *reputation,* I felt decidedly ashamed.

Dirty.

My dad looked at me sternly and said, "You must *never* have boys in your room with the door closed."

"But we were listening to records," I argued. "I always close the door when my friends come over and we listen to records."

Mom: "Inga, it's very important not to get a bad reputation. Letting boys in your room and closing the door is one way to get a bad reputation."

Dad: "When your girlfriends come over, you can close the door, but when boys come over, keep it open."

Little did my parents know, it was me and my *girl* friends who engaged in sexual activity. At age ten I'd *remotely* entertained the notion of kissing boys, while at least three of my girlfriends and I had figured out how to make each other come by the time we were seven.

I've had the satisfaction of clueing my mom in, but I wish my dad were alive so I could say, "Yo, Pops, if you were *really* concerned with my chastity, you shouldn't have let certain friends spend the night with me, ya fool."

This isn't to preface my anger toward my parents for instilling in me shameful associations about my budding sexuality.

They Did the Best They Could.

I quelled any animosity I may have felt toward them the time I saw this real old Japanese print of two people having rapturous sex while their three children peacefully played a game with marbles at their feet. It is the epitome of the family-at-home-together picture. The kids don't care that the parents are fucking because fucking is as much a part of life as playing with marbles. They are completely unconcerned with what their parents are doing because *it's no big deal.* They're just fucking. The parents are playing a game that somebody taught them how to play. By the time those kids got big, they'd know fucking like they knew the soft, glassy chink of marbles colliding.

This was not my reality.

When my mother was pregnant with Nick, the youngest of her brood, she described how sexual intercourse created the magic of a baby in her belly.

"You and Dad have done that *four times*?" I asked, thoroughly disgusted.

People helped me out when it was time for me to walk and to ride a two-wheeler. Everyone I knew encouraged me to talk, use the toilet, sing, draw, swim, read, write, and make lots of friends.

I am very fortunate and grateful that I got helped out quite a bit.

There was this one—rather crucial—part of my being, however, that was pretty much left to the elements. I didn't get nearly as much encouragement learning how to express myself sexually as I did learning how to pronounce big words.

When I became sexually active with men, sex wasn't what I wanted *at all*. I wanted love and affection. I had fun having sex with my girlfriends, but it was just that: fun. Suddenly, it seemed one day I was supposed to reenact this with boys, and it just wasn't the same, spontaneous, jiveass, wanton fun. It's quite the bummer—not to mention life-threatening reality—that I didn't figure this out 'til after I'd tested sheets with surfers, vatos, punks, nerds, and a rather sadistic wrestler-chiropractor.

I didn't even really think about my formal, heterosexual awakening until years after the fact, when two of my hometown friends and I talked about it.

Why did we fuck those boys who never exactly made our clits pound out the "Bohemian Rhapsody" in the first place? What were we doing? Did we love ourselves at all? We certainly mustn't have, or we would *at the very least* have practiced safe sex. Why didn't we understand that our quest for love and affection could have easily killed us, and why didn't it? Was the Goddess magnanimously smiling upon the truly ignorant?

Toni Childs sings this really cool song I wish I had heard when I was seventeen. It's called "I Just Want Affection," and it's one of many beautiful songs on the album *The Woman's Boat*. This song taught me about the difference between erotic closeness and fucking.

Lots of girls grow up thinking the way to be loved is to fuck because our culture holds that affection is part and parcel to gettin' down. But in my mind, and in the minds of many, many cuntlovin' women I know, it is dimly related, but not the same thing at all.

Had I been left to my innate feminine wiles, I would've found a much safer and supportive way to procure affection, love, and acceptance, starting with myself.

The happy ending is, though, that through trial, error, forgiveness, and willingness to accept my ignorance, I learned that I'm the Cuntlovin' Ruler of My Sexual Universe.

Which leads to the story of Mademoiselle Precious, my cousin's daughter.

When Mademoiselle was seven, her parents granted her a premier waltz with independence: a visit to the city to stay with my musical love and me for a week one summer.

We were a little nervous. Neither of us had been around kids for long, parentless durations of time. Our home was not designed around the premise of a child's entertainment requirements. We didn't even have a television set. What if she was bored with our lives?

But we needn't have worried. Mlle. Precious loved all our friends. She loved going to the coffee shops, the river, everywhere we took her. She loved the Free Box in our apartment building and insisted on visiting it first thing every morning.

We all got along quite famously.

One day, my musical love said, "I've seen Mlle. Precious jiggling under her covers on the couch. Do you think her parents have talked to her about masturbating?"

I said I didn't know.

"Do you think you should talk to her about masturbating?"

I thought about how embarrassed I was that time my sister barged into the bathroom while I was whacking off with the shower massage. I also thought about how I probably wouldn't have had such a baggage-load of negative beliefs to dispel as an adult if just *one measly person* had told me it was fine and dandy to bandy my clit when I was a kid.

But, *jeez*, talking to Mlle. Precious about masturbating? What if it embarrassed her? What if it scarred her for life and it would be all my fault? What would I say?

I said I didn't know again.

It was quite the preoccupational quandary in my mind all day long.

We went to the river, played in the mud and the water.

When we came home, my musical love made phone calls and Mlle. Precious and I took a bubble bath. We were busy getting clean and shiny and, suddenly, it just jumped out of me.

I said, "Hey, Precious. I don't know if you ever do, but if you ever play with your wahchee [that's what her family calls cunts], I just want you to know it's okay."

She turned crimson, looked at me and then down at the water. "I don't do that. I don't play with my wahchee."

Shit.

Goddamn.

I spluttered, "I *know*. I mean, it doesn't matter. I just wanted to tell you that *if* you ever *did*, it's all right. Everybody plays with their wahchee, I swear to god."

She glared at me. "Well, *I* don't."

I hastily changed the subject and we splashed more bubbles to life.

After a few minutes, Mlle. Precious says, "Everybody plays with their wahchee?"

My heart leaped in my chest. Oh, how I smiled inside.

"Yeah. Everybody."

"Do you?"

"Yup."

"Does your musical love?"

"Yeah."

"My mom?"

"Probably. I mean, I would *imagine.* Just about everybody does, Precious. And it's *perfectly fine* if you do, too. Even if people tell you it's bad, they're just scared or stupid. It's not bad at all and *everybody* plays with their wahchee."

She laughed crazy, absolutely thrilled, and yelled, "Everybody plays with their wahchee?"

I screamed, "Everybody plays with their wahchee!"

We chanted, yelling at the top of our lungs, "Ev-ree-body plays with their wahh-chee! Ev-ree-body plays with their wahh-chee! Ev-ree-body plays with their wahh-chee!"

My musical love, still on the phone: "Jesus Christ! What are you two screaming about? What the hell's a wahchee?"

We laughed and splashed and chanted and flooded the whole bathroom.

I hope this experience has a positive effect on Mademoiselle Precious's sexuality. I hope she remembers all her life that there's not a problem in the world with her jilling off. However, even if our conversation gets lost in her shuffle of growing up, our little talk heartened *me* tremendously. I felt like I'd righted an inadvertent wrong committed against me when I was a little girl.

Felt the cards of karma riffle into place.

In my cosmology, Wilhelm Reich holds the distinction of being the only male psychoanalyst who could knock on my door and be invited in for tea.

Reich's books were banned in America for many years, while he himself was ostracized—even imprisoned—by the US government during McCarthy's scary reign.

He challenged the puritanical ideas about sexuality in our culture. In laywoman terms, Reich believed humans store emotions in our muscles. During orgasm, muscles in the body contract, then relax, thus releasing emotions. Reich asserted that all aspects of healthy human psychology are dependent upon one's sexual expression.

When you cry, laugh, or feel free as a bird after coming, it is partly because you just released a bunch of yucky crap that's been building up inside your body for days, months, years, possibly your entire lifetime.

A moment of epiphany on this subject occurred after six months of Reichian therapy. I was at the beach, thinking and watching the waves. The revelation assailed me quite suddenly, as revelations are wont to do: each wave is an orgasm. Sometimes they're big. Sometimes they're small. Sometimes they tear faces of cliff from the earth's surface. If the ocean did not have waves, it would be a big, salty lake. A lake is a still pool of water. Personally, I don't venture into water that doesn't move. Bored, malevolent monsters live in bodies of water that do not move.

When women function like the ocean, we live happy, healthy lives. Holding on to stuff that does not serve us in our present situation creates actual, physical blockages within our bodies.

Bored, malevolent monsters.

Which, on the individual level, manifest in bitterness, stifled creativity, sexual perversion, and unwillingness to trust, love, and/or touch.

Collectively—when an entire society is sexually repressed—phenomena such as war, rape, racism, greed, and wholesale shitty behavior are considered acceptable.

It is difficult to strip away cultural thought patterns and stereotypes to arrive at the pulsating naked core of Woman: Cuntlovin' Fucklove Prophetess. I realized the enormity of this very task on New Year's Day in 1995.

I was walking down the street when a gentleman whose family and tribe have lived in the Pacific Northwest for thousands of years asked me for some spare change.

Because of the rising cost of living, I don't believe in spare change. As I handed him a dollar, he peered into my eyes and, smiling, asked, "Hey, did you get Any for New Year's?"

I was just about to say, "That's none of your fucking business, dickhead," but his eyeballs caught me off guard. He didn't have perving eyeballs. He had very nice, open eyeballs with a pretty glint in them. He was just good-naturedly asking me if I rang in the new year with a celebratory tumble in the sack. And, as it happened, I actually did ring in the new year in just such a manner.

So I said, "Yeah."

The gentleman positively *beamed*. He said, "Hey! Me too! Ain't nothin' like gettin' Some on New Year's to humble ya, know what I mean?"

As I walked home, I thought about this man and his message. I thought, sex truly is humbling. I thought, sex, birth, life, and death are all humbling. Most of all, I thought how thankful I was to this gentleman for giving me a beautiful message about sex, something seldom resonated in society. I tried to think of all the positive, reinforcing messages about sex I have access to on a general basis whenever I leave my home or otherwise subject myself to this culture.

The only one I readily managed to summon was the words of a very nice Lummi gentleman on New Year's Day in 1995.

All my life, I've absorbed stimuli about sex from my culture, family, friends, and teachers. Most of this information has been hopelessly gnarled all up with violence, racism, power, purity, shame, denial, guilt, humiliation, victimization, objectification, rejection, and unimaginative stereotypes of sexual identity.

Probably even more stuff than that.

It all, all, all, all, all, all, all, all, all stems from fear of women and our enormous sexual power.

When we were children, one of my older brother's favorite means of torment was to sit down near me, cut a *foul* noiseless fart, and wait. As soon as he ascertained that I'd detected his gastric horror, he'd restrain my hands so I could neither run nor cover my nose and diabolically whisper, "Silence is deadly."

Though his farts miraculously never threatened my life, I agree with this sentiment wholeheartedly.

Since the early days of the church, women had been barred from speaking in the house of God as well as preaching, teaching, or speaking in public: "As in all the churches of the saints," wrote St. Paul, "wives should keep silence in the churches. They are not permitted to speak, but should be subordinate, as even the law says. If there is anything they desire to know, let them ask their husbands at home. For it is shameful for a woman to speak in church." This prohibition grew out of the synthesis of separate traditions, the Greek, which taught that women were by nature inferior to men and therefore should be their subordinates, and the Biblical, which suggested to many readers that women be perpetually silent as a punishment for the sins of Eve, whose garrulousness brought disaster to all mankind: "The curse of God pronounced on your sex weighs still on the world. Guilty you must bear its hardships," wrote Tertullian in the third century, "You are the devil's gateway . . . you softened up with your cajoling words the man against whom the devil could not prevail by force." Over the centuries these themes hardened until silence became a virtue particularly recommended to women. "By silence, indeed, women achieve the fame of eloquence," wrote one Renaissance commentator. (Brown 1986, 59)

The enforced silence of women allows men's fear of us and our sexual power to reign unchallenged. Thus the wisdom of brilliant people such as Audre Lorde is not venerated, and we are still sent to schools where idiotic puds like Aristotle are worshipped.

A-hem:

Just as it sometimes happens that deformed offspring are produced by deformed parents, and sometimes not, so the offspring produced by a female are sometimes female, sometimes not, but male. The reason is that the female is as it were a deformed male; and the menstrual charge is se-men, though . . . it lacks one constituent, and only one, the principle of Soul. . . . Thus the physical part, the body, comes from the female, and the Soul from the male, since the Soul is the essence of a particular body. . . . Females are weaker and colder in their nature, and we should look upon the female state as being as it were a deformity, though one which occurs in the ordinary course of nature. (Aristotle, as quoted in Brown 1986, 188)

To the best of my knowledge, it wasn't until 1968, when Valerie Solanas published her *S.C.U.M. Manifesto,* that this par-ticular form of intolerance was duplicated with any serious eloquence:

It is now technically possible to reproduce without the aid of males (or, for that matter, females) and to produce only females. We must begin immediately to do so. Retaining the male has not even the dubious purpose of reproduction. The male is a biological accident: the y (male) gene is an incomplete x (female) gene, that is, has an incomplete set of chromosomes. In other words, the male is an incomplete female, a walking abortion, aborted at the gene stage. To be male is to be deficient, emotionally limited; maleness is a deficiency disease and males are emotional cripples.

The male is completely egocentric, trapped inside himself, incapable of empathizing or identifying with others, of love, friendship, affection or tenderness. He is a completely isolated unit, incapable of rapport with anyone. His responses are entirely visceral, not cerebral; his intelligence is a mere tool in the service of his drives and needs, he is incapable of mental passion, mental interaction; he can't relate to anything other than his own physical sensations. He is a half dead, unresponsive lump, incapable of giving or receiving pleasure or happiness; consequently, he is at best an utter bore, an inoffensive blob, since only those capable of absorption in others can be charming. He is trapped in a twilight zone halfway between humans and apes, and is far worse off than apes because, unlike the apes, he is capable of a large array of negative feelings—hate, jealousy, contempt, disgust, guilt, shame, doubt—and moreover he is *aware* of what he is and isn't.

While Aristotle is lauded in our culture, Valerie Solanas is considered—when she's considered at all—to be a terribly unhinged individual who died homeless on the streets of San Francisco in 1988. Whereas, if you changed the pronouns throughout her manifesto, and backdated it a couple of decades, you'd probably have the ramblings of a brilliant, Pulitzer Prize–winning male scholar.

See how that works?

Women and silence have been historically mashed together like potatoes and cheese. Our true erotic nature is not exalted. Rather, it is mutated into some manageable illusion created and sustained by men. Meanwhile, the Washington Monument attests to the grandeur with which male erotic nature is glorified.

This same pattern is found in the scant funding for both breast cancer research and the risk of female-to-female transmission of the HIV virus versus the gazillions of dollars poured into research for prostate cancer and the risk of male-to-male transmission of the HIV virus.

In an interview in *BUST* issue 10, the beautiful, genius porn star Nina Hartley describes what's at stake here.

I got the first edition of *Our Bodies, Ourselves* for my 13th birthday and it was the most powerful book I'd ever read next to *Sex for One*, which saved my life. Sex is enlightening. The reality is that once a woman knows that the pleasure goddess is at the end of her arm, then she can swing her hand in front of her crotch anytime and woops! there it is, anytime she wants. It's really easy—let's see: teddy bears, washing machines, Jacuzzi jets, vibrators, cunnilingus, fucking, OOO, lots of things can do it. Women are denied pleasure because pleasure is very, very powerful, very, very potent. (93)

Women reach orgasm via our clitoris, through contractions of the muscles deep within our cunts, or by stimulation of our G-spots. Sometimes all three or any combination. Women ejaculate. Fingers or other apparati strategically placed up a woman's ass can lead to ten-minute-long multiple orgasms. Women can come just by looking at—or imagining—some major turn-on for a while. Women can come over and over, one orgasm right after the last. Women have orgasms in many, many different ways.

Men, on the other hand, come when their cock is stroked via a hand, mouth, cunt, or anus. Many men can also achieve orgasm through stimulation of their prostate gland via their asshole. Sadly, though, the general feeling among straight men is, "I ain't no fucking faggot, so keep clear of my ass." Thus, a lot of men deprive themselves of this (I've gathered) highly pleasurable sensation.

After a man comes, he's usually spent for at least fifteen minutes, and, generally, that's it for the session. This, of course, is in the event that he has not studied any Tantric-type breathing and muscle control practices, which the vast majority of men in our culture don't have the opportunity, inclination, or self-discipline to explore.

As a dick is a finite structure, with a visible beginning and end, so too is the potential for a male orgasm.

As a cunt is infinite—how many bloody mysteries and future generations are hiding up there, somewhere?—so too is the potential for female orgasm.

I'm setting my imagination free to roam here, but if I were a man, and had no *biological* idea what it was like to have such a complex orgasm mechanism as a cunt—with *so many* intricate, endless, and fascinating possibilities for achieving pleasure—I'd be pretty nervous making love to a woman. And I might find millions and billions of ways to camouflage my nervousness rather than be like Jesus and just humble myself.

Aristotle opted to obsessively devote his life to the creation of an elaborate belief system based on total cuntfear rather than simply face reality. That seems like pretty nervous behavior to me. Ditto Sigmund Freud—the Rush Limbaugh our society actually takes seriously.

You might as well throw pretty much all male politicians, military leaders, industrial revolution kings, mafia dons, bankers, artists, and executives in there too.

After all, if Rockefeller, for instance, knew how to please a woman, he'd hardly have transferred so much nervous sexual energy to proving his virility—in the guise of Standard Oil—to every woman, child, and man on the planet.

In this culture we preserved the words, laws, codices, artwork, religions, music, and mergers of a bunch of nervous, insecure lovers. Evidently, there is no shortage of them. Then we went and hailed them as Geniuses of Our Time. Men have gone to exorbitant lengths to camouflage—rather than reckon with—their cuntfear for thousands of years. The naked female form is idolized, obsessed over, and blamed for any maltreatment it meets. There is a veritable surplus of references that state how sinful, impossible, miraculous, or wrong it is for women to experience sexual pleasure.

Retarded male sexual power is expressed in maneuvers people have come to look upon with unerring respect, such as warring, ruling, or becoming heads of production companies in Hollywood.

In offense to women who positively *refuse* to remain silent, some women are placed on pedestals in poses of righteousness for holding our tongues (no pun intended) in religious, political, artistic, economic, and legal arenas. The women on the pedestals, then, provide a twofold service: (a) presenting physical evidence that men have no interest in holding us down, and (b) serving as points of reference for other women who want to be "heard" in this society.

This isn't to say there aren't countless numbers of women fighting our hearts raw in all of the aforementioned arenas. If we're vocally pro-woman or speak in favor of healthy human sexuality, our silencing (i.e., the end of our careers, à la the brilliant, courageous, stunning Dr. Joycelyn Elders) is imminent.

Because we are invalidated for speaking our truth or, worse, are mute from the get-go, men never face how amazing our cunts are and, further, never reckon with the infernal jealousy they have that we can come in so many ways, so many times in succession.

We young women of Arabia recognized that the men of our land would never pursue social change for our sex, that we would have to force change. As long as Saudi women accepted their authority, men would rule. We surmised that it was the responsibility of each individual woman to ferment desire for control of her life and other female lives within her small circle. Our women are so beaten down by centuries of mistreatment that our movement had to begin with an awakening of the spirit. (Sasson 1992, 75–76)

Things *are* gonna change, and cuntlovin' ladies all over the world *are* gonna make it happen. Just as soon as we accept the fact that our cunts are the Holiest of Grails, the Hopefulest of Diamonds, the Goldenest of Medals.

Claire Cavanah is one of the owners of Babeland, a woman-positive sex paraphernalia/erotic multimedia store with branches in Seattle, Washington, and New York City. I interviewed her about women's fears of our own sexuality:

A lot of straight men come into the store because their partners won't come with them. I guess a lot of women can't imagine a place where there's so much freedom and peace involved with finding out what they want and then getting it. Getting what you want sexually is a huge achievement, and it seems to frighten a lot of women. They're afraid that if they see how much fun and pleasure they can experience by incorporating a vibrator or dildo into their sexual activities, they won't need their partner anymore. They're afraid to be free. It seems many people have this weird desire to *set-tle*. It's hard to keep growing, to constantly find out more. For some women, the desire to grow stops even before they learn how to come.

Obstacles such as these would not exist in a society that required students to read Audre Lorde's "Uses of the Erotic: The Erotic as Power" in high school.

The erotic is a measure between the beginnings of our sense of self and the chaos of our strongest feelings. It is an internal sense of satisfaction to which, once we have experienced it, we know we can aspire. For having experienced the fullness of this depth of feeling and recognizing its power, in honor and self-respect we can require no less of ourselves.

It is never easy to demand the most from ourselves, from our lives, from our work. To go beyond the encouraged mediocrity of our society is to encourage excellence. But giving in to the fear of feeling and working to capacity is a luxury only the unintentional can afford, and the unintentional are those who do not wish to guide their own destinies. (Lorde 1984, 54)

Let's, shall we, go ahead, drop all the bullshit and get down to the nitty-gritty reality that you and your cunt are the Cunt-lovin' Rulers of Your Sexual Universe.

Because I have no idea what turns you on, what (if any) sexual hang-ups and/or fetishes you may have, whether you come via penetration, clitoral stimulation, a G-spot massage or by tickling your bellybutton at 1:18 p.m. with a redorangeyellow sunset rose in full bloom, I'm gonna skip all the guesswork and go right to sources. You answer all your own questions, make all your own guesses, and explore your own sexual expression.

If you have a really hard time letting go of cultural mindsets you have learned about sex, I highly suggest opening up a dialogue with your women friends or family members. Find out what the women in your immediate community have been taught and how they process and deal with negative shit. Refrain from focusing conversation on your *lover(s)*. Keep everything real nice and personal.

I could underscore the point until profits from the feminine hygiene industry were placed in a college fund for young women and *still* I don't think I'd do justice to precisely how *profoundly* exchanging stories, fantasies, and problems with women has improved the quality of my life.

Though some close and others open, woman-positive sex stores abound in North America. A woman-positive sex store is *not* a porno shack with twenty-five-cent semen-encrusted peep booths in the back.

I've been in four: Babeland in Seattle and New York City, Good Vibrations in San Francisco (they have multiple locations), Grand Opening! in Brookline, Massachusetts, and It's My Pleasure, in Portland, Oregon (unfortunately, the last two are now closed). The experience was always illuminating and great fun. All are/were owned by women *full-on dedicated* to redressing sexual stereotypes that keep folks down. The atmosphere in each of these stores is: "Come on in and browse at your leisure, ask questions, take a vibrator for a test drive in our private boudoir. Most importantly, enjoy yourself." All are stocked with state-of-the-art sexual apparati, beautiful, informative, and erotic books, videos, calendars, comics, photo-journals. Every staff member is patient, sensitive, and totally helpful. *The women who work at these stores are hired for their ability to be fully supportive of women who manage to shove aside their embarrassment and shame to ask, "Where the fuck is my G-spot and why should I care?"*

Other wonderful stores include Come As You Are Co-operative and Good For Her, both located in Toronto, the Smitten Kitten in Minneapolis, Early to Bed in Chicago, Eve's Garden in New York City, A Woman's Touch in Madison, Wisconsin, and Sexploratorium in Philadelphia.

That covers a lot of geography. Pile all your friends into a car and barrel ass to one of these stores. Plan a trip! Whee! Spend the weekend contemplating, discovering, and achieving your orgasmic potential.

The women who work at woman-positive sex stores are warriors in their own right and have dedicated themselves to freeing women's sexual, erotic nature.

They love you!

They want you to make all them cuntdreams of yours come to 3D, pulsating, glorious, sweaty life.

Buying things online (exclusively, SheBop and SheVibe. Most of the stores mentioned also have online catalogs.) is nice, but the in-store experience is edifying as a library and good for your soul.

The generally recognized sexual revolution in the '60s was mostly about men justifying their desire to fuck as many women as humanly possible. A common term arising from this era, after all, was not "husband swapping." The sexual revolution that's long overdue is about women loving themselves alone, with another, whenever, however, forever.

Or at least:

Until death do you part.

Acrimony of Cunts

My mind is very logical. Thoughts are a kind of math to me. Well before undertaking the task of writing this book, I understood that certain very specific elements must be present in order to make a whole.

The element of Whoredom tripped me up a little. Rape—an element you will be coming upon shortly—rather hurt. Never did I remotely entertain the notion of omitting either of these elements.

I make this little introduction because I *positively adore* and *consistently seduce* the idea of leaving this chapter—concerning the element of Acrimony—out, out, out. Chills of *ecstasy* shimmy down my spine when I think about putting a big, fat, red X over this chapter.

However, my mind is sometimes just this *very weary* high school algebra teacher and will not withstand such tomfoolery.

It was very difficult for my sister and I to acknowledge the insidious nature of acrimony that was (and still can be) present in our relationship. Jealousy, cattiness, and general shit-ass vibes were some of the crapola emotions we learned to harbor during our socialization in a culture founded upon destruction. It required *months* of conversation focused on total honesty, acceptance, and love to even approach overcoming negative patterns we grew up with in our personal relationship.

The idea of acknowledging the presence of acrimony among *all women* is pretty dang-awful daunting to me. It extends far past jealousy, cattiness, and general shitass vibes into highly oppressive forms of ageism, classism, homophobia, objectification, and racism.

I held my sister in my arms on her ride home from being born at the hospital. My sister and me go way back. You, on the other hand, only met me a few short chapters ago. But in comparison to *my* position, *you're* sittin' tight. I have absolutely no idea who you might be, and I'm about to start talking shit to you about nasty things you may perpetuate.

Big sigh.

Still, I know for a fact that being honest and forgiving about acrimony in my personal relationships has freed me and continues to improve the quality of my life intensely. I am privy to the ways acrimony manifests between women in our culture and inevitably conclude this sense of freedom and life improvement can be true on the much broader cultural level as well.

In an interview, the singer-songwriter Fiona Apple described a shitty period of her life—which she knew she had to experience in order to survive on her terms—as her "dog years."

In the exact same spirit, I present *Cunt*'s dog chapter.

One time I had an Iranian dance teacher named Jaleh. After class, we'd often have lengthy discussions about culture. As a result of these conversations, I developed a new perspective on the standard by which freedom is defined in my country.

I used to think women in fundamentalist Islamic countries, or societies where genital mutilation is practiced, have it *way worse* than us ladies in the West. American women can *generally* wear what we want, fuck who we want, love how we want, and work where we want.

You know, experience "freedom."

Coupled with her religious and political beliefs, that nagging inspiration known as survival forced Jaleh to flee Iran. There were many things about her country she detested with all her might and mien. Malevolence toward women is one thing that ain't veiled in Iran. Iranian women are shamed, silenced, or killed for many vagaries Americans guilelessly take for granted. Iranian women are very consciously aware of gender-explicit oppression.

Therefore:

with so much more at stake, Iranian women have each other's back:

on the street,

in stores,

at celebrations,

everywhere.

When Jaleh first got here, she *completely freaked* about the mean-spiritedness American women project onto one another in our day-to-day lives. She eventually learned to live with a dull thud of longing for the *general*, loving, woman vibe that was once part of her normal reality. Loss of this closeness truly tore her heart asunder, and Jaleh wondered about the sacrifices American women make at the behest of our "freedom." What I learned from Jaleh distressed me greatly because I couldn't *imagine* something so precious as an everyday closeness with women, founded in the common knowledge that we all want to survive and thrive in a patriarchal society.

In my country, women don't seem to like each other much at all.

Sucky, sucky, sucky vibes.

I was offered another profound perspective on the actual reality of American women when I interviewed Soraya Miré, a Somali woman who made *Fire Eyes,* a deeply moving, powerful film about genital mutilation.

In countries like mine, the law is *blatantly* against women. What we do have, though, is love and *community.* You never think only of yourself, you always think of your neighbors and family, too.

The problem with a lot of Western women is they think they can *help* me, that they *know what's best* for me. Especially feminist women. They come into conversations waving the American flag, forever projecting the idea they are more intelligent than I am. I've learned that American women look at women like me to hide from their own pain. They can't face their pain, and mine is so obvious, they think they can help me without looking at themselves. But many women in this country are empty. They desperately try to find something to fill the empty space inside them—the loneliness deep inside. In my country, this kind of loneliness does not exist.

In America, women pay *the money that is theirs and no one else's* to go to a doctor who cuts them up so they can create or sustain an image men want. Men are the mirror. Western women cut themselves up voluntarily. In my country, a child is woken up at three in the morning, held down and cut with a razor blade. She has no choice. Western women *pay* to get their bodies mutilated.

When you base your whole self-image on a man—on another human being—how can you expect that person— whether it's a man or a woman—to respect you? How can *you* respect yourself when you do not *have* love and respect for yourself?

One of America's finest cultural phenomena is something called *The Jerry Springer Show*. This is an arena akin to the Roman ones where prisoners fought to the death. On *The Jerry Springer Show*, the audience watches people on a stage emotionally and physically maul one another. The viewers at home watch both the audience and the people being mauled. It is the pinnacle of voyeurism, where love, American style, is dissected and pinned down in its most caustic glory.

The Jerry Springer Show is one of my all-time favorite contemporary American anthropological studies.

The show titles change from episode to episode:

"I Want My Man to Stop Going to Strip Clubs."

"I'm Pregnant with His Child and Want Him to Leave His Wife and Three Girlfriends Because I'm More of a Woman Than They Are."

"Gee Honey, Your Mom, Sisters, and Best Friends Sure Are Awesome Good Fucks."

The title never matters because it invariably leads to women physically and verbally attacking each other over some ugly-assed schmuck whose main talent in life is pitting women against each other to bolster his sense of manliness and self-worth.

The Jerry Springer Show is a highly charged and concentrated reflection of a much broader and generally subtler consciousness under which *all* American women—regardless of sexual orientation—exist.

It's easy enough for the viewers and audience members to look at the woman on the stage and really, really wonder if she's ever even *heard* the term *self-esteem*. It's even easier for lesbians to pass judgment on the hapless straight ladies who expend so much energy on something of such dubious merit as a man's unsullied attention, but I've yet to encounter a tribe within *any* community that is not similarly rife with cruelty, possessiveness, jealousy, betrayal, power trips, and general shitass vibes.

Some say this is inherent to love, but I say it's inherent to socialization in a destructive cultural setting of ageism, classism, homophobia, objectification, and racism.

As Soraya Miré points out, American women indeed learn to look at our pain in others rather than deal with it as a reality in our lives.

America is a collection of many tribes unified under every conceivable banner—from blood and geography to the Selena fan club and Harley-Davidson motorcycles. Within these tribes, women *may* find inner sanctums of cuntlovin' support.

What interests me, though, is the *standard* of how we perceive community and the ways we judge women based on very negative thought patterns we've adopted to survive in this society's environment of out-and-out destructive tendencies. As it stands, American women have no frame of reference for relying on each other—cultivating trust, love, standards of beauty and sexuality, economic power, and sisterhood.

The fucked-up elements of destruction we learn to view as acceptable are all founded in the exact same basic consciousness, or, rather, lack thereof. Ignorance is the most valued consciousness in America. It rends deep chasms of total distrust and perpetuates mean-spiritedness bar none. Education, therefore, is the panacea for undermining all manifestations of acrimony in our society.

Every way we see, hear, feel, taste, and smell is a *self-reflection*. Our perception awake and asleep is what we, we, we *choose* to perceive. The way we react to any stimulus is the way we *choose* to react.

For a long time, I had a problem with women I perceived as privileged. Rather than harbor and nurture this negative feeling—which would, ultimately, only constitute a bummer in my personal life—I got into reading biographies. I read books about Imelda Marcos, La Toya Jackson, Princess Diana, the Kennedy women, and Marjorie Merriweather Post.

It's not like I'm this massive Imelda Marcos fan now, but I have solid ideas about what her life was like when she ruled the Philippines. (And if you think ol' Ferdinand ruled, you be wrong.) Imelda Marcos is no longer just some greedy, capitalist shoe fetishist to me. She is a woman who developed her own set of survival skills, which I clearly do not identify with. Learning something of her childhood and life, however, has made it very difficult for me to pass judgment.

I never imagined Imelda Marcos would communicate any information I would consider valid in my own life, but she taught me a whole new way of looking at women. Imelda wore make-up twenty-four hours a day, seven days a week, with four complete changes, every six hours. She inspired me to appreciate the intricate cultural art form of presentation. The lengths to which she went to be considered beautiful are astonishing. I have complete respect for dedication, precision, and commitment, regardless of the fact that Imelda's particular brand represents an insidious form of cunthatred.

Women choose to be catty, cruel, prejudiced, competitive, or jealous of each other partly because we grow up learning that negative behavior toward women is perfectly acceptable and partly because it is a difficult *task* to see ourselves in our perceptions. Seeing ourselves requires effort and commitment.

This unwillingness to see ourselves is greatly exacerbated by the fact that we, quite often, do not see even a remote semblance of ourselves in the images of women commonly found in our society. The women presented to us in ads, TV shows, movies, and music videos are powdered and coiffed under standards set by male associations of what is and isn't beautiful.

As a result, many women are scornful and lay blame on women who work in any of these false-image-creating industries. But women who base identity and economic security on a specific standard of "beauty" exist in an industry that is rife with cuntfear. Women choose to work under self-esteem-corroding conditions such as these because cuntfear is highly valued in our society and corporations are willing to pay women exorbitant sums of money for glorifying illusions of beauty men can deal with.

One of my dearest friends used to be one of them fancy übermodels. This experience psychologically damaged her to the degree that I know she would be terribly hurt if I stated her name. I spent a weekend with her a few years ago, and she dug out her modeling portfolio for me to look at. The photographs showed this totally posh babe being either sporty, babyish, scary, or spicy. I would never, ever, ever, *never* have recognized my dear friend as the woman presented in her portfolio. "They made me," she said. "That was my 'talent': allowing the people who run companies to make me look the way they wanted me to look." When my friend told photographers at shoots that she was interested in photography, they laughed at her. After she quit modeling—and used all that money she saved up as a tidy little nest egg—she became a successful, award-winning art director, designer, and photographer.

It doesn't get anybody anywhere to diss models, actresses, dancers, and women in general who identify with this male-made standard of beauty. If real images of powerful women being cuntlovin' and beautiful are what women want, the advertising, television, motion picture, and music industries must first be infiltrated and revolutionized from the inside out.

It is less *directly* painful to *ourselves* to respond negatively to women than to honestly figure out what other women represent inside of us that we either dislike, fear, wish we "possessed," or are afraid to love.

Another one of my friends used to be almost pathologically uncool about large women. She was rail thin and readily admitted her own fear of being "fat" was the problem. Once she told me, "I think, in a way, I'm jealous because fat women *potentially* love themselves no matter what society says, and I, obviously, do not."

After this conversation, I bought her a bunch of postcard reproductions of paintings depicting large, voluptuous women in erotic poses. She put some of them up in her bathroom. As time passed, her attitude about women and body image evolved, and she also gained weight. These positive images of women *aided* her in developing a new, healthier perspective, but it was her own courage to be honest with herself that really spurred along positive change in her life.

It is nice to get in the habit of consciously stopping yourself from wishing ill tidings on a woman and asking, "What of myself do I see here?" When you can honestly respond to that question without perpetuating self-judgment or nastiness, you is a cuntlover on high.

Adding to the acrimonious nature of growing up in a society that breeds destructive behavior is the fact that the United States is home to more ethnicities than can be found in any other single country on the entire planet. Most nations have the relative luxury of being populated by a few distinct ethnicities. I have a friend who is Chinese and Greek, with smatterings of Swiss, Chicana, and East Indian blood. She grew up speaking Mandarin and English. I know Korean Jews and African American Irish folk. America's ethnicity is the whole kit 'n caboodle, all mixed up in every imaginable combo.

Our national cultural heritage is gloriously schizophrenic.

The result of living as women in an acrimonious, multiethnic nation is a subconscious negative preoccupation when dealing with each other. It thus quite naturally escapes us that while we are so preoccupied we forsake our collective power of sheer mass.

This is a bummer for a number of reasons.

American women cannot so much as stand on the same escalator without the presence of discord—much less design and implement cuntlovin' economic and legal systems, run huge cuntlovin' corporations, and make sure all of our children are loved, protected, fed, clothed, educated, and tucked into bed with a sleepytime story that has a happy, cuntlovin' ending.

A significant portion of the acrimony is rooted in economics.

White people took away the home of Native people who lived on this land since *The Beginning*. White people said, "Sorry, it's this thing called economics, and your home since *The Beginning* is now on our property."

White people stole African people from one place and took them to another, far, far away. White people said, "Sorry, it's this thing called economics and you are not a human being anymore, you are our property."

White people snagged Mexico and named it things like "Southern California," "New Mexico," and "Texas." White people said, "Sorry, it's this thing called economics, and we'll grudgingly let you live here but you hafta remember: It's our property."

White people corralled all the Japanese people who were born in this country same as anybody else. White people said, "Sorry, it's this thing called economics and what was your property yesterday is our property today."

So I figure right off the bat: a lot of women in America were raised by mothers who have good, solid-assed reasons for entertaining acrimonious vibrations toward *Las Blancas*.

Good.

Solid-assed.
Reasons.

There is a saying.

It goes, "If you don't face the past, you hafta keep living it."

White women are not readily compelled—much less forced—to face the past. In a white-dominated society, women of color are not generally accorded this option. At some point in life, all children realize skin color plays a major role in one's destiny of survival in this society. Little white girls learn that skin color is a nonissue when one is white. Little girls of color, however, must, at some point, grapple with *why* skin color affects destiny so dramatically. This often leads to facing the past.

I do not think it is culturally healthy or cuntlovin' that facing the past is not *everyone's* responsibility.

One day my friend Harper handed me a piece of paper. She said, "I wrote this at work this morning," as if it might perhaps be a things-to-do list. But it wasn't a things-to-do list at all, and I asked her if I could put it in my book.

It is a fascinating Sunday, or at least seems like it should be. I have been reading *Essence* magazine (the first time in a few years) and something in it inspired me to think of new projects to work on. One is the idea of where you come from,

and if you can really go far without establishing in truth—
or just in any manner—that sense of belonging somewhere.
Like when that man from India was so insistent about asking where I am from, and I ended up at slavery, and I think
it was the first time I *really felt* slavery. I mean, I recognized
that some of my ancestors had been slaves, but until that
day I hadn't felt connected to it past the color of my skin
and feeling disgust at the mistreatment and the scope of the
cruelty that humans have inflicted on each other—and also
embittered in that slaves weren't even allowed the consideration to be recognized as human beings by the colonizers
or slavery owners. It was like remembering the tiny pieces
of scenes, sound bites and music from the mini-series *Roots*
that I viewed before my bedtime as a child . . . a sort of
far away horror story. In history lessons this story became
worse, with descriptions of the tools used for torture, the
neckbrace with bells to keep track of slaves who'd tried to
escape, the length of the ships, the number of those herded
into the holds, the vomit, the smell, the disease, the death
and the wounds—and sometimes mentioned, the note of
survival, that continual note of survival that is allowing me
to write these words. And more than that note of survival—
also my denial and my ability to avoid the remembering because of the pre-recognition of how it makes me sick about
humanity in general.

I know I do this about many atrocities.

It wasn't until that day, on my way to Seattle, at a gas
station with the two East Indian men I barely knew, as my

friend pumped gas, that one of the men asked me where I was from, and I said, "Iowa and D.C." And he said, "No, where are you FROM?" And I said, "Iowa and D.C." And he said, "No, where are you FROM?" And I said, "Iowa and D.C." I explained how I was born in Iowa but had grown up mostly in D.C. "No, ORIGINALLY," he said. Finally understanding that he perhaps made no assumptions that I was a descendant of black slaves, I started to explain there was this thing called slavery in this country and . . . But he was very insistent and interrupted me. "Yes, but YES, WHERE ARE YOU FROM, *your people*?" And I said, "Africa and Germany, but *I don't know,* exactly." As my friend—a white friend—returned to the car, the conversation ended. An uncomfortable silence surrounded me as the conversation turned to the tourist sites in Seattle. I felt lost. I realized this man I had spoken to very likely *knew* what his family was doing in the 1400s. He knew where he was from and where he was grounded, all those miles away from his home. I had just always accepted that I was black in America, and to me, that meant being of questionable mixed heritage, as diverse as the skin tones that defined blackness to me. But this acceptance had never brought me to that question of where I am FROM. And to come to that question in a car at a gas station somewhere between Olympia and Seattle on some random gray day left me silent and lost and feeling the reality of postcolonialism and the reality of the slave trade for the first time in my life.

It is a source of great sadness that my friend is forced to identify with such an ugly treatment of her people in history. If you ever get into reading history, though, you will see how pretty much all cultures on the planet have pasts filled with bloodshed, rape, war, enslavement, torture, and other symptoms of a destructive patriarchy encroaching on and dominating everybody else.

There is much sadness in this world.

If you have the courage to ask, Rigoberta Menchú, Sojourner Truth, Wilma Mankiller, Jacqueline Woodson, Mary Crow Dog, and Kathy Acker will tell you:

There is much sadness in this world.

During the '60s and '70s, Steve Biko was one of the leaders in South Africa's Black Consciousness Movement. In the biography *Biko*, by Donald Woods, I found that Black Consciousness and cuntlove share many of the same basic principles. Biko, as quoted in Woods, writes, "Many would prefer to be colorblind; to them skin pigmentation is merely an accident of creation. To us, it is something much more fundamental. It is a synonym for subjection, an identification for the disinherited" (Woods 1979, 37).

I can relate to this because the presence of estrogen in my body is a synonym for subjection and identification for the disinherited.

However, America was colonized by male and white people. *All women* experience alienation due to the overwhelming *male* standard based in this history. Women of color experience alienation for the overwhelming *white* standard too. I consider it perfectly acceptable to expect men of all ethnicities and classes to educate themselves and take responsibility for their individual role in women's oppression. I likewise consider it perfectly acceptable to expect white women of all classes to take responsibility for our individual role in the oppression of women of color. Women of color *have no call* to trust white women until white women take a gander at the world around them, investigate, learn, and annihilate ignorance founded in being white in a society where the perspective and voice presented to the general public is white.

Still and too, acrimony between white women and women of color is but one of many pits in our potentially delicious cherry pie. Within each tribe, racial acrimony is present. Acrimony is a way of general socialized American life until you decide you don't want it that way no more. All races of people are divided and isolated from one another.

It is the house that Jack built.

Chinese women might harbor negative stereotypes about Filipina women, who may not think nice things about Jewish women, who might grow up thinking ill of Muslim women, who may think lesbians are the scourge of the earth, who might think women married to Promise Keepers are the incarnation of evil, who may think teenagers who get abortions should be sentenced to hard labor at juvey.

And on and on.

In school we learn that one of the best survival strategies is being part of a clique. With our friends, we create a little, tiny world with codes of conduct, morality, dress, communication, ethnicity, and sexuality. We then learn to judge everyone else who is not part of our little world by the standards that are acceptable to us. This is called "divide and conquer" and happens to be exactly how male white patriarchal society operates. When you choose not to see how you, yourself, perpetuate this social model, your world assuredly becomes—or remains—small, "safe," persnickety, judgmental, and uninspiring.

How else could Bill Gates decide it was a good idea to build such a temporal item as a sprawling multi-million-dollar house for his three-child nuclear family in a society where kids in schools hafta *share* textbooks published in 1987? In his little, tiny world, it is acceptable to squander money and responsibility in this manner. I consider it an embarrassing display of karmic retardation when someone invests so much money in something that could *burn to ashes in a fire,* while human beings continue to starve and go insane on the streets.

We learn to justify many preposterous actions within the small worlds we are encouraged to create throughout life.

You can't be a solitary human being. [We're] all linked. . . .
Because of this deep sense of community, the harmony of
the group is a prime attribute. And so you realize that anything that undermines the harmony is to be avoided as much
as possible. Anger and jealousy and revenge are particularly

corrosive, so you try . . . to enhance the humanity of the other, because in that process, you enhance your own. (*"The Progressive* Interview: Desmond Tutu" 1998, 19)

We are *all* raised under the influences of negative standards set by our culture. We naturally fail to note that all the women around us are dealing with the exact same things, in entirely different ways.

If you want to find out how your oppression infringes on your freedom, walk into the bathroom, stare deeply into your eyes, and face your pain without blame. Don't go feeling sorry for them ladies in Saudi Arabia and Pakistan until you do this first. Don't be dissin' on übermodel types with silicone titties until you do this first. Don't sneer at women from a class or ethnicity different from your own, at lesbians, bi women, straight women, fat women, skinny women, old women, or young women until you do this first.

There will remain much sadness in the world until people are willing to rise to the task of facing the world's pain in the bathroom mirror.

American culture is very, very, very, very, very beautiful.

I am thankful and happy to live in a society where so many perspectives and bounties of educational resources are available. My society honors the public library system. I have *every* opportunity to learn about things of which I was raised to be ignorant.

Wheee!

In one American afternoon, I might encounter Cibo Matto sounding out from a used bookstore, a Peruvian band attracting a crowd on the street corner, Missy Elliott pulsating from one of those cars that are really state-of-the-art sound systems on wheels, while a queer Lithuanian-Basque Vietnam vet caterwauls Barbra Streisand songs in the doorway of an office building.

Wheee!

I believe it is possible for women who live in this beautiful culture to access a forsaken—but still inherent—love and respect for each other based on the sole criterion of what our cunts have been through for the past few thousand years.

Which segues into a commandment the bible, koran, and torah writers plumb done forgot to include . . .

Rape Not Cunts

While writing about orgasms at four o'clock in the morning, I ran out of soymilk for my coffee. I was tired. I needed a bike ride and coffee to keep da pace. At ten a.m., I would've encountered no internal deliberation. The wee-dawn hours, however, are definitely past curfew time for women on solo ventures.

Still.

I didn't want to drink my coffee black. I didn't want to be afraid of going to the grocery store just because I have a cunt.

So I:

1. Put a beanie on my head to camouflage my femaleness, at least from a distance.
2. Did the ol' once-over in the mirror to ascertain that my sweats were baggy enough to hide the contours of my fine, round, womanly ass.
3. Tied my running shoes nice and tight, in case I might have to kick or bolt.
4. Donned a loose, black, butchy-poo jacket.
5. Stuffed the five medium-sized rocks I keep on hand

for excursions such as this into the pockets of said jacket.

6. Made sure the tires on my bike had enough air in them, in the event that I'd have to race to safety.

All six of these steps are part of a survival tactic I have incorporated into my lifestyle because: *I can't stand the fact that the danger of having a cunt is threatening enough to keep me from doing as I please.*

Though I've lived away from home for over a decade, my mother still has a tizz when I go out by myself after eleven p.m. So I don't tell her it drives me insane to allow the possibility of being raped to dictate my will.

I Do the Best I Can.

My friend Esther, who lives in the same apartment building, gets off work at three in the morning. She rarely goes to bed before eight. The last step in this particular survival tactic is calling her.

"Esther, I'm going to the store. If I'm not home safe and sound in fourteen minutes [we have it timed], come find me. I'll be riding up Olive and down Broadway."

"Okey-dokey. It's 4:18. Go. Oh, wait. Pick me up a pack of smokes, will ya? Go."

Esther and I have never discussed my motive for calling and letting her know I'm going to the grocery store. One night, the need simply arose. How telling it is that *not once* did it occur to Esther to question me. As women raised in a violent, patriarchal culture we inherently understand the risks one may encounter when one has a cunt.

I ride my bike to the grocery store. The cashiers are used to seeing me at unseemly hours. They let me park my bike inside, by the greeting cards. I feel safe in the grocery store, but at the same time, I know not to assume this to be a fact.

I go to great lengths to make it seem like I'm not fettered to the violence—and subsequent injustice of the American legal system—that my cunt can potentially inspire.

But I ain't foolin' nobody.

Certainly not myself.

I'm fully privy to the reality that my cunt's presence on my body can inspire people with cocks to attempt to exert their power by attempting to humiliate me. I have no illusions about what happens to women in "the wrong place at the wrong time." I have seen too many movies, read too many newspapers, watched too many episodes of *Unsolved Mysteries*.

I know too many women who have been raped.

I do not pretend too realistically that I am free to go where I please. At least, not without taking extreme precautionary measures.

Purchasing soymilk for my coffee at four o'clock in the morning, then, is an act of rebellion.

A foolhardy and mundane one, perhaps.

Like I said, I Do the Best I Can.

When I was twenty, my mother told me she had been raped. Five years passed before I mustered the courage to write about it.

It is highly distressing to learn the sacred, holy place where you lived during your first nine months on this planet was ruthlessly pillaged long before you were conceived.

It makes you wonder if there exists a safe place.

She was nine.

She was nine.

My mother was nine.

Over a Christmas holiday, Mom and I were talking in the kitchen. I don't remember that we were discussing anything in particular. Liz popped her head in to say goodbye. She was going to a party dressed to the nines in a satin slipdress.

Our mother stopped in mid-innocuous-sentence and stared. Liz and I stared back. Mom looked down at her hands. (Momspeak interpretation: **Something Is Up.**)

Big sigh.

"I really wish you wouldn't go out dressed like that."

In the past, my sister and I would have rolled our eyes at each other and made light of it. Mom said things like this pretty much whenever she saw us dressed scantily for a party. This exchange had taken place hundreds of times.

But we could tell from her voice that tears were welling up in her eyes. This wasn't something we could shrug off as Mom's "overprotectiveness." There was suddenly a **Big Problem** in the kitchen.

Liz put her purse on the table and felt for a chair.

Neither of us could tear our eyes from our mother.

"Mom . . ." my sister spluttered.

I whispered, "Mom, what's wrong?"

Both of us were crying, but we had no idea why.

Nobody went to any party that night.

Two men saw her walking home from school in her Catholic girls' school uniform. The temptation was too much for them. The men pulled her into some bushes in Hyde Park and raped her.

Our mother, our, our, our beautiful mother.

Two men did that to her.

She was nine, she was nine.

She had no words to correspond with the defilement. She didn't come across sufficient vocabulary for an entire decade. She walked home, changed her clothes, and never breathed a word to anyone until she was in college. In the meantime—that is, throughout her adolescence—my mother relied solely on rape's best pal, silence, to help her survive this experience. She buried her silence deep because what else could she do.

When the Goddess eventually blessed her with two daughters, oh, how she watched us.

She said, "You two always thought I was paranoid, but how could I tell you why I was like that, how could I hurt you when you were so little and free? Then as you got older, I didn't know *when* to tell you. I knew it would make you cry like this."

We sobbed from the pits of our guts.

The whole time we were growing up, she attended seminars and clinics focused on rape to help her deal with the pain she sequestered in a dark region of her heart when she was a child. She had to learn how to control her fear that "something would happen" to my sister or me.

Hawk, mother hawk.

A new panorama slammed into my heart. I remembered years and years of relentless warnings: "Don't take shortcuts," "Come straight home from school," "Never walk past vans," "If a car is following you, cross the street and run to a neighbor's house. If you aren't near a neighbor's house, run into the middle of the street and scream 'FIRE!' at the top of your lungs."

A childhood memory assailed me.

I was eight. One morning, my friend Kit and I went to the mall to buy our moms gifts for Mother's Day. We ended up dawdling awfully long, and I didn't get home until dinnertime. My mother was standing in front of our house. There was no color in her face. Her eyes were blind terror. She swept me into her arms and hugged all of the breath out of me. Then she slapped me across the face.

It stung.

My father was cruising the neighborhood in a cop car. He came home and immediately grounded me to my room for a week.

My mother didn't utter a word.

That week I brooded in my room.

I thought they were overreacting.

In other words:

Because of the action of two completely unknown males in the year 1948, I was slapped across the face and grounded to my room for a week in 1974.

A different way of looking at this is:

I was raised by a woman who was held down in a park and raped when she was a little girl. Whereas the consequences of this event became, for Liz and me, a Grand Duchess Overtone in our upbringing, the two men who raped our mother have no idea either of us exist on the planet to have been raised under the shadow of their action.

A further perspective might be:

A man could, feasibly, sacrifice his coffee break raping a woman.

That woman would then spend her entire life dealing with it.

So would her daughters.

So would theirs.

This distribution of power is not acceptable.

The Lakota believe a people cannot be vanquished unless the spirit of woman is broken.

Though rape is viewed merely as a crime, it is the fundamental, primal, most destructive way to seize and maintain control in a patriarchal society.

When wars are declared, everyone involved in the declaration assumes women will be raped. Invading soldiers do not necessarily rape women to hurt us, per se. Women are raped to stymie the morale of husbands, fathers, and sons. Women's bodies are considered solely in regard to how they affect men. In the context of war, rape literally plants the seed of the invader in the body of a people. The secret weapon of war is spiritually crippling an entire nation of human beings and generations to come by sexually assaulting as many women and girls as possible.

Men use our bodies to bear witness to their power.

America was founded on the bodies of women: African women, Jewish women, Native women, Latina women, Chicana women, Asian women, European women. Grandmother, grandmother, grandmother, grandmother, grandmother, grandmother, grandmother.

Guatemalan, Bosnian, Vietnamese, Iraqi, Afghani women know war.

Pretty much every nation in this world was established by war.

How many women do you think that is?

In 1993, a woman named Mia Zapata, the lead singer of a rock band called the Gits, was found dead in Seattle, Washington. I lived in Seattle and wrote for a local weekly newspaper at the time.

It sucked very hard.

I clung to the fact that newspaper and word-of-mouth accounts did not mention the word *rape*. *Strangled, murdered, killed*. Those words were already quite unbearable. No sooner would the word *rape* flit through my mind than I'd remind myself none of the newscasters mentioned it.

I felt the world could still seem a halfway decent place so long as Mia Zapata wasn't raped.

I never knew her, never went and saw her band. Never listened to her music, not even after she died. But Seattle's a small city, and we shared a number of friends. She was generally associated with things like outspokenness, creativity, powerful expression, talent, and loving inspiration.

She was strong.

A Whore found
her body
in
an
alley.

I knew no woman who was not profoundly grief-stricken by her death. This was the feeling *before* the word *rape* was associated with Mia Zapata's death.

In the autumn following Mia's death, I interviewed the band 7 Year Bitch in the very tavern where Mia spent her last night. That is when I learned, once and for all, beyond a shadow of a doubt, yes, Mia Zapata was raped.

Even though women are raped and murdered every day, I tried really, really hard to pretend it didn't happen in my world, where I live, to women I see when I'm walking down the street each day.

I don't do that anymore.

In the final analysis, it took far more negative energy to live in denial than to face my fear and acknowledge the astounding prevalence of rape in my culture.

Now, I routinely assume that if the cancer of a man's soul condones the murder of a living, breathing, hoping, loving, fighting, singing, dancing, searching, yearning human being, the chances are pretty slim his cancer has spared his cock.

Now, when I hear of a man murdering a woman, I assume that he raped her unless I read the fucken coroner's report myself.

A definition for *martyr* according to my trusty 1965 *Random House Dictionary* is: "One who is put to death or endures great suffering on behalf of any belief, principle or cause."

The greatest purposes martyrs serve are teaching, inspiring, and giving strength to those who live on after their death.

In contrast to the killing of Dr. King or Malcolm X, there is little to support the idea that Mia Zapata was raped and murdered because of her personal (that is, political) actions as a woman. Nevertheless, her unspeakably tragic death is symbolic in that very mien. Ms. Zapata was a pillar of strength—a living, thriving, raging testimony of the power of unleashed artistic expression.

That she was killed in a horrible way psychologically tortured an entire community of women. Mia Zapata's life and death moshed into a collective consciousness.

Being part of a community that was grieving the brutal murder of one of its priestesses had a massive impact on my life. I could no longer contain my fear and rage. This was sickeningly exacerbated by another incident, which took place a few months later.

A woman parked near her apartment building late at night. As she was getting out of her car, she noticed two men up to some kind of mischief. She judged the distance to safety and thought she could negotiate it.

She was wrong.

The two men grabbed her, put her in her car and drove away. They cruised 'round the city for hours, taking turns raping the woman in the back seat of her car. When they were done, they took her to a high school field, stabbed her in the head repeatedly with a Phillips screwdriver, and left her for dead.

She did not die.

She had to learn everything all over again. She will probably never function in the way she had once always assumed she would.

One kinda takes it for granted that because one learned to read in first grade, one probably won't ever have to learn to read again.

For many, many women in the Pacific Northwest, it grew increasingly unavoidable to confront the issue of rape in our culture.

Directly after Ms. Zapata's death, the organization Home Alive was founded. Its mission statement reads:

> Home Alive is a collective of performance and visual artists (and other freaks) hell-bent on fighting all forms of violence and oppression including rape, domestic abuse, gay/lesbian bashing, racism, etc. We support people choosing any form of self defense that is necessary to survive in any given situation. Examples of self defense are verbal boundary setting, walking friends to cars or houses, locking doors, planning escape routes, de-escalation techniques, using pepper spray, physical striking techniques, fighting, yelling, martial arts, knives, guns, other weapons—ANYTHING that keeps us alive.

> Since the brutal rape and murder of Mia Zapata on July 7, 1993, we are dedicated to presenting an on-going series of high intensity music, art, spoken word, theater, film and video events that raise money to provide our community with free and affordable self defense workshops, educational material, resource information and a nagging reminder that none of us are safe.

In Seattle, Olympia, and Portland, self-protection classes became de rigueur. In Portland, a beautiful compilation album called *Free to Fight* was released. Home Alive later released a compilation album, *The Art of Self Defense,* featuring the work of many regional and national artists. Creative expression rolled to a boil, and women performed en masse. Rage crested at the forefront of songs, words, movements.

A lot of brilliant women all thinking about the same thing at the same time is very powerful. This is how change happens. Rather than underscore this to queendom come, I dedicate the next few pages to the voices of some of the women who lived in the area at the time.

Because I didn't know Mia, I didn't feel the intensity of grief a lot of people around here felt, but it made me really paranoid to the point where I felt I was losing my mind. For about three months, I lived in a state of terror, where I became afraid of everyone I knew, everyone I met, everyone I saw. I even became afraid of myself. I felt this vast rage, like I wanted to kill someone, but I didn't know who. That was very frightening. I'd never felt like that before.

But what I did was, I wrote a play called *Again.* It was all about sexual violence and abuse and the fact that your own sexuality seems to invite danger. I spent a lot of time asking myself how I can still be a sexual person, while at the same time warding off dangerous situations. Having my sexuality at the surface is very important to me, and I'm not willing to give it up. Somewhere inside myself, I suddenly believed that in order to get through this life without being raped, I had to give up my sexuality.

So, I wrote *Again*. I didn't pursue having it produced because I wasn't sure that it wouldn't make people feel more afraid and disempowered, which is not what I'm trying to do with my work at all.

Recently, my friend was telling me he was reading this book about serial killers. When he'd read about half of it, he threw the book out the eleventh-story window of his apartment because he felt it was some kind of evil totem. He wasn't learning anything from it, it was only exacerbating a fear he already had, and the book was debilitating him.

The way he described it to me sounded like that terror I felt after Mia's death, but also what I felt like when I was finished writing *Again*. It helped me, the individual, deal with my fear, but as a piece of art, I felt more like it would debilitate society in general.

There wasn't enough hope in it.

I still have so much fear of my sexuality. I hope to someday produce something to honor my sexuality, but right now, my relationship with my sexuality is colored by how other people respond to it, which I distrust greatly.

People seem to have a hard time responding to a woman's sexuality without having the desire to literally touch it. I guess in some ways, sexuality implies that, but I don't think sexuality necessarily invites someone else to participate. I don't want people to interpret my work as an invitation to fuck me.

I did read *Again* a few times, at a couple small theaters and a nightclub. There's one part where the woman character is describing what she finds erotic to a man who wants to have sex with her, but she does not want to have sex with him. She talks about listening to the rain gush into a gutter, watching a woman dip her finger in her latté and lick the foam off her finger, and someone taking their shirt off and having another one on underneath. She's telling him all these things that have nothing to do with intercourse, and often nothing to do with other people, in an effort to explain her idea of sexual eroticism to him.

After I read this at the nightclub, a friend of mine told me an acquaintance of his came up after my performance and said, "Who's that? I'd like to bone her." I was amazed. Was this guy listening to what I was saying? The character was telling a man exactly what she did not want from him and this guy thought I, the writer, would want that? That I'd want to be "boned"?

In *Letters to a Young Poet,* Rilke says, "The highest form of love is to be the protector of another person's solitude." That's what I want. For other people to love each other without having to *partake* in them, to *possess* them, to allow them to be their own inside their solitude, to protect that. I wish people respected each other's aloneness. I wish I could write something very beautiful and erotic without worrying about people wanting to use me to fulfill some fantasy—which I have no control over, and often, has nothing to do with me—inside themselves. (Kristen Kosmas, writer and performer)

When Mia died, it was like, "This is something that happens to *other people.*" I mean, it happens all the time. A woman is raped in this country every four minutes, but for someone you know to be raped and murdered, someone so strong . . . It's hard to talk about the effect Mia's death had on other women in the community. Mia's rape and murder wasn't just one isolated event, unto itself. It happened in a really vocal, outspoken community of women, who were already trying to find their voice. A lot of people say, "I didn't know her, but I felt moved to do something about her dying the way she did."

There's also a general, unifying feeling of rage in the community. Rape and murder will inspire that, regardless. Like [the young woman mentioned earlier who was abducted by two men]. She's still alive, and there was a huge response to her attack.

I teach self-defense in the community to instill in women the idea that no one has any more or less power than anyone else. What happened to [the young woman mentioned earlier], to Tanya Zolah Lippe [a Seattle writer who committed suicide in 1995], Kristen Pfaff [Hole's bass player, who overdosed on heroin] and Stefanie Sargent [7 Year Bitch's guitar player, who also overdosed on heroin]— it's all related in the sense that within the span of every minute, a woman dies in some fucked-up way, based upon her belief that she is powerless.

I started performing because I had to. It was a natural progression of what I was already doing. I make a difference and have an effect—it's not that I think people will see me perform and view violence against women in a completely different way, but I am definitely part of a larger thing which effects change. Often people either don't want to, or aren't used to seeing women angry. Not emotional, not upset, just angry. Not reactionary anger, necessarily, the anger of just being a woman. My anger serves me. It gives me a lot of energy. Sometimes, it hurts, which is the flip side of the same coin. But, I'm happy. I like my life. I like being free to express my rage. (Cristien Storm, spoken word performer, self-protection instructor, cofounder of Home Alive)

My life profoundly changed [after Mia Zapata's death] because Home Alive started out of that, and it's been one of the major focuses of my life.

My personal habits have changed dramatically as well. I used to hop on the bus alone late at night, walk around late at night. I don't do that at all anymore. I always ask my female friends how they're getting home at night and if they don't have a ride, I'll drive them. I never leave my friends without asking them if they need a ride home and they do the same for me. The whole "Okay, see you later, bye!" thing just does not happen in my life anymore.

Self-defense is something you have to work on consistently and practice. Cristien [Storm] is a fine example of a woman who practices self-defense. I never took self-defense before Home Alive started.

I've still never shot a loaded gun, but I've taken gun classes. I respect other people's choices to have a gun in their life and use it as a form of self-defense. I know a lot of women who have guns and that's their business. I don't feel comfortable with guns. However, we live in a society where guns are quite prevalent. You never know when there's gonna be a situation where a gun might be present, so you might want to know how to use one.

A big part of the philosophy of Home Alive is that people have to make their own choices about self-defense. Anything they're comfortable with, that makes them feel safe and keeps them alive is the right choice. (Gretta Harley, musician, cofounder of Home Alive)

A couple of years ago, I woke up at three in the morning to this knock on my door. My friend was standing there, scared and crying. She hadn't been feeling well and couldn't sleep, so she had gone for a walk. She was walking by the park a few blocks from here and this car started stalking her. Later she didn't know why, but she thought she'd be safe if she hid in the women's bathroom. He found her and went into the bathroom. They struggled for a while and I think she did the "I could be your sister" thing and he finally went away. That's when she came to my house. I imagine her walking those three short blocks and how frightened she must have been. Later on, we had to go back to the bathroom to find her glasses, which she lost when she was struggling with the man. That was very terrifying, even though there were three of us.

The next night was the Olympia Arts Walk and the streets were full of people walking around town. I'd been projecting images on the arts center's wall across the street from my apartment building, so we worked feverishly all that afternoon making a slide show to let people know what had happened the night before. We projected a description of the man and his car, when and where he tried to attack my friend. It was really strange to see people's reactions to it because since we didn't have much time, the images were really cartoony so people kinda laughed until they understood we made this because our friend almost got raped the night before, three blocks away from where they were standing. Then they were like, "Oh, that's right over there."

No matter how strong you are, no matter how safe you are, no matter how lucky or crafty you are, you still might be put in a position where you could get hurt. That kinda might be depressing to some people, but I think as long as you're aware of that reality, you might actually make it to the moon if you're a rocket scientist. [Laughs.] You might survive.

Also, realizing that you might not have everything you need to survive makes it more likely that you'll seek out other people to help you. Like when my friend came to my door that night. She could've run up to the park and screamed, knowing someone would've opened their window and helped her, but she knew we'd hold her instead of just providing her with a place to be removed from the danger.

I thought about that a lot when I was working on the *Free to Fight* album, which is this really great collaboration project Candy Ass Records put together. It was so cool when I got this lovely letter from Donna Dresch, saying they were gonna be putting out this record and asking me to contribute. I was like, "Oh, wow!" I don't really know how the whole thing came about, but it seemed like a great idea to me, an amazing thing to be a part of.

Anyway, during the *Free to Fight* tour, there were self-defense workshops before each show. Self-defense is something I've never taken the time out to learn, but this was really cool because it was right there. It was very beautiful. Everybody lined up in three rows, the whole room was shouting in unison. Three girls would go up at the same time and do the move while everyone else yelled and cheered them on. So many voices. It made me so happy. The workshops made people feel good about themselves, like, "I can do this!" It wasn't like, "You better do this because the world's scary and people are out to get you." It wasn't inspired by paranoia or anything. It taught me that I already do a lot of these things, I just never thought of it as self-defense before. Everybody has their own way of defending themselves, they just never think of it as such. Simple things like walking tall, talking loudly, crossing the street.

Last night I was at a show in Seattle. I went outside to get some fresh air and there was a girl standing there near

me. These two guys walked up and asked her what was going on inside and all these other questions. They weren't
being assholes or anything, but I stayed near, even though
I'd gotten enough fresh air. I didn't want to leave her alone
outside with these two guys. I stood there until they left and
then I went back inside. That was self-defense. (Nikki Mc-
Clure, performance artist)

If the violent rape and murder of one woman has an impact on the lives of thousands of her sisters, then at the very,
very least, she did not die in vain. Unfortunately, for every
solitary woman whose death inspires something other than
cavernous silence, millions of women are raped, maimed, mutilated, and murdered without garnering so much as a paragraph in the local newspaper.

There is no Howardina Stern on the airwaves every morning
instigating passionate, proactive, cuntlovin' dialogues about
rape in our culture. News helicopters hover over the scenes of
bank robberies and traffic accidents, not parks where a woman
was raped. Cities bestow awards of valor to fire fighters and
good Samaritans, not women who elude, maul, or successfully
prosecute would-be rapists.

On the back cover of Migael Scherer's courageous and
brilliant book *Still Loved by the Sun: A Rape Survivor's Journal,* Ursula
K. Le Guin says, "The power of the harasser, the abuser, the
rapist depends above all on the silence of women."

Contemplate the simplicity, depth, and truth of this statement:

The power
depends
on the silence.
Silence is our focal point of attack.
Silence is the unlocked door through which intruders enter and pillage the sacred temple of womankind.

The threat of rape lurked around my childhood in relentless warnings and admonishments. When my mother told me she had been raped, I understood the source of the fear I grew up with.

Like many women, it saddened me to feel "lucky" that rape remained a threat, but not an actual occurrence, in my personal life. I was further saddened by the fact that the very reason, I believe, neither my sister nor I have been raped is in part because of our mother's experience. She actively, consciously, ferociously protected us. Long before we knew our mother had been raped, Liz and I developed a sixth sense for dangerous situations. I am thankful for that. I believe it has aided me on a number of occasions. I wish, however, it was not initially inspired by fear and feelings of powerlessness.

Fear and powerlessness.
Silence.
Rape.

Cunthatred.

It's time for this to end.

When I started this chapter, I was re-studying Pippi Long-stocking. Partly because of my childhood, I would like to for-mally invoke Ms. Longstocking's attitude to serve as the Grand Duchess Overtone for the duration of this book:

"Have you ever seen hair like hers? Red as fire! And such shoes," Bengt continued. "Can I borrow one? I'd like to go out rowing and I haven't any boat." He took hold of one of Pippi's braids but dropped it instantly and cried, "Ouch, I burned myself."

Then all five boys joined hands around Pippi, jumping up and down and screaming, "Redhead! Redhead!"

Pippi stood in the middle of the ring and smiled in the friendliest way. Bengt had hoped she would get mad and be-gin to cry. At least she ought to have looked scared. When nothing happened he gave her a push.

"I don't think you have a very nice way with ladies," said Pippi. And she lifted him in her strong arms—high in the air—and carried him to a birch tree and hung him over a branch. Then she took the next boy and hung him over an-other branch. The next one she set on a gatepost outside a cottage, and the next she threw right over the fence so that he landed in a flower bed. The last of the fighters she put in a tiny toy cart that stood by the side of the road. . . . The boys were absolutely speechless with fright. (Lindgren 1950, 32–33)

There are two things women can do to facilitate the end of rape as an inevitable—even acceptable—aspect of our culture. The first is relatively easy, but the second will take a bit of serious cuntlove to come to fruition.

One out of eight movies produced in Hollywood contains a rape scene. In American cinema, rape scenes tend to be violently eroticized and often have nothing to do with the main plot of the film. When viewing a rape scene, scads of men feel confused and disgusted with themselves if it turns them on.

Eugene Chadbourne, a columnist for *Maximum Rocknroll* eloquently discussed a male perspective on Hollywood rape scenes. In response to *The Accused,* he stated:

After more than an hour of the film, the audience is shown the rape. There she was, Jodie Foster, stretched out on top of a pinball machine with a bunch of assholes holding her down. The first few shots of her breasts and the man kissing her and slurping around were undeniably erotic. . . . I kept wondering why I was turned on. I explained it to myself that I just knew it wasn't a real rape, [but] . . . if the whole center of the film, a supposedly brutal and disgusting rape, turns on even one person in the audience just a little bit, then the film has completely missed its mark.

A few weeks later, I saw an Australian film entitled *Shame*. This was also about rape . . . the differences between these two films were many, but one basic thing was that the makers of *Shame* chose not to show the rape, the makers of *The Accused* made it their climactic scene. (Chadbourne, March 1990)

Another non-Hollywood film that deals with rape in a responsible way is *Bandit Queen,* which is based on a true story. The protagonist, Phoolan Devi, was raped for a number of days by high-caste men in an Indian village. The camera focused on the door of the room she was kept in, with images of man after man entering and exiting. The point of her assault was clearly, horrifically made, and there was absolutely nothing erotic about it. (Her gang was allegedly responsible for later killing all of these men.)

It must be noted that this scene utterly humiliated Ms. Devi and she worked to have the movie banned in India. Whereas to my blighted Western imagination this scene was notable for its subtlety, the movie actually served as a further assault on Ms. Devi. For this reason, I can no longer recommend viewing *Bandit Queen*. Read the book instead.

On July 25, 2001, after becoming a Member of Parliament in Uttar Pradesh, Phoolan Devi was assassinated outside her home in New Delhi. A moment of silence, please.

In general, with the exception of a few films—*Thelma & Louise* comes to mind—rape scenes found in American cinema are filmed from the p.o.v. of men, who evidently experience some kind of personal gain by humiliating women. I do not know if the men who make movies enjoy humiliating individual actresses, or if it is a symbolic show of power over women in general. I do know that too many movies contain scenes that deal with rape in an unrealistic, male-fantasy-based manner.

Women viewers subjected to such scenes may experience any emotion between utter indifference and profound grief. It is safe to assume, however, that underneath any emotional response is a basic assumption of powerlessness. We are powerless to help the woman on the screen, unable to change her destiny, we cannot kill the piece of shit who violates her. We are forced to watch the pillage of one of our sisters unfold under the charmed auspices of something executives in Hollywood refer to as a plot.

Perhaps also, we are unwilling to take responsibility for something we are brought up to think of as inevitable.

The last rape scene I ever saw was in *Last Exit to Brooklyn.* The gang-rape of Jennifer Jason Leigh's character physically sickened me. When someone tells me about a great new movie, I almost always ask if there's a rape scene in it. Once this information is obtained, I can gauge whether or not this might, indeed, be a great new movie. Boycotting movies with rape scenes has enriched the quality of my life.

I don't need to see that shit.

And so, I don't.

We do not need to see our sisters up there on the screen being overpowered and assaulted by bad, scary men. We do not need to see good, righteous men saving our sisters in the nick of time or achieving "justice" for us in the courtroom.

It does not serve us.

There are a couple of options here.

Option 1

If you know a movie will contain a rape scene, forgo seeing it altogether. If you unwittingly go to a movie that contains a rape scene, leave the theater and demand your money back from the manager. Let the manager know you will not pay to see women raped. Write a letter to the president of the movie theater's distribution company. Feel free to incite your friends. Especially if you're a teenager and you organize a huge protest. The ten o'clock news likes nothing more than high school girls causing a ruckus in the name of social change. Even though it may seem like a faraway, remote place, Hollywood is a very small town with very big ears.

Movies featuring women who are strong, ass-kicking controllers of destiny are not so hard to come by these days, so it's not like such a boycott would encumber our moviegoing habits. There are plenty of wonderful films to choose from. It's far healthier to watch *The Long Kiss Goodnight* five times than to bother yourself with *Showgirls* or *Kids* once. *La Femme Nikita* and *Gloria* are excellent classics. *Set It Off, Freeway, Girls Town,* and *Bound* are part of a very welcome influx of excellent, cuntlovin' movies produced in the 1990s.

Option 2

Plan to attend movies that you know contain rape scenes. Go with a bunch of your friends. Once the rape scene is under way, stand up and scream. Freak. Loudly narrate your own version of what is happening on the screen:

"Now she is pounding his face into the metal stairs of the fire escape. Her shoe is off. Ooo! Spiked heel to the temple!!! Look at all that blood oozing from his head!" Etc. . . .

When the scene is over, march to the manager. Demand your money back based on the affront to women you were forced to witness. Continue making a huge, articulate scene in the lobby. When all your friends get their refunds, leave quietly, but continue to be cranky about it.

If our buying dollars are not squandered on that which does not serve us, sooner or later, the gentlemen in Hollywood may see the light. However, in the not too unrealistic event that gentlemen in Hollywood never see the light, our money can be used to generate more movies that serve us. There is an *entire regiment* of women in the motion picture industry struggling very hard to deliver such products to us. Let us, shall we, constructively focus on this branch of American cinema. At the same time, we also can choose to offer constructive and loud criticism to the present movie machine that makes billions of dollars off us each year.

You may have already figured this out, but the whole reason I ever felt inspired to sit down and write this book originated with the rape of my mother. I couldn't think of any other way to exact vengeance on the men who hurt her, my sister, and me so deeply.

I have thought long and hard about why women are objects of violence.

I've been through the Blaming Men phase and then I passed on to the Blaming Women phase. Neither phase did me, as an individual, much good. So then, I guess for sheer lack of imagination, I blamed myself. That didn't last long though, 'cause one night I was falling asleep and this cherry '68 Impala Lowrider cruised around in my head, and it had a bumper sticker that said:

Blame is lame with a "b"

So I thought to explore an option I hadn't considered before. I decided to love myself. To love my cunt. To love everything it does and represents.

That seemed to do a lot of good and led me to ask myself:

What is the result of women loving our cunts, en masse?

There is no place for rape in a society filled with women who love our cunts. Women can be kicked when we are down, but no one is stupid or strong enough to kick us when we are standing up, all together.

This may sound idealistic in some regards, but cuntlove envisions no mass utopia. Cuntlove is about the individual and her community. Cuntlove is about the power of you, your sisters, cousins, daughters, and intimate friends. Cuntlove is not distant rhetoric found in books and debate halls. Cuntlove is in your head, on your heart, between your legs.

Aldous Huxley, a white male writer with the ensuing sense of entitlement for which white males are famous, said, "Liberties are not given, they're taken."

In the past, women have relied on individual men and patriarchal judicial systems to fight rape.

Unfortunately, this nets exactly the same result as when I got my brothers and sister to lean toward the Baskin-Robbins as our family car approached that big, gorgeous pink-'n-white "31 Flavors" sign.

At the time, I thought the sudden redistribution of our body weight would affect the momentum of our Volkswagen van, forcing the parent driving to involuntarily swerve into the parking lot. Sometimes our parents stopped in and we all got ice cream cones, and sometimes they did not. Even though I once believed my siblings and I contributed to the former destiny by leaning toward the Baskin-Robbins, I'm willing to face the fact now that it was, ultimately, always Mom and Pop's call.

Women can continue to sit in the car and lean, or we can climb over into the front seat, yank the person controlling the vehicle out of the way, and make a sharp-assed left into the Baskin-Robbins parking lot.

This involves something I warmly refer to as:

Cuntlovin' Public Retaliation
(CPR for short)

In a climate of cuntlove, if a woman in the community is raped, other women react.

We understand there is no such thing as an isolated attack on an individual woman. We understand that a Haitian American sorority girl, a Norwegian Filipina construction worker, a Chumash Cree librarian, or a Jewish Whore is *us*. **CPR** is not at all dissimilar to a mafia philosophy in which a sister's rape is a rape of the family and cannot go unpunished. Someone has offended the honor of our family. Naturally, then, we do something about it.

In a climate of cuntlove, no one feels "lucky" it was "some other woman" who got raped. There is no such thing as "some other woman" when you have compassion and cuntlove for yourself.

The basic premise of **CPR** is publicly humiliating rapists. Because rapists count on a woman's shame and silence to keep them safe and on the streets, it seems to me that an undue amount of attention focused on rapists would seriously counter this assumption.

CPR can be employed when a woman is sure of her attacker's identity. Because most attacks are *not* perpetrated by strangers, this is a highly relevant factor.

There is safety and power in numbers.

A group of two hundred women walking into the place of employment of a known rapist would have an effect. If each of these women were in possession of a dozen rotting eggs that were then deposited onto the rapist's person, the rapist might well come to the conclusion that he had committed a very unpopular act, one that was not appreciated by the community. If a rapist had to walk through a crowd of angry, staring, silent, or quietly and deadly chanting women to get to his car in the grocery store parking lot, he might feel pretty uncomfortable.

Cuntlovin' Public Retaliation has limitless possibilities.

CPR actions can be executed without breaking too terribly many laws and without becoming violent—the latter being true especially if women only are present. Unnecessary violence is for stupid, unimaginative people. There are far more damaging ways to punish someone without invoking violence.

Cuntlovin' Public Retaliation serves history as well as the future. Women who have been raped may find enormous satisfaction and healing by acting out in a setting with other women who are present in total support, rage, and love. In this context, we are offered a liberation from silence, self-blame, quiet acceptance, or any other negative reaction we have—in the past—believed we needed for survival.

Men should not be included in **CPR** actions. Excepting situations where men have been raped, the general male response toward the rape of a friend, relative, or lover is outraged, self-righteous indignation. I've seen this reaction a number of times and believe men react this way because it gives them a chance to prove to themselves what good nonraping men they are. If men really and truly want to be "good," they can stand in the background and quietly support their women friends and relatives while we stand up for ourselves. They can chip in money to charter the buses we may need to transport everyone to the **CPR** site.

We don't need men to protect us.

This is between women and rapists.

More to the point, this is between women and ourselves.

Here is physics: a positive action yields a positive reaction.

At present, the cultural reaction to rape is generally a negative, shame-filled silence.

Fine, let the culture react that way.

We have the power to put something else there. Women can react in our own poetic, imaginative way, utilizing the resources in our community. We have power in numbers and many, many means of communication.

Yes, indeedy.

It's time for a cool change.

Any rapist would feel pretty dang upset to see his car packed full with rotting fish heads and Limburger cheese. Especially if it was a Jaguar XJS. Also, especially if the 542 women responsible were crowded onto the street where he lived, insisting that he move himself and his stinky car to another locale.

Nobody likes to be pelted with 2,060 bloody tampons.

Wouldn't you just hate like the devil to be pilloried, smeared with dogshit, forced to kneel in front of a high-powered microphone on a raised platform, and apologize to the ten thousand women who solemnly marched by you? Boy, that would be an unpleasant day that you might not forget right away, huh.

Perhaps some communities of women would be interested in constructing huge severed penises and burning them on a rapist's front lawn.

Cuntlovin' Public Retaliation is a valid cultural custom. Different tribes decide how to implement this custom in the community.

It could be highly effective.

Most importantly, with a little love, communication, temporary organization, and networking, **Cuntlovin' Public Retaliation** is very, very possible.

It's also very, very up to you.

PART III

RECONCILIATION

Recently, I saw a lady wearing a T-shirt that read, "In the post-patriarchy, I'll be a post-feminist." I realized that just a few short years ago, our vocabulary had no need for either of these terms, and I smiled.

It was the same week *nuestra* Mary Magdalene was on the cover of *Newsweek*. The pope is evidently receiving thousands of petitions daily from Catholics all over the globe, asking him to indoctrinate *nuestra* Mary as co-redemptrix—Jesus's "equal."

Each passing day heralds the emergence of yet another athlete, rock star, activist, artist, or politician who reminds women we can do pretty much whatever the fuck we want.

Signs of the dawning postpatriarchal age are positively rampant.

My 1965 *Random House Dictionary* reveals the following about the word *reconcile*:

1. to render no longer opposed; bring to acquiescence or acceptance (usually fol. by *to*): *to reconcile someone to his* [sic]

fate. 2. to win over to friendliness; cause to become amica-
ble: *to reconcile hostile persons.* 3. to compose or settle (a quar-
rel, dispute, etc.). 4. to bring into agreement or harmony;
make compatible or consistent: *to reconcile differing statements.*
5. to reconsecrate (a desecrated church, cemetery, etc.). 6.
to restore (an excommunicate or penitent) to communion
in a church.

The definition most pertinent to this book is number five:
to reconsecrate a desecrated church.

The religious ritual of submerging a newborn child in a
bowl of water inside a house of god is an attempt to simulate
the power all women are potentially born with. If it is reasonable for the patriarchy to call these houses of god "churches,"
then it is reasonable for me to believe that both the individual
female body and the body of womankind are churches too. *And
I do.*

Fixing up our church, as well as the reference point of worship
inside our hearts, is therefore a timely thing to do.

The following items comprise a church:

1. Protection from potential hostilities represented
   by opposing belief systems. Our mission to educate
   ourselves and children the way we want.
2. All mediums of art and literature depicting a cor-
   responding creed and collective consciousness. Our

immolationless stained glasses and holy scriptures that we design to our specifications.

3. Resources. Cash flow. Passing around our tithe baskets to fill our coffers with our money, honey.

For the reconciliation of our church, we will use cunt-lovin' perspectives on protection, representational art, and money. I start with protection because it flows nicest after the subject of rape.

Aggro Beyond Your Wildest Dreams

I will kick your fucking ass.

—ancient Goddess mantra

Mapping Out a Belief System

The first thing you need to protect yourself is a womanifesto. My friend Ashley turned me on to the importance of womanifestoes when she said:

"I like them because they tell me what I think."

Defining and articulating your beliefs serves you in any context. By taking that a step further and causing those beliefs to exist in the material world, you contribute to a social climate of cuntlovin' evolution.

I offer my womanifesto on self-protection to perhaps give you some ideas about how you might write yours. A womanifesto does not have to be written. It can be a song, dance, painting, or whatever medium stirs passion in your heart. I strongly suggest creating your own womanifesto before moving on to the next section, "Kickin' Ass Like There Ain't No Tomorrow."

• • •

THE WOMANIFESTO FOR THE
CATEGORICAL NEW FREEDOM LADY

when you see a really drunk girl leave a bar alone late at night and you follow her and make sure she gets into her taxi all right, that's self-protection.

when you aren't afraid of looking like a supreme chickenshit and ask your friend to go into a public bathroom with you because it creeps you out, but not for any tangible reason, that's self-protection.

when you are in the music store and you pick a CD by women musicians who have your back instead of by a bunch of boys who hog all the airtime on the radio, that's self-protection.

when you are sitting on the bus and the man who sits next to you gives you a bad vibe and you get up and move to another seat without giving a rat's ass about feeling like you're being rude, that's self-protection.

when you find out which politician is supportive of women, lesbians, and motherhood and vote for her, that's self-protection.

when you look at all the beautiful women on TV and in magazines in the grocery store and think they are part of a weird industry run by men with major, major dick complexes, that's self-protection.

when you boycott all media not responsive in every way, shape, and freudian slip to women's rights, that's self-protection.

when you make a conscious effort to spend your money in establishments owned by women, that's self-protection.

when you tell your dude if he can't hold his wad until you're damn well ready to come then he's gonna hafta invest in a strap-on dildo of your choosing, that's self-protection.

when you ask for a raise, that's self-protection.

when you insist everyone re-read *Pippi Longstocking* again, that's self-protection.

when you and your friends concoct plans of poetic guerrilla terrorism against a teacher, fellow student, coworker, or boss who sexually harasses women, that's self-protection.

when you decide it's in your best interest to worship a Goddess who innately respects women, that's self-protection.

when you cook a gourmet, five-course meal no one but you will partake in, that's self-protection.

when you "accidentally" spill your drink on a man at a party who looks at your body rather vulpinely, and you don't in the least appreciate it, that's self-protection.

when you educate yourself about clitoridectomies, infibulation, forced prostitution, rape as a war tactic and a way of controlling women, the Nation of Islam, Judaism, Christianity, and prepatriarchal religions, the Inquisition, women painters, photographers, filmmakers, poets, writers, activists, politicians, sex-industry workers, historians, archaeologists, and musicians, that's self-protection.

when you read, then watch *Bandit Queen*, that's self-protection.

when you massage your friend because she's PMSing hard, that's self-protection.

when you keep a tire iron by your front door, that's self-protection.

when you buy a pull-up bar and install it in a doorway you pass constantly so you end up doing pull-ups all the time, even though you used to think you couldn't do pull-ups, that's self-protection.

when you dance, run, jump, buy yourself a birthday cake even though your birthday's five months away, cavort, kiss all the girls you love to love, laugh, sing, shout, jump rope, ding-dong ditch the house of someone who gets on your nerves, swing, climb trees, pick your nose in public, daydream, eat with your fingers, break something on purpose, fart loud, skip, and pin your friends to the ground and tickle them, that's self-protection.

every time you look in the mirror and your heart races because you think, "i'm so fucking rad," that's self-protection. protect your self.

• • •

I wrote that when I was twenty-eight. I went through a lot of re-conditioning on my own terms before I had the knowledge to sit down and compose those thoughts off the top of my head.

I grew up in a relatively small town in the Central Coast region of California. The *president of the Elks* spoke at the high school graduation ceremony I boycotted. Cruising up and down the main street in a car, going to the mall, and attending drunken date-rape festivals called "parties" were the culminations of social interaction.

I was never entirely comfortable in this setting.

Until I was eighteen and left "home," I was constantly at odds with this culture I grew up in. The older I got, the more clearly I saw what was supposed to be looming ahead for me as a woman.

I wanted nothing to do with any of it.

This conflict became increasingly unsettling with each passing year. I did not want to keep my mouth shut and act ladylike, stop having sex with my girlfriends, or respect the idea that all of my teachers were smarter than me. Dealing with such opposition on a day-to-day basis disrupted the momentum of womanpower I was born with. I struggled to keep my power somewhat apace with my life. This proved difficult, as I expended a large amount of energy defending my own concept of the woman I wanted to be. Furthermore, deprived of the experience I needed in order to *know* exactly what "the woman I wanted to be" *meant,* things were not only difficult but mind-bogglingly complex as well.

At one point in my life, I detested the adage "What does not kill me will only make me stronger."

But it is true.

When I was a kid, I was on the swim team, played tackle football, and moto-mud bicycled. My friends and I endlessly plotted live-action *Charlie's Angels* episodes, including our edited-in couplings between 'Bri and Jill. Underwater Tea 'n Smash Party in the ocean always ruled. I loved the "Heidi" look and wore dresses with my waffle stompers. I was a late bloomer in terms of clearly established gender roles.

Largely through the teachings of my philandering, sexist father, who did not want me to grow up prey to men like himself, I became a premature and great advocate of vigilante-type behavior. I heartily beat the shit out of any mean boy who made the sorry mistake of pulling my pigtails or pushing any girl's face into the water fountain at school.

My mother, for obvious reasons we've already discussed, had no qualms about this sort of behavior. Fighting with girls was not cool (and seldom occurred), but she didn't give a rat's ass if I beat the shit out of a boy.

My older brother was not only bigger than all the boys at my school but also acted in the role of sparring partner in our perpetual sibling battle for turf, rights, and privileges. Childhood with my brother provided an ongoing study in the velocity of a strategically placed kick, the rhythm of a punch in the gut, and the mother lode of reactions elicited from a well-timed, ear-splitting scream.

Between the (albeit dubiously inspired) sense of entitlement fostered by my parents' philosophies and the practical, tactical skills I derived from life with my brother—not to mention the wolf-pack mother mentality I found in such sister bad-asses as Deanna Alvarado and Hannah Class—the mean boys at my school were resoundingly pummeled whenever a girl reported untoward behavior to one of us.

A most satisfactory arrangement, as far as I was concerned.

Then I grew up.

The mean little boys who taunted and teased and harassed little girls also grew up.

We all grew up.

The taunting, teasing, and harassing evolved into rape, passive-aggressive control lurking behind proclamations of "egalitarianism," sexual harassment, and collective beliefs of male superiority.

I experienced damnable levels of confusion going from a little girl who accepted highly suspect gender roles to a young lady suddenly in possession of a very specific set of restrictions and scriptures.

One of the many, many, many scriptures imposed upon me once I got big was: "It is your duty to ignore mean boys and their games."

And, see, given the latitude I enjoyed throughout my early years, I just had a very difficult time ignoring this kind of stuff. But now that I was big, even if I tattled (a wimpy manipulation

I rarely resorted to as a child), no one listened or cared. If I retaliated, I got in trouble, lost jobs, made enemies.

Oh, how I sometimes longed for those days on the playground when kicking a mean boy's ass was a mundane occurrence in any given school week.

It became my reality to let mean boys slide. Though I did not like it, I also didn't see much in the way of options. The operative words here are *I didn't see.* Before any option-seeing went down, I had to *really see* my own fears.

It was a *struggle* to see options.

I looked very, very painstakingly.

I came to terms with the reality that in the eyes of an overwhelming percentage of the population, my sole purpose on the planet was to make dicks ejaculate, either for procreation or recreation. Being reduced to this identity every time I ventured out in public was an affront I chose to ignore for a long time. It is still a drag to see men looking at me in terms of their dicks and to know that no matter what I accomplish as a person, or how I live my life, this will probably not change significantly in my lifetime.

If I had not avidly, passionately, relentlessly sought options, I am sure I would have gone insane. Regardless of whether *I* ever recognized the existence of options, they were always there. Like a faithful old family dog, my options waited for me to recover the survival skills I relinquished in adolescence.

Kicking Ass Like There Ain't No Tomorrow

It got to a point when I reasoned, if I take my survival into consideration every time I leave the sanctity of my home—if, indeed, my home sometimes seems to be a fortress that deters enemy forces—then aren't I kind of like a soldier, and isn't my life kind of like a war?

It plain and simple dawned on me: somebody here was seriously out of the loop. There was no circumventing the fact that I had allowed my nice wolf-pack-mama girlhood survival skills to languish.

A sad—but certainly not irrevocable—mistake I made in order to survive into adulthood.

So let's see.

The first thing a soldier does is train. In boot camp she learns physical tactics and the psychology of her enemy. She meditates upon all the nuances that come into play in the battle of how a life lived in fear is a life half lived.

In the Army of Me, self-protection class was appointment number one, dee-dee-dun.

After I published an article about rape, a cartoonist named Ellen Forney wrote a letter to my editor. Ms. Forney eloquently pointed out my responsibility to urge women to learn how to protect ourselves rather than merely publish essays about all the things we had to fear in this world. In the letter, Ellen described her pivotal experiences learning and then teaching self-protection. Her letter fully inspired me. I asked if she'd be interested in teaching a class if I organized it, and she graciously agreed.

Ms. Forney taught us about using our voices and deflecting verbal assaults before venturing into physical maneuvers. I was all geared up to kick me some ass; it was surprising to discover such a fount of strength and release simply by listening to women talk about how we deal with everyday situations that rankle the psyche in a slow and eroding process.

I learned a lot of physical tactics in this first self-protection class. More importantly, it became clear that these skills exist as part of a larger philosophy of self-protection that is explored and practiced by each individual woman, on our terms, at our pace.

Ellen's class ruled, and my second self-protection class kept the ol' synapse pulsations spurring along.

The next course I took was Model Mugging. It's a form of self-protection developed by a group of martial arts experts. A woman in this group had been raped. This, in itself, is not terribly unique. However, she was an eighth-degree karate black belt. She knew a martial art very, very well, but she did not know how to protect herself in the specific context of sexual assault. The group decided to pool their expertise and design a way to teach any woman, regardless of agility, prowess, or strength, to protect herself.

They did an awesome, good job.

Model Mugging was intensive and expensive, and all my ass-kickin' dreams came true because there were *actual, live human men* in padded outfits that I got to pound on. My job in this class was to use my power to change the physical course of another human being who, for all intents and purposes, meant me harm. Even though I was in a room with nineteen other women and rubber mats were spread out all over the floor, the reality was daunting. *These men were present to attack and react.* We twenty women were present to react and attack.

Attack, attack, react, react over and over and over.

Certainly on par with the joy of actually downing the big, burly, padded dudes was watching other women negotiate power against them. This was when I *really understood* there are as many different definitions of self-protection as there are cerebral filing systems. No one reacted to the exact same situation in the exact same way, even though we were all being taught the exact same tactics.

A womanifesto and self-protection classes (note the plural form of *class*) are fantastic starting points for powerful reconditioning. Define what you believe. Train your mind and body to react to detrimental situations in a powerful, assertive way. These two survival tactics are, however, just that: *tactics.* They *help* your brain to think differently.

Remember back yonder when I induced an abortion without going to the vacuum cleaner? Remember how the herbs I took aided me in directing *my own focus*? The same concept holds true here (and at many other outposts in a cuntlovin' lady's life). Training requirements aren't fulfilled by attending a course every Wednesday night for eight weeks. Self-protection is a *way of thinking, constantly,* each and every moment of your life. Classes help. Entertaining proactive dialogues with the women you love helps. Womanifestoes help. Lotsa stuff helps. *Nothing* is as valuable as implementing new learning tools and committing to your focus for *the rest of your life.*

I advocate self-protection as a lifestyle philosophy—modus operandi. I don't believe that wielding a can of pepper spray, a switchblade, or a gun is on par with existing on the planet with a self-protection lifestyle at the forefront of one's being.

Neither do I in any way oppose the use of weapons as self-protection. When one chooses weapons to protect oneself in this world, it is of *utmost importance* to learn *formal, rigorous safety and precision techniques in the specific context of protection from physical and/ or sexual assault.* Deer hunting and gang banging are probably not gonna prepare your spirit, mind, or body for a potential sexual assault.

The most reliable weapon is your mind. When women relinquish the power of our minds to objects that can inflict debilitating pain or death, we weaken our position. A quick, resourceful, well-trained thinker is a *much deadlier opponent* than someone who projects power into a deadly instrument.

A quick, resourceful, well-trained thinker with a deadly instrument in hand is then Warrior Goddess incarnate.

Hee fucken hawww.

Cross that bridge when you get to it.

In the meantime, the most wonderful way I have found to train my mind for assessing situations and reacting with the resources I have available to me is on a checkered playing board that has two sets of sixteen figurines carved to represent different qualities and nuances of power.

Chess Is Our Friend

I am thankful to Boaz Yakin, a gentleman who made a movie I will watch anytime, anyplace. It's called *Fresh*. In light of its *phenomenal* importance, the injustice of *Fresh*'s poor distribution makes me almost pass out.

Fresh is an adolescent young man growing up in a situation rife with predators. His environment is predatory, his inherited socioeconomic latitude is a predator, and all but one of his role models are predators. Fresh's sole nonpredatory role model is his father, played by the incomparable Mr. Samuel L. Jackson.

Fresh lives in a foster home. He isn't supposed to see his father, but he does. Every week, they play chess together in a park. I said Fresh's father is not a predator, but that's not altogether true. He manifests his predatory traits on the chessboard, in the game he lives and breathes.

The story of Fresh unfolds around these weekly chess games with his father. Territory being what it is, both on the chess board and in life, Fresh's father routinely wins the game. Meanwhile, in his day-to-day life (of which his father is completely ignorant), Fresh faces responsibilities and situations that would cause chronic intestinal complications in the hardiest CEO at IBM.

Fresh meets his father in the park every week and plays this very old game. It is kind of a ritual. His father says things like, "What kind of player am I? Am I an offensive player or a defensive player? Right, I'm neither. *I play my opponent.*"

With all his heart, Fresh listens, looks, learns. The gift of chess and its lessons in strategy may be all his estranged, alcoholic father has to offer him. It is also more valuable than an eight-digit trust fund.

Fortified with nothing more than a psychology that assesses and undermines their *individual* ways of operating, Fresh pretty much mauls every predator in his life—without personally committing a single act of violence. He learns how to *think like the predators.* You know who reigns supreme, or the movie wouldn't be called *Fresh.*

Fresh has become one of the biggest role models in my life. I constantly ask myself, "How would Fresh deal with this situation?" When I'm reacting like a dork in response to some damn stimulus or another, I say, "Fresh wouldn't do that in a million years." Perhaps most significantly, Fresh reminds me to get off my ass and play chess every chance I get.

My father taught me how to play chess when I was five. I played quite often with my sparring partner—er, brother. Just as I had grown up and left my survival skills in the hinterland, I likewise stopped playing chess at some obscure point in adolescence. Whenever I had the opportunity to play chess as an adult, I met a fierce resistance inside myself. I didn't like the competition, the cutthroat vibe.

After Fresh came into my life, I managed to shred this resistance asunder. However, it turned out most of my opponents were of the male persuasion. With precious few exceptions, my girl friends either never learned how to play or said the same thing I always said, "I used to play when I was younger, but I haven't played in a long time." As if not having played "in a long time" is somehow grounds for continuing this trend. Throughout my non-chess-playing rehabilitation, this response started sounding like, "I used to enjoy honing my strategy and getting what I want by employing my vast intelligence, but that stuff just doesn't interest me anymore."

Chess is a psychological exercise. It whets the brain for every conceivable means of self-protection.

When my pieces are threatened, my brain is presented with a puzzle. I must come up with a way to counter—with a ruse, sacrifice, or threat of my own. No apologies. My A-1 priority is devising any plan in the whole wide world that does not involve retreat. Unless it diverts my opponent's attention from how devastatingly I plan to fuck them over on my next coupla moves, retreat is an absolute anathema.

Each person I play chess with tells me about their way of surviving in the world. If I piece together an overall view of their modus operandi, I win. When I sit across the board from someone, I'm engaged in more than a game. I silently beseech, "Tell me how you survive." Each opponent I play offers yet another survival strategy for my cerebral filing system.

Chess teaches how to deal with threatening situations and individuals *in the midst* of taking territory for oneself. The chances of being caught off guard have discernable boundaries. Predators become opponents instead of scary monsters over whom one has no control. When played on a regular basis, chess melds into one's consciousness. It becomes evident that one is never not playing this game.

Chess fortifies the psyche. When interwoven with physical and psychological training, it keeps a lady on her self-protective toes.

This game matters.

Get good at it and then get better.

Play chess with your friends instead of watching the M Tee Vee. Organize all-girl tournaments at your school and all-women tournaments at your work. If you're not kickin' everybody's butt, then put a lot of thought into why they're kickin' yours. Play yourself. Play your mom. Invite a woman you think you can't stand to play a game with you. Play chess at a coffee house with someone you would never otherwise interact with. Have email chess challenges. Tell your boss if you beat her at chess she hasta give you a raise.

Get on down and get back up again.

Play chess every day.

Predators Are Our Friends

I founded a direct-action antirape warfare group called Mobilizing Our Neighbors and Sisters to Eradicate Rape (MONSTER). More accurately, I thought up a clever acronym and organized a space for women to come together and address the issue of rape as a cultural oppression tactic used to control women. The group of women involved did all the founding.

MONSTER's objective, decided upon after much discussion and debate, was to be a primarily nonviolent vigilante group that (more or less poetically) terrorized known sexual predators in our community, educated people about rape, and provided a safe, supportive environment for women to devise and carry out nefarious plans of poetic attack.

As with every activist group on the planet, MONSTER consisted of a balance of two creeds. One was of the passive, leaflet-plastering, networking persuasion, while the other had a much more aggressive, predatory nature.

For many weeks, I interacted with this group of bright, imaginative, angry women and listened carefully to both systems of belief. Although I was a subscriber to the predatory creed, I came to have a deep understanding of the women who wanted to act out in a more genteel manner. The argument ran along the lines of "We don't want to act like predators because then we are lowering ourselves to the level of a rapist," which is as valid an argument as can possibly be. This would invariably provoke the "nature versus nurture" argument and someone would cite the ferocity of a Serengeti mother lion or an arctic mama polar bear.

As is evidenced by MONSTER's eventual objectives, compromises were reached, leaning toward the predatory.

What I learned from this experience was a pretty solid foundation for *Cunt*: when women 100 percent define anything—from simple words to complex institutions—the meaning or outcome inherently serves us *most* satisfactorily. Period.

It is very simple, but a lot of work.

A predator, as defined by our society, is a bad man who will hurt you.

Ouch.

A predator, as defined by MONSTER, is a nice lady who proactively protects herself and the women in her community.

Whee!

Both definitions are sound.

MONSTER's cuntlovin' definition doesn't attempt to make the former one null and void. It sits right along next to it, happy as the day is long. Practically *the instant* we actually defined *predator* for ourselves, the group's Kali the Destroyers piped down a few notches, while *nuestra* Virgens de Guadalupe started baring teeth.

Fucken refreshing, you know?

Predators are important people. Why else would there be one in almost every movie and story throughout history. Take away the predator, and where does that leave the koran, bible, torah?

Nowhere, that's where.

Predators are not the problem.

I, for one, don't *feel* like going out into the world and making sure all the predators who focus on women are put behind bars or executed or whatever. In this cuntfearing society, there's plenty more where they came from. Some Sisyphean tasks can be fun, but that's not one of them.

It is impossible to change the fact that sexual predators are a product of our society, whether they are incarcerated or free to roam. And, *damn*, it sucks that no incantation from heaven and hell combined will undo the deeply rooted damage rape has already done to the collective consciousness of womankind.

Dang, that's all impossible, so forget it.

Say goodbye to the impossible: toodle doo.

It is possible to change our way of reacting and dealing. Without silence, the *cycle*, the *livelihood* of violence toward women, goes haywire. Women break the cycle, and the situation then belongs to us.

Our ball, our court, our move.

As I see it, the major problem facing us ladies is not all the horrible shit that's been happening to us for the past two thousand-odd years.

Nor is it the perpetrators of the horrible shit.

The problem is we don't seem to think we have much of a predatory disposition. This is heartily reinforced by our culture, which unduly punishes women who are caught acting out in a violent, predatory way. It frightens people very, very much when women do violent things. The United States legal and judicial systems are hardly exempt from this fear. Jails are populated with women who murdered the lovers, friends, or male relatives who assaulted us or our children for years. If it is at all possible to completely avoid contact with the judicial sector of society, I suggest doing so with vigor.

Physical violence is something one resorts to only when it is the very, very, very best way to safety. Violence is not a defining trait of a lady predator. It is certainly imperative to know how, when, why, and where to be violent. It is also imperative to know how, when, why, and where to get away before a situation has the chance to escalate.

Lady predators are cuntlovin', imaginative women. We therefore manifest our predatory stance in just such a manner. We're not too shy to be highly visible. We'll scream "My Country 'Tis of Thee" to drown the voice of Loudmouth Asshole who is trying to impress his friends by telling everyone on the street the effect we do/do not have on his dick. We're not too proud to be invisible, either. We know that for Mr. Obviously Fucked-Up in the Head, "Amazing Grace" sung soft 'n low under our breath miraculously makes him forget we're crossing his path.

Lady predators get all our friends to confront the dickwad who bugs us at work or at school. We ensure employers know which of their employees is a date rapist and picket the place if the boss does not respond accordingly. We publicly humiliate the man who rapes our daughter, sister, lover, mother. We organize into mama wolf packs with a rabid sense of humor. We have Abusive Husband Treasure Hunts on Super Bowl Sunday.

We interrupt the game.

It

is

funner 'n shit.

Who to Include

When the general public asks me what *Cunt* is about, I used to say, "It's a women's studies book," and change the subject. By the "general public," I mean those who unquestioningly exist in a culture of consumerism, the teevee, and denial. Most folks of this stripe aren't attracted to the ideas in my book, so I don't see much point in engaging about it.

Upton Sinclair said, "It is difficult to get a man to understand something when his salary depends on his not understanding it."

(Forgive him the male-centered language; he was six feet under by the time the Summer of Love rolled around.)

I study occupational vocabularies so I can convincingly fabricate an identity when I am in social situations (like weddings) where the fucken annoying question "And what do *you* do?" is likely to come up.

Lately, I've been an underwater welder and a cake designer.

Don't get me wrong.

I'm not a reticent person. It's just that the corporate work ethic has completely infiltrated US culture and created a pathologically unhealthy atmosphere for self-actualization and

open-mindedness. I'll talk a blue streak with self-actualized/
open-minded folks. I can spot a self-actualized person from a
mile away and have gotten into breathtakingly beautiful cunt-
versations with open-minded cowboys and marines.

Once I was in Flagstaff and my buddy Dawn Kish asked
some friends of hers if they had read a book called *Cunt*. One of
them, a man, kinda chuckled and said, "No. What's it about?"

Without missing a beat or even looking askance at me, she
said, "Freedom."

I was delighted. Dawn inadvertently provided me with
something to say to members of the general public who manage
to find out I wrote a book called *Cunt*.

So, freedom.

The all-purpose, common-denominator, one-word syn-
opsis of *Cunt* that I like best. *Cunt* is a product of my freedom
and my need to be in a free world with free people.

I lived in a small town for the first nineteen years of my life,
and I was not free there. It was no secret to me. Towns like
Santa Maria are tried-and-true petri dishes for cultivating incredibly oppressed adults.

When I was growing up, *feminism* and *vegetarianism* shared
similar, extremely peripheral roles. I could probably have given
you a definition for both terms, but it never occurred to me
that *feminism* and *vegetarianism* were *actual realities* that happened

in the lives of *actual people*. I had absolutely no experience with either term until I was almost twenty years old, when people started calling me a "feminist" and I found out how grocery store chickens die.

As a teenager, I had one, and I mean ONE, resource informing me that there existed sound-assed reasons for feeling imprisoned in my community—an album called *Penis Envy* by the UK band Crass.

It was, evidently, enough to kick-start a life of political resistance that shows no signs of petering out, but really, *Penis Envy* was all I had. The end. Nothing else.

Crass is a social movement/band of vegan anarchist punks who created their own record label, a community center/school, and other such amenities in the early era of the punk movement. *Penis Envy* sent me scurrying to the dictionary, puzzling together phrases like "rituals of repression." I listened to that album every day, over and over.

Loudly.

In my room with the door closed, but thudding.

How does one go from being a pissed-off little punk rocker holed up in her bedroom to being a pissed-off writer who gets to experience fucken rad things like freedom?

It's a long process. I live in flux. Nothing stays the same here.

By the time I sat down to write *Cunt,* I was at a point where I'd read a lot of books, interviewed a lot of people, written poems, songs, articles, and stories, and, *crucially*, had almost ten years experiencing life in communities where women were, for example, on stages talking/singing/rapping serious-assed shit and starting night patrols to see people home safely. I was sick of being pigeonholed as a "feminist" just because I asserted myself. I was also angry about the prevalence of and ambivalence toward sexual assault (among many other things). I wanted to write a book that could, feasibly, speak of freedom to all girls and women.

And—in my wildest dreams—to boys and men as well.

What I did not consider—and this is totally a result of my socialization—is that the world is made up of more than women and men, boys and girls. In writing *Cunt,* I completely overlooked the realities of gender-variant people.

This was brought to my attention a year after the first edition of *Cunt* came out.

At the 1999 Michigan Womyn's Music Festival, issues of transgender inclusion exploded within the queer community. As the story goes, some transladies attended the festival that year, thus defying the festival's "Womyn Born Womyn" policy. While one of the "trans-gressors" was taking a shower, other festival attendees saw her dick, and people freaked out and started running around screaming "There are PENISES on The Land!!!"

(I am not making this up.)

A few months after this brouhaha, I started being questioned about my "position" on trans-inclusion. In particular, some readers had problems with the sentence "All women have cunts," which appeared in the introduction to the first edition and led many transfolks to feel expressly (and rightfully) excluded from *Cunt*.

The events in Michigan set off a firestorm, and I was pressured to defend my book in ways I'd never anticipated. I was confused—kicking myself for inadvertently alienating an entire sector of humanity and, at the same time, being patient because learning never ends.

Learning is endless.

A woman named Zabrina Aleguire from the wonderful land of North Carolina wrote me a long, incredibly intelligent email about gender and trans-inclusion.

Here is an excerpt:

> *Dear Inga,*
>
> *Tearing through your book* Cunt *was incredible for me—an experience I've wanted to share with many other gals. . . . I'd like to thank you for helping me get back in touch with my body, my passion, my silliness, and my fighting feminism. Your book helped inspire me and some other cunt-lovin women to resurrect women's health and art collectives, in the tradition of groups like Magical Pussy from Chapel Hill.*
>
> *In addition to letting you know how much your words have inspired, ignited, and entertained me and my friends, I want to share some thoughts about an omission from* Cunt. *What I'm talking about is transgender identity and gender nonconformity. In the intro to the book I was stopped short by the words "womankind is varied and vast. But we all have cunts."*

Do we? I thought. Aren't there women without cunts? Or, what about the tranny boys in my life who have cunts but don't consider themselves women—despite years of assigned female gender? I wanted their inclusion in this declaration of independence, this feminist manifesto. And yet, "the anatomical jewel which unites us all" and "the only common denominator . . . that all women irrefutably share" didn't seem to imply that room for inclusion. . . .

I'll tell you about my experience being a bridesmaid in my friend's huge country-club, limousine-princess, "you don't want to know how much I paid for this gown" wedding. It was the first wedding I'd been to since coming out the year before and subsisting on a really small salary doing queer activist work. By the time we reached the reception, I was feeling so strange amongst the wealth and heterosexism that I was almost physically ill. But I burst into a smile when I saw our waitress Joy. Noticeably a male-to-female trans-woman, Joy had short hair, a bunch of earrings, long press-on nails, and a long, pleated black skirt. She was our headwaiter for the wedding party table, and I felt relieved and a little less isolated to know I wasn't the only queer in the ballroom.

Then other guests noticed her. Little cousins and the groomsmen began whispering, pointing, and asking, "Is it a boy? Is it a girl?" Then she became a snicker, a joke, a snide remark. Some were "weirded out." Some were "appalled." Some were "disgusted." Toward the end of the evening the intoxicated matron of honor, Cynthia, exploded, "I don't know what the hell he's doing! I'm gonna call him George. Why does he call himself Joy?

It must give him joy to wear a skirt." She spat her words. "He's sick! . . . That man/woman whatever." I stood by stunned and pissed off by such a venomous diatribe against Joy, who was quite lovely—and a helluva good waiter at that. Looking back I wish I had asked Cynthia what made her so angry. Instead, I have just been wondering the question on my own since. . . .

My guess is that Cynthia was feeling it that weekend—the pressure of conformity. Compared to the bride, nothing about herself must have felt good enough—not her house, her car, her job, her husband, her family, her appearance. Damn, I was feeling it too—inadequacy, comparison, even shame. And there was Joy, intentionally, blatantly not conforming in an environment where Cynthia required it of herself and doubted her own worth among the wealth, beauty, and (perceived) acceptance of those around her. This experience illustrated to me how we stick to gender conformity as strongly as, if not stronger than, any other norms. We get hell when we—as women or men or trans or androgynous people—diverge from those norms. It's in these moments that I see how tightly feminism, queer, and trans liberation are connected.

Our culture's stringent male/female gender codes are inextricably linked to our oppression as women, our materialistic capitalist culture, and the rigidity and denial of self-expression that is characteristic of white people (particularly those holding on to significant power). We are culturally accepted and even celebrated if we stay within established power differentiation. That's how Cynthia gets hers—being a seasoned hetero beauty. That makes her "better" than people like Joy. How dare Joy challenge *the system that Cynthia knows deep down has gotten her at least somewhere, with a husband, a sorority membership for life, and a home of her own away from that crowded middle-class house of her childhood in the Midwest.*

In my mind it makes sense for feminists and progressive transgender folks to be united—and in many of our communities this is the case. But there is still such serious division, as we see from the Michigan Womyn's Festival. I think it's work like yours that can help bridge this division. Clearly there needs to be more challenge put to feminist communities who don't acknowledge transidentity as authentic, as well as to transgender communities who don't engage with gender privilege and oppression. From what I have observed, your ability to inspire cuntlove in so many people makes me think that you can really help this effort. I look forward to hearing back from you.

In solidarity,

Zabrina Aleguire

I feel really blessed that such an incredibly smart person would take time out of her life to write me such a beautifully articulated letter.

Thank you, Zabrina.

This multifaceted issue raised a lot of questions in my heart. I called my friend Lynnee Breedlove, a woman who—as lead singer for the band Tribe 8—has had her dick sucked on stage by hundreds of people. This surely merits an entry in the

Guinness World Records by anyone's standards except for, evidently, the people at Guinness.

Anyway, I needed answers and Lynnee is a person who often has good ones.

And she did, but not like how I thought her answers might go.

She said:

> ### "It's question time, pal.
> ### It's not a time for answers.
> ### It's a time for questions."

This was one of those moments when gold lamé banners unfurl from the sky in my mind and trumpets blare in the dawn's early light of my consciousness and I say, "Oh. But of course."

Question time.

What if someone who was born a "boy" feels like a "girl" almost always?

If s/he dates girls, is s/he heterosexual or homosexual?

What if someone who was born a "girl" feels like a "boy" five months out of the year like clockwork?

If s/he dates girls is s/he bisexual?

What if someone who grew up to be a "man" felt like being *more* than a woman every Friday night at the local cabaret?

What if this "man" was happily married to a woman and had three kids?

What if this "man" was happily married to a man and had three kids?

What if someone who grew up to be a woman felt like being a man when she went out for solo nights on the town?

What if, as this man, she developed an endearingly cantankerous personality? And what if she loved this personality and loved having two completely different sides of herself that she manifested through changes in dress, thinking, environment, and comportment?

What if a kid felt completely NOT the specific gender that society assigned him/her throughout life, and so decided to get an operation or take hormones when s/he grew up so that his/her physical appearance would mirror the self-image s/he holds dearest to his/her heart?

What is wrong with any of this?

What, exactly, does it mean to be a "woman"?

What, exactly, does it mean to be a "man"?

Why shouldn't one's gender be as fluid as one's life should be, if it's a happy life, I mean?

If it's a life where freedom happens.

I wrote *Cunt* from my experience as a white woman who grew up on the West Coast of the USA in a working-class single-parent home. I grew up in a culture that hates cunts, hates women, hates everybody who isn't white and/or white-identified, and hates all of us over here in what Eddie Murphy and I lovingly refer to as "the faggot section" (*Eddie Murphy: Comedian*, 1983).

When I found out that the word *cunt* once held emphatically nonderogatory meanings in cultures all over the world, I saw this huge link in the way both women and this word have been denigrated over time. It took *thousands of years* to get women to believe we were such silly things as "the weaker sex." I was seeking freedom from this history for myself and for everyone who is afflicted with it. My experience of being a woman was, and is, greatly influenced by my cunt: a maligned part of my body that bleeds, that can be raped, that was the focal point of two harrowing vacuum abortions; a cunt that produces grand, smashing orgasms.

I never thought my cunt was what *made me a woman*, but I knew that many of my experiences as a woman were (and continue to be) centered around my cunt.

I considered defying society's prescription for how we treat our bodies to be a revolutionary act of nonconformity. It is *political resistance* to learn self-protection, to masturbate, to fuck whomever you want, to take control of your body's functions and fluids. All of these things are in direct opposition to how society deems we should act and feel. I still believe this with all my heart, but in the last few years, I've been inspired to think about gender variance in a broader context. This has really shaken up my whole notion of how I perceive the world—and my book.

As a child, I took umbrage at being repeatedly told I was "such a pretty little girl until you open your mouth," but I was also perfectly content doing things little girls weren't "supposed" to do, such as fighting, cussing, and challenging my teachers. Through all of this, though, I never felt a conflict about my assigned gender.

I knew I wasn't like the "good" girls at my school, who cried if you hit them with a muddy dodge ball. I knew I was a "bad," "loud," and "aggressive" girl.

But still, a girl.

Before people started asking me about trans-inclusion, I simply took it for granted that I was a biological woman. When I stopped to think about it on a daily basis, however, I seldom consciously think, "I am a woman." I am most often aware that I am a woman when I feel threatened or when someone—through actions, body language, or words—points out that I am a woman.

When I am riding my skateboard late at night and see a group of (potentially drunk, repressed, and sexually frustrated) men outside a bar on the sidewalk, I feel like a woman. I am faced with a number of choices, all based on survival. Should I cross the street? Should I yell, "Coming through, fellas!" and plow forward? Should I turn back and go around the block before they notice me? Should I hop off into the street and coast around them?

At decision-making times like these, I am acutely aware of being a woman.

When I am in the airport and a security person hollers, "FEMALE," so I can be wanded, I feel like a woman.

When I am on my period and aggressively shun loud-mouthed men and their radio stations, I feel like a woman.

In the final analysis, I think of myself as *a woman* only in specific circumstances.

The rest of the time I am just me.

Me, asking questions.

Me, in flux.

Isn't this the same for most people?

I mean, when you stop to think about it.

Whenever I go to the Midwest I feel very comfortable because I always think I am surrounded by dykes. To me, women in the Midwest are much sturdier and more assertive than women in other regions of the United States. I know it is irrational for me to feel this way, but I am presently conditioned to view dykes as sturdier and more assertive than everyone else. This is not to say that I don't know a lot of kickass straight ladies and prissy lesbians, but in general, queer women are not people one wants to tangle with. Same with women in the Midwest. Hence, my comfort level rises there. Does this mean that women in the Midwest challenge gender roles more than women in other places?

No.

It means my perception of gender is in flux and affected by context.

In my experience, there is a certain demographic of gay men who are obsessive about their appearance, endlessly yap into cell phones, and walk around like they are very, very busy, all, all, all the time. Subsequently, in Los Angeles, I often make the mistake of assuming straight men are this specific kind of flaming gay man. I am conditioned to perceive a certain kinda guy as a certain kinda gay, and I see this guy all over LA. In any other part of the country, he probably *is* gay, but in LA he is likely an ardent heterosexual.

Does this mean that men in Los Angeles challenge gender roles more than men in other cities?

Fucken, fuck no.

It means my perception is in flux and affected by context.

Everybody's perception is in flux and affected by context.

Gender is fluid and gender norms vary fantastically.

So when we talk about gender, we are all talking about something endlessly fractalized and fascinating, to say the least.

I was born a woman and I live as a woman. In certain contexts, I deal with prejudice because I do not conform to what a woman "should" look like. I don't shave very often. I keep my fingernails clipped shorty short. I ride a skateboard. I often wear what many consider to be "men's" clothes and footwear. All of this is subtly—and not so subtly—unacceptable to many people.

In general heterosexual society, I sometimes feel ill at ease, but no one gawks at me or says stuff like, "What are you?"

In the queer community, I am more or less a plain jane, a runna-the-mill white dyke who shops at thrift stores.

This has led me to wonder what it would be like to be treated by the queer community the way blindly heterosexual society treats me. What if I didn't conform to gender norms upheld by the queer community?

Well, a coupla things have given me some insights on what my life might be like.

The death of Sylvia Rivera led me to some pretty ugly aspects of history.

According to legend, Ms. Rivera was known as the person who instigated the Stonewall riots in New York City. This is something of a myth, but I like tall tales.

They say that when the cops raided the famous Stonewall Inn in June of 1969, Ms. Rivera threw a brick/her shoes/a bottle at them, thus inciting what would become a nationwide fight for queer—but, as we shall see, not tranny—rights.

What really happened is she, along with the whole crowd, reached critical mass and everyone got sick of the same fucking brutalization at the hands of the NYPD at the exact same time.

After Stonewall, she went on to become this huge activist and revolutionary. Along with Marsha P. Johnson and Angela

Keyes Douglas, she was pivotal in organizing the Gay Liberation Front (GLF) and the Gay Activists Alliance (GAA). In 1970, she and Ms. Johnson started an organization called STAR (Street Transvestite Action Revolutionaries).

It kinda pissed me off that I never heard of any of these truly heroic women until I got five or so emails telling me that Sylvia Rivera had died. (Peacefully, in the hospital, surrounded by loved ones.)

I searched her name on Google and ended up at trans-history.org.

Here I learned that Ms. Rivera—a tireless crusader for queer and tranny rights—*lived on a fucking wharf* in New York City for a year and a half because she was also a crack addict and Rudy Giuliani's administration rendered her (and many others) homeless. During this time, Marsha P. Johnson was murdered. Her body was found in the Hudson and the police, insisting she committed suicide, refused to open any kind of investigation. Marsha P. Johnson was Sylvia Rivera's mentor and best friend. As far as I can find, the gay and lesbian community offered absolutely no support in pressuring the NYPD to open an investigation into her death.

For the rest of her life, Sylvia Rivera would wear a button photo of Ms. Johnson on her outer garments.

I do not doubt that Ms. Johnson was murdered because her loved ones said she was not suicidal, she left no note, she was on her way home from the 1992 Pride March in NYC, and murder seems to be a pretty common way to die when you are transgendered.

For instance, on June 20, 2000, it was widely reported that cabbies and street vendors *cheered* while witnessing the brutal stabbing murder of twenty-five-year-old Amanda Milan in front of the Port Authority Bus Terminal. Though there was no way for the police to claim Ms. Milan killed herself, newspapers (such as the *New York Times*) nevertheless served her the profound postmortem injustice by reporting that "A man was fatally stabbed in Midtown Manhattan yesterday after a dispute with two other men, the authorities said. . . . The victim . . . was found on the sidewalk . . . dressed in women's clothing and stabbed once in the neck."

If you look up some photos of the stunningly gorgeous Ms. Milan, you will see that it would require an entirely deluded stretch of imagination to mistake her for a "man."

Six months prior to her death, one of Ms. Milan's dearest friends, Simone, died after being thrown from a five-story window in San Francisco. Two years before that, their friend, Kim, who rounded out this triumvirate of soulmates, was found mangled beyond recognition at the bottom of a cliff in Australia.

She was identified by the serial number of her breast implants.

Do a web search. Google will give you over seventeen million hits for "transgender murder."

I have a very difficult time believing Marsha P. Johnson decided to end her life by drowning herself in the Hudson River, no matter what the NYPD says.

Here's the part where I got really, really pissed off:

I found out that, as a queer biological woman, I inherited a part in a legacy of totally shunning and despising people like Sylvia Rivera and Marsha P. Johnson. It seems that in the 1970s, feminists, lesbians, and gay men were vociferously intolerant of transgendered people. Before founding STAR, Sylvia Rivera and Marsha P. Johnson were edged out of the GLF, an organization that they had been *instrumental* in forming. In a stunning betrayal, the GAA wrote an antidiscrimination bill presented to the New York City Council that excluded transgendered people.

Being totally, totally shafted by a community that you poured *all your activist genius into* would be incredibly heartbreaking.

It seems to me that everyone in the queer community has a bit of accountability to face up to here. I truly believe that if Ms. Rivera and Ms. Johnson were accepted, respected, and supported for the work they were doing (and continued to do, despite setbacks like micro-marginalization within a marginalized community, poverty, and homelessness), it is possible that both of them would be alive today, helping younger generations learn how to fight and kick ass and stand up for ourselves.

Because of our own ignorance, fear, and prejudice, we have probably lost many leaders of this caliber.

Another woman who fell prey to trans-exclusion was a recording engineer at Olivia Records. In 1977, Sandy Stone was one of the most brilliant recording geniuses in the business, and Olivia Records was an all-women recording studio. They were poised to turn a profit for the first time that year, but a bunch of separatist types (which comprised a very vocal demographic in the 1970s women's movement) found out that Sandy Stone was transgendered and threatened to boycott Olivia Records. The record company reluctantly fired Ms. Stone.

This story is notably ironic:

During the 1999 Michigan Womyn's Music Festival, a rumor somehow got out that members of the Butchies supported trans-inclusion while also respecting the Michigan Womyn's Music Festival's policy that only "womyn born womyn" attend this yearly event.

The Michigan Festival policy led to a nationwide trans-activist boycott of the Butchies and all other bands on the Mr. Lady record label. (Although, I must say, I don't see how punishing Mr. Lady for the MWMF's policy is fair. Wouldn't this reasonably lead to a boycott of every band, performer, and organization that attends the festival?)

I think it is very interesting that twenty-odd years after one women's record company was boycotted for *including* trans-women on their staff, another women's record company was boycotted for honoring a festival's policy that *excludes* transfolks.

That seems like 180 degrees to me, so it's time to start another chapter of history—one that is totally trans-inclusive.

The reason I didn't know about Sandy Stone, Sylvia Rivera, Marsha P. Johnson, or any of these women is that they've been airbrushed out of queer, feminist, and US history. To find out about them, one has to research *transgender* history. (And I highly suggest you do so, starting off with those three luminaries.)

This answered the biggest question I was asking when I started getting my "trans-inclusion position" email queries: Why *did* I exclude an entire sector of the population when I was supposed to be writing a book about freedom for all?

The answer is, simply, I didn't know.

And why didn't I know? Why did an avid reader like myself never come across references to transhistory?

For the exact same reason that "feminism" and "vegetarianism" were peripheral to my life in Santa Maria, California: it's not—or at least, when I was writing *Cunt,* it wasn't—a topic that came up much.

It's, uh, excluded.

The identities, realities, experiences, accomplishments, and history of transgendered folks are not acknowledged in the marginalized cultures of queers and feminists and are pathologically feared in the "general" culture of the United States.

Time after time, in its effort to appear "normal" to blindly heterosexual society and thereby gain "equal rights," the queer community has kicked its own in the ass. Tranny folks have been the lightning rod for straight *and* queer wrath because they shake up ideas about—to paraphrase a talk-radio windbag— the way things oughta be. Like Cynthia in Zabrina's wedding experience, if you can't put someone in an easily identified box, then how do you know where *you* fit in?

The comedian Margaret Cho said something wonderful in the June 2002 issue of *Lesbian News* in an interview with Kathleen Wilkinson: "If you are a woman, if you are a person of color, if you are gay, lesbian, bisexual or transgender, if you are a person of size, if you are a person of intelligence, if you are a person of integrity, then *you* are considered a minority in this world." Margaret Cho is always saying wonderful things.

I would like to mention here that most of the people who have challenged me about trans rights have been white. I am not aware of the ways in which race factored in to Ms. Rivera's and Ms. Johnson's exclusion in the queer community (both were women of color). I do not doubt, however, that it did indeed factor in.

I have had many conversations with many, many people about how the white queer community exoticizes, marginalizes, and stereotypes queers and transfolks of color. I am not paying lip service to racial complexities by mentioning this. The infernally kaleidoscopic nature of race and the perception of race are confounding, to say the least. Rather, I would like white trans-activists to look at how they themselves may perpetuate ideas of exclusion and "otherness" by taking whiteness for granted.

I don't know how anybody—transfolks, queers of all colors, people of color, white women, feminists, fags, retirees, farmers, workers, really, I could go on—can stand around with our heads up our asses, expecting rights to be handed to us on a silver platter, when we are so terribly busy oppressing as we are oppressed.

But this is, like I say, a subject for a book.

Throughout the annals of queer and feminist history, transgendered folks have been misrepresented, feared, and marginalized to the point of perceived nonexistence.

Through dialogue, grassroots efforts, and legislation, trans-exclusion seems to be on its way out the door. Activists have been fighting since the millennium began, and laws upholding gender rights have passed throughout the world.

In the spirit of Sylvia Rivera mythically instigating the Stonewall riots by throwing a brick/her shoes/a bottle at cops, things changed in 1999, by a single event in an outdoor shower area, by the laughter inspired at the thought of people freaking out and yelling, "There are PENISES on The Land!!!"

People may not recognize this as a historic event quite yet, but after the festival that year, transfolks and their allies started calling people (like me) to task in the queer and feminist communities.

Trans-inclusion has since spiraled out from "The Land" into the general public. People don't necessarily understand, and transpeople are still targeted for violence and humiliation, but folks are gaining knowledge. Gender-variant children are being listened to by their parents and respected by their peers and educators, public bathrooms and gyms are recognized as potentially unsafe places for transpeople, the US military embraces trans-inclusion, nine countries (Pakistan, India, Nepal, Germany, Canada, Bangladesh, Malta, New Zealand, and Australia) offer gender-neutral options on official forms, and celebrities and athletes have publicly come out as transgender.

It's a start.

Like Lynnee said, we're in question-asking time, but a few answers have come to the fore.

Who Remedios Varo Is

*If you would understand a people, look
at them through the eyes of the poet,
the musician and the artist.*

—Cynthia Pearl Maus, *The World's Great Madonnas*

When I was ten, the Fam took a trip to LA to see the Treasures of King Tut exhibit. At this time, my art world consisted of paintings, pictures, books, records, and the radio. (My father's tyranny is in evidence here. We didn't have a television set in our house for *simply ages*.) Art was furthermore associated with making a huge mess that was magically sanctioned by most all authority figures.

Art was a wonder to perceive, and I perceived it at complete and utter face value. This is to say, I very much enjoyed art but did not attach a symbolic interpretation to either my own or other people's.

The King Tut exhibit forever altered this tabula rasa.

I remember gold.

I remember gold, and I remember four women who guarded the box where King Tut's body lay. They were gold, of course, and stood with arms to their sides, hands outstretched hip high, palms perfectly at my eye level, staring me down. Their eyes never left anyone in the room. They saw all. They were impassable. Their gaze was searing and irresistible, like licking a nine-volt battery.

My parents and siblings wandered off. I was not interested in anything else the King Tut exhibit had to offer, so installed myself with the sentinels until it was time to go.

I knew little of Christ, much less anything that went on Before Christ, but it was quite obvious those sentinels were *obscenely* out of their element in a museum in Los Angeles, California, circa AD One Thousand Nine Hundred and Seventy Whatever. And yet, through what I later recognized as the wanton pillage mentality of my culture—in this context, innocuously referred to as "archaeology"—there they irrefutably stood.

Magnificent overseers of an entire civilization, brought across oceans on a boat steered by the victors of history's present telling.

I felt incredibly minute and *of the flesh* in their presence. It was important to remain in contact with what was in the pocket of my shorts: half a bag of M&M's and two green plastic army men I'd fished out of my little brother's mouth on the drive to LA. I think the contents of my pockets comforted me, because fear was certainly present.

The sentinels possessed incomprehensible powers for thousands upon thousands of years. They were *alive* under the desert sands of Egypt long before even my *grammy* was born. And now, standing in this weird museum room, they were not only alive but *pissed as hell* to be taken from their place.

I could not stop digging the amazement of this whole situation.

I was too young and impatient to understand what compelled people to create all that gold stuff, and too uninterested in the museum itself to put much thought into the little explanatory plaques affixed near each piece, but I knew God when I saw Her.

This, I understood.

This, I respected.

This was a whole new slant on art.

I grew up and found out three more things about art:

1. The individual artist is a *medium* for making representational and deeply meaningful symbols of the community's collective consciousness, whether they are symbols of the community's religion, love, hurt, power, hate, hope, dreams, fables, foibles, or on and on and on.

2. Some cultures know this, think it's divine, and respect the importance of art and artists as perfectly natural manifestations of innate human life, growth, and expression—without insanely glorifying

huge, corporate-induced false images of individual superstars.

3. American culture is not one of them.

One kind of art occurs naturally in the course of everyday life and does not generally involve widespread cultural glorification. My mother's Thanksgiving dinner is art. The one Aunt Genie creates is of a completely different genre, though she utilizes the same basic components. The dashboard of Liz's car is art. Shells and goddesses and pretty rocks are arranged in a specific way that holds meaning for anyone who is privy to the need for protection when navigating an automobile. Grammy's wildflower and bird sanctuary garden is art. She designed it. It is a reflection of her and her community. It is symbolic of the culture she lives in.

Another kind of art is the art people make and *intend* to be considered art as symbolic representation. Art such as this moves you for certain very specific reasons directly related to your history and experiences, and moves your girlfriend in a thousand and one absolutely different ways.

This art includes paintings, metalwork, sculptures, murals, photographs, dances, poems, stories, storytelling, essays, plays, screenplays, movies, videos, ads, buildings, fashion designs, performances, puppet shows, monuments, pornography, erotica, music, spoken word, and so on.

Both kinds of art represent a culture, a collective consciousness, and the passions of an individual. Grammy's wildflower and bird sanctuary garden is as monumental as Toni Morrison's epic *Beloved*.

On a scale that measured love and pain,

they'd proportionately weigh the same.

The difference between these two kinds of art is:

I know my grammy's story and the average onlooker does not. I've developed an emotional bond with my grammy since I was born. Therefore, I walk into her garden equipped with a lifelong perception that is in continual evolution. I am thus able to identify with her garden utilizing symbolism unavailable to most everyone else.

Beloved directly, out and out tells a story. The words of the story are arranged with high regard for the common bond of humanness that each and every reader shares. Everyone who can read is equipped to identify with *Beloved*.

Beloved taps into the collective consciousness of a community that spans the entire planet.

Grammy's garden doesn't echo out much farther than Sweet Home, Oregon.

Art imitates life as life imitates art. Art and the community are whirling dervishes unto one another. Takes two to tango. It doesn't matter which one causes and affects the other, or when, or why, or how. This came first: the chicken or the egg.

There is, of course, a huge problem here.

Throughout the history of Western civilization—and by this term, I mean the destructive, competitive, capitalist, patriarchal, filthy-rich, white, male social system that threatens to consume every other culture on the planet—what is considered "art" has been presented by and for far less than half of the human community: the white, male portion. Art that our culture takes seriously, invests in, and reflects upon was created by men. Women do not belong to the "art" community, as it presently exists.

In what is considered the art community, the enormous contributions of artists such as Yoko Ono and Octavia Butler are methodically and unquestionably overshadowed by those of the Andy Warhol/Stephen King ilk.

In the early '90s, I attended college at one of America's most *liberal, progressive* institutions. There, my friend Ashley turned me on to the surrealist painter Remedios Varo.

One quarter, Ashley took a course in "art history." She asked her teacher numerous times throughout the quarter to include Ms. Varo's totally brilliant, fabulous, and inspiring work in the program. The teacher resolutely overruled this motion, time and again. His argument was that there must be a solid reason why Ms. Varo's work was not "good enough" to be included in any of the art history books he had ever seen. Because none of the sources this teacher deemed reputable recognized Remedios Varo, why on earth should he?

Catch-22, deedle dee-doo.

In her second autobiography, *Beyond the Flower*, Judy Chicago provides a simple, astute answer:

> Historically, women have either been excluded from the process of creating the definitions of what is considered art or allowed to participate only if we accept and work within existing mainstream designations. If women have no real role *as women* in the process of defining art, then we are essentially prevented from helping to shape cultural symbols. (Chicago 1996, 72)

As I learned in a beautiful book entitled *Spider Woman's Granddaughters*, there is a name for this: intellectual apartheid. In her brilliant introduction to *Spider Woman's Granddaughters*, Paula Gunn Allen speaks as a Native artist working in the white American literary world, but her profound truth is applicable to many artists existing in many worlds:

> Intellectual apartheid . . . helps create and maintain political apartheid; it tends to manifest itself in the practical affairs of all societies that subscribe to it. Contrary to popular and much scholarly opinion in Western intellectual circles, aesthetics are not extraneous to politics. And because political conquest necessarily involves intellectual conquest, educational institutions in this country have prevented people from studying the great works of minority cultures in light of critical structures that could illuminate and clarify those materials in their own contexts. The literatures and

arts of non-Western peoples have thus remained obscure to people educated in Western intellectual modes. Moreover, non-Western literature and art appear quaint, primitive, confused, and unworthy of serious critical attention largely because they are presented that way. (Allen 1989, 3)

Men forge merrily along, continuing to get 99.9 percent of the credit for doing pretty much everything. When the glaringly obvious retardation of this situation is pointed out, the ensuing rebuttal tends to be that men just unanimously happen to be the most fabulously talented creators on earth. Thus, everyone who is not a man fails to get due credit.

For women painters, for instance, to be included in the history of art in modern civilization, it must first of all be established that we *exist*. This places the artwork *in the hinterland* of the artist's gender. Women artists are required to explain our presence, to defend our identity, to speak for our multitudes, and men are not.

Meanwhile, reproduction upon reproduction of women in various stages of undress litters "art history." Women artists are airbrushed out of art history and still endure alienation and invalidation, yet images of women positively abound as the focal point of men's artwork.

In this kind of setting, one learns that Salvador Dalí is deemed an uncontested surrealist master (though he readily admitted his obsessive reliance on a woman named Gala for inspiration), while you probably don't know who I am talking about when I name a chapter for Remedios Varo, one of the most freaking genius surrealists of the twentieth century, who relied on herself for just about everything.

In 1989, the Guerrilla Girls—a proactivist group that will be discussed at length in just a few short pages—addressed the question, "Do women have to be naked to get into The Metropolitan Museum?" Here are their findings:

Asked to design a billboard for the Public Art Fund [PAF] in New York [City], we welcomed the chance to do something that would appeal to a general audience. One Sunday morning we conducted a "weenie count" at [T]he Metropolitan Museum of Art in New York, comparing the number of nude males to nude females in the artworks on display. The results were very "revealing." (Guerrilla Girls 1995, 61)

They designed a billboard depicting a reproduction of Ingres's reclining *Grande Odalisque*, with a gorilla mask on her head and a dildo in the hand draped over her hip. Accompanying this image was the following statement: "Less than 5 percent of the artists in the Modern Art Sections are women, but 85 percent of the nudes are female."

Alas, the Public Art Fund and the Guerrilla Girls' *Odalisque* were not meant for each other.

The PAF said our design wasn't clear enough and rejected it. We then rented advertising space on NYC busses and

> ran it ourselves, until the bus company canceled our lease,
> saying the image . . . was too suggestive and that the figure
> appeared to have more than a fan in her hand. (Guerrilla
> Girls 1995, 61)

The difficulty in locating art made by women artists compared with the *impossibility* of avoiding artwork created by men reflects *how women live* in this culture.

It is the absolute normal reality.

Cultural symbols that hold deep representational meaning for the community are shaped by the victors of history's present telling. The victors have a time-tested interest in controlling women's bodies, decimating civilizations, playing cops and robbers, keeping people of color and white women in our "proper" pigeonholed place, and glorifying themselves through power plays with each other.

These interests are serviced through most television shows, movies, songs, and music videos readily available. The interests of the victors project and reinforce absolutely *nada, zilch, nothing, zero* that serves women.

Yet we view and absorb this art every livelong day.

And it hurts us.

Ouch.

Every day.

Here is a paragraph from the 1997 handbook for the Michigan Womyn's Music Festival:

If you play recorded music that can be heard by others, please make it music with womyn-only vocals. We come here to enjoy a womyn-only environment, part of which is hearing only womyn's voices. This is not a judgment on men or music, but a strong, positive desire to spend these few special days surrounded only by the sounds of womyn.

Valid criticisms aside, at its very best, the Michigan Womyn's Music Festival was *simultaneously* an unparalleled spiritual experience for—I'd be willing to wager—every woman who attended. It was a weeklong world created not so much without men but with women. Women cooked the food, played the music, guarded the gates, and drove the shuttle buses twenty-four hours a day. We could see, speak, smell, taste, and touch nothing but women. Every structure, artifact, and song was of women's creation. It is not often one has the opportunity to exist in an entire community of women, wholly untouched by men, even for a day.

The only men who set foot on the festival grounds do so to empty out the PortaJanes.

It can change a lady forever.

When I step outside my home, I am besieged by the creations of men. They designed the cars driving down the streets; indeed, they planned the placement of the streets. Because architecture is one of the many, many fields considered "male dominated," I trust that most of the buildings and residences I see come from the blueprints of men's minds. Ditto landscaping. The probably male-designed movie posters at the bus stops usually feature men and, if not, represent the labor

of male producers, directors, sound engineers, and camera operators. If I turn on the radio while I am driving down
this male-made street, the voices of men selling their products and singing their songs about how much they love/hate/
want to fuck women will promenade into my male-designed
automobile.

It is not difficult to appreciate the art of men.

In fact, it is dang-ola a chore to altogether evade it.

For two years in college, I read only books by women. I did
not watch television or read magazines in the checkout line. I
studied paintings, photographs, sculptures, and films created
solely by women.

George Bush Sr. got hisself inaugurated, Ted Bundy
counted down the days to his execution, and Somalia cried out
in pain, but I was in Zora Neale Hurston's world. Leslie Marmon Silko kissed me goodnight. Sister Rosetta Tharpe sang
lullabies into my sleep. Diane Arbus scared me giddy. Maya
Lin was the Cinderella of my heart. Käthe Kollwitz made me
cry and cry and cry.

It was only an experiment. I only meant it to be one of
those let's-see-what-happens-if-I-do-this kind of things. But
it turned into sort of a habit. I fully immersed myself in the
expressions of women, exclusively, and felt so comfortable, I
guess I just didn't leave.

I wouldn't venture to advocate a supreme, *lifelong* militancy
about the gender specifics of art appreciation. I recently finished Laurence Leamer's eight-hundred-plus-page book *The*

Kennedy Women: The Saga of an American Family. Chet Baker croons through the speakers as I write. The taxidermy manual I read last month was written by a man, but I've forgotten his name, Jesse Charles or something. As far as I'm concerned, Samuel L. Jackson is a demigod and I'm never-endingly inspired by the garden of Mr. Young-Park, who lives next door.

It's not a bad idea, however, to focus *solely* on the artistic expressions of women for *at least* one year. That way you notice not only the horrifying prevalence of male artistic expression much more but the mother lode of inspiration and brilliance our grandmothers, mothers, and sisters have produced.

I loathe special sections for women just as much as the next lady. It will forever bug the shit out of me that there's a W before "NBA." This designation makes certain we know that all basketball involves men, unless it's this special, *exceptional circumstance* that can only be qualified as "women's basketball."

Schools have classes called "women's studies" and "African American literature" because the standard for *existence* set by white men has yet to be rescinded in this age. "Normal" history is the history of a certain class of white people, from the perspective of men. All the other histories are precisely that: other.

I wish that when I said "rock star," the kneejerk status quo association was Me'Shell "Brilliant Goddess Lovechild" Ndegeocello instead of Keith "Piece of Shit" Richards.

I wish when I queried "great American writer?" most people standing on the street would respond, "Oh, yes, well, *obviously* Flannery O'Connor and Louise Erdrich," instead of, "Why, John Steinbeck and Ernest Hemingway, of course."

But that is not the case at all.

There is subsequently an unfortunate—yet urgent—need for something I'll refer to as a "Cuntlovin' Women's Art Movement." At least, until our culture no longer recognizes women within a male paradigm and language and perception have broadened enough to imply the (art) world's inclusion of and dependence upon women.

Also, not to sound like a total wet blanket.

The *multitude* of acclaimed cuntlovin' artists bustin' fine round womanly asses getting honest reflections of us into the world *thrills me beyond measure*. Women populate the stages, giving acceptance speeches for Nobels, Grammys, Pulitzers, and Guggenheims like never before. With each passing year, it grows easier and easier to immerse oneself in the expressions of women.

The singular detail here is to *immerse* yourself in the expressions of women; to *create* a Cuntlovin' Women's Art Movement with your friends, sisters, lovers, and daughters; to be part of the community that defines art.

Cuntlovin' Women's Art Movement
Item CWAM-1: chant

> You are what you eat.
> You meet who you greet.
> You head where you tread.
> You dead when not fed.

Cuntlovin' Women's Art Movement
Item CWAM-2: womanifesto

the never-ending "she taught me" womanifesto
. . . diamanda galás.
she taught me.
all the pain and joy of the whole wide world is inside my body.
my dna never forgets.
her voice in my body is the inquisition, all slavery ever, all rape, all war, AIDS. her voice brings all
that pain into my body—which hurts—but the fact
that she offers me the opportunity to physically perceive the complexities of this pain, which exists in
the world in her voice, means it exists in the world in
my body, too. knowing this, the ball's in my court to
take responsibility, which gives me power.
all the pain and joy of the whole wide world is inside my body.
my dna never forgets.

leslie marmon silko.
she taught me.
if i want it to, history can mean his story. but mostly
and much moreover, history means hi, story.
she said hi, story, and i understood what the vietnam war was from her perspective, which mirrors
my own much more closely than the textbooks i
read in school. she told me cowboys and indians are

people i see in my everyday life, the *nahual* flies overhead, slavery is a business based on male sexuality,
and home is where the heart is.

if i want it to, history can mean his story. but
mostly and much moreover, history means hi, story.

pippi longstocking.
she taught me.
don't you worry about me, i always come out on top.
she reigns supreme over the police, mean boys, pi-
rates, nosey parkers, uppity snoots, the education
system, monsters, and rascally impositions of her
culture. the wonders of just simply being alive in the
world are limited solely by her imagination. she was
one of the first fashion inspirations of my life, and
when i grew up, her stories became the vortex of my
feminist rhetoric. don't you worry about me, i always
come out on top.

remedios varo.
she taught me.
i am what i eat.

she painted pictures of magic happening, which
are also what her paintings, themselves, are. her life,
her cosmology, and her product are three mirrors
peering into one another at the same time, infinity.
her precise science is based on the findings deep
inside her consciousness and it is irrefutable. what

comes from her is what she is because she is what she comes from.

i am what i eat. . . .

Cuntlovin' Women's Art Movement
Item CWAM-3: Guerrilla Girls

The Guerrilla Girls have been an exemplary part of this culture for over a decade. Here is their mission statement:

> The Guerrilla Girls are a group of women art-ists and arts professionals who make posters about discrimination. Dubbing ourselves the conscience of the art world, we declare our-selves feminist counterparts to the mostly male tradition of anonymous do-gooders like Robin Hood, Batman, and the Lone Ranger. We wear gorilla masks to focus on the issues rather than our personalities. We use humor to convey in-formation, provoke discussion, and show that feminists can be funny. In 10 years, we have produced over 70 posters, printed projects, and actions that expose sexism and racism in the art world and the culture at large. Our work has been passed around the world by kindred spirits who consider themselves Guerrilla Girls

too. The mystery surrounding our identities has attracted attention and support. We could be anyone; we are everywhere. (www.guerrillagirls .com)

The Guerrilla Girls are one of the most internationally recognized activist groups on the planet. Though they'll never get due credit, the Guerrilla Girls' poster style is a huge inspirational prototype for the strong-image/in-your-face text combo that has become formulaic in everything from Nike ads to blockbuster movie trailers.

Their tactics are clever, humorous, and highly effective. They attack specific issues at specific locations. Guerrilla Girl propaganda is clearly and concisely worded. The vivid, often co-opted images grab the attention of non-English-speaking people, those unable to read, and the completely jaded, alike.

Were the Guerrilla Girls originally a bunch of seventeen-year-old kids who bullshitted a mission statement into being, got their act together, and poetically terrorized the art world after they finished their homework every afternoon?

Are the Guerrilla Girls really a smattering of disgruntled career gals who realized how very, very pissed off they were that they had "sold out" instead of pursuing their passions as artists?

Are Chelsea and Hillary Clinton Guerrilla Girls?

How weird must it be for men who work with women in New York's finest museums and galleries *not to know* if one of their colleagues, bosses, or subordinates is one of an increasingly powerful group of women who undermine everything they allegedly work toward together during business hours?

It is very delicious that so much surrounding this group is a matter of conjecture.

Here's a conservative guess:

The Guerrilla Girls originated as seven to twenty-eight women who decided to do something together instead of sitting back and witnessing the horror.

Talk about an inspiration to the nation.

Here is the recipe for starting an activist group in your hometown:

a. pictures

b. words

c. a reproduction and distribution system

d. women friends with imagination, focus, and motivation—especially ones who work at Kinko's

Put it all together.

On your marks,

get set.

Go.

Cuntlovin' Women's Art Movement
Item CWAM-4: disbursement of revenue

Get CDs and books at the library when appreciating the work of men. Rent their movies. Watch their sporting events on TV.

Buy CDs and books by women. Go to the theater to see films by women, and purchase videos for your gorgeously expanding library. Buy tickets to our basketball games.

Disburse revenue into the women's art world in your community and afar. Each cent spent on work by men is money taken away from the Cuntlovin' Women's Art Movement.

Who Mammon Is

The ceiling isn't glass, it's a very dense layer of men.
—Anne Jardim, author

I love money.

I love money so much I can hardly contain my passion for it.

Money rules.

Besides shelter, featuring a warm cushy bed, heat, electricity, a pot to piss in, and a floor to watch my period blood drip onto, money equals: time to work on my book; presents for people I love; a sumptuous, satin-lined, floor-length, pink, polyester fur coat with matching bikini; mango mochi ice cream; a telephone line and email account; a three-hour luxuriation and massage at the communal women's baths; new books and CDs; industrial-sized rolls of double-sided tape; sheets of stickers with my face next to an alien's; fancy dinner dates; and that divine three-tiered cocktail table at the antique store.

Lordisa yes, money is grand.

Making,

managing, and

generating

yet more money in a cuntlovin' way that makes me smile from earlobe to earlobe is an absolute different story.

There are two ways to make money in a capitalist, patriarchal setting:

1. Fuck other people over faster and more efficiently than they fuck you over.
2. Whore.

I'm too much of a sucker for the wrath of karma to excel at number 1, so that leaves number 2. In this context, Whoring consists of selling some aspect of one's being in order to survive. Sometimes this is selling one's dexterity at the espresso machine, and other times it's selling one's ability to seduce people into buying things they don't want. Sometimes we think we can escape corporate Whoredom by becoming artists or owning our own businesses.

But no.

To make money, we gotta associate ourselves with a corporate pimp somewhere along the food chain.

This ain't circumventable.

Any kind of Cuntlovin' Women's Economic System that's implemented in this society will have to answer to the capitalist patriarchy because the buck stops there. It is downright illegal

to ignore the IRS. Please inform me if there's a single behe-
moth insurance company owned and operated by women, but
I'm quite certain the New York Stock Exchange floor has never
been grid-locked by cuntlovin' ladies vying to invest in the education of our children.

So be it.

At the 1997 Michigan Womyn's Music Festival, I met a writer
for a popular American magazine. We got to talking and duly
realized that we totally disagreed on pretty much every mien
of existence. This in no way hampered our mutual fascination
and respect for one another.

I will never in my life forget her candor when she said to
me (of all people) in an unabashedly woman-centered community (of all places), "I am totally seduced by male power."

In context, it was one of the most brutally honest statements I'd ever heard—even though (and indubitably because)
I could not relate on any spectrum of cognizance. She'd put
great and highly intelligent thought into her choice for survival, which involved investing all of her power and trust in the
capitalist patriarchy economic model.

Which makes perfect sense.

The proof is in the pudding.

The largest, most successful women-owned companies in the
United States are cute little unicorns that play in the rainbow

compared to the village-stomping dragons like Microsoft, GE, and Disney.

I ain't never heard tell of an internationally recognized multimedia production company, chain of car dealerships, real estate conglomerate, advertising agency, or garbage-collection firm owned and operated solely by women. There are no states with women in all positions of political office, from the governor on down to the postmaster in each city. If mafias are needed to keep the economy humming along, there certainly aren't any matrifocal ones testifying to the truth of this.

This has been the economic reality since time out of my grammy's mind. Past and present cuntlovin' businesses are inherently at odds in this reality. Subsequently, they must fight like the devil to remain solvent.

Cunt would never have become a product accessible to consumers if it weren't for the rippling effect of one woman's struggle and tenacious dream. One woman's unwavering standard to employ and serve women creates a cuntlovin' consciousness that bolsters every person who works for—or comes in contact with—her company. Rest assured, pretty much any product purchased from a cuntlovin' business benefits all women in a similar manner.

Cuntlovin' businesswomen are consistently on the economic defense because—at present—we aren't the ones who foment the rules and codes of supply and demand. Women have no modern history of managing commerce on the civic, county, state, or federal level.

I am a sharecropper on the patriarchy's land.

I can dress this up with all the modes of independence imaginable, but if I want my mail every day, I am at the mercy of the United States Postal Service. The electricity for my computer is compliments of the Pacific Gas and Electric Company, which still often boasts repair signs that remind me of the fact that this society is run by a series of "Men Working."

Furthermore, individual women are systematically shot down when we make a stand in the name of anything that defies the white male standard of existence. To my dying day, I'm gonna be cranky about the fact that Dr. Joycelyn Elders got canned for testing our society's puritanical tolerance level about sexuality.

Women who acquire the courage, will, and/or money to secure positions of high-octane power and prestige *must conduct business* within the same "mainstream designations" found in the art world. Likewise, to become and remain a hugely successful organization, woman-owned companies must alienate women.

Marjorie Merriweather Post, for example.

Her father, C. W. Post, of Raisin Bran fame, was right there at the crest of the breakfast and advertising economic revolutions here in America. He insisted his only child be involved in the intrigues of business. Marjorie was raised much differently from how other girls of her generation were raised. She grew up with a sense of entitlement and independence, believing her gender was certainly no hindrance in getting what she wanted. Undoubtedly, this is more a reflection of C. W. Post's money, whiteness, and love for his only child than of the philosophies of the women's movement at the time. The result was, nonetheless, a strong-willed woman who controlled a huge corporation after her father kicked. Almost until the day she died, Ms. Post ran the family business, and she did so under the same model as every other "successful" corporation in America. Men held positions of power and decision. Women were secretarial mom-wife-Whore-sis sycophants.

I reckon if the breakfast-cereal industry hadn't been revolutionized by C. W. Post and the Kellogg brothers until, oh, say, 1960, and Marjorie Merriweather Post was raised in the '70s and took over in the '90s, Postum Cereals would've ran its course along pretty much the same gender lines. There would, as a concession to existing mainstream designations, perhaps be a smattering of men and women of color and white women secreted away in a few executive positions.

It's doubtful that Marjorie would have employed only women, provided child care, self-protection courses, profit sharing, investment groups, and generous retirement plans for her employees. Neither would she have played Tori, Nina Simone, Me'Shell, Shonen Knife, Sinéad, and Yma Sumac over the factory loudspeakers to boost morale, meanwhile revolutionizing the advertising industry's image of women and children with her sheer buying power.

Good businesswomen just don't take risks like that.

So let's, shall we, define risk:

A maneuver that has neither a past nor a guaranteeable future generating profits is a risk.

It's a risk for women to run the show because the show was designed to be run by an elite group of white men.

Women will never be an elite group of white men, so the show was not designed to be run by us.

Deedle dee-doo, Catch-22.

When I feel defeated or frustrated or just dang upset because there is simply no sidestepping this shitty reality, I sometimes call my sister. She says, "Count your blessings, ya lucky hooker. Don't be bitter. Your face gets all ugly when you're bitter."

I represent maybe 0.0001 percent of cuntlovin' ladies throughout history who have been and continue to be bored to death with the plights of this reality.

Sometimes, though, I *feel* like being bitter because I wake up in the morning and just have to face the fact that within this economic model, *it makes perfect sense* for Kevin Costner to spend more money on a single, fully lunkheaded movie that contributes absolutely nothing to society than the entire nation of El Salvador sees in one year.

My face gets all ugly and I call my sister and she reminds me I'm a lucky hooker when I think about the multitudes of women who are creating desperately needed and appreciated products that have no *physical place* within the capitalist, patriarchal economic model and—like women artists—struggle to prove our *existence* long before advancing upon the struggle to *survive*.

I work with a woman named Kathleen Gasperini who publishes *W.i.g.* (*Women in General*) magazine. *W.i.g.* focuses on giving women a place to write about our fabulous lives and adventures living them, the music and sports that move us, our poetry and stories, interviews with other women living their fabulous lives, and our battles with cancer, violence, poverty, racial and sexual hatred, drugs, and/or eating disorders.

Ms. Gasperini has a difficult time finding investors because her magazine does not reflect standard "women's interests" found in other culturally accepted "women's magazines."

Here is what potential investors say to Ms. Gasperini, "There's no section for your magazine in the stores. It can't be in the sports section. It's not just about fitness and health. Neither is it for new mothers, brides-to-be, lesbians, or feminists. If you focused more on fashion and make-up, we'd be happy to invest because then we'd know how to market it and people would know where to find it."

The fact that *W.i.g.* is one of a handful of like-minded, brilliant magazines—*Bitch, BUST,* and *HUES* come readily to mind—doesn't seem to inspire any thoughts about a market of consumers who represent an acute demand for what these magazines supply.

Once upon a time, Kathleen Gasperini spent two months begging her printers to be patient for the money she owed them, because a gentleman who runs a major magazine publishing company had expressed an interest in investing in *W.i.g.* Week after week they played phone tag; Kathleen's heart lodged in her throat.

When she finally met with him, he had the following nugget of inspiration to impart:

"You are the wrong gender for what we are focusing on at this time. The market is going crazy for young men right now."

Circulation for the first issue of *W.i.g.* was five thousand.

Circulation for *W.i.g.*'s fourth issue was fifty thousand.

For a market that does not exist, fifty thousand consumers is a pretty heady figure, considering *W.i.g.* sales depend upon word of mouth in lieu of national advertising and promotion. Stores do not have a section for magazines such as *W.i.g.* because it is by, for, and about women, on our terms.

Our culture does not provide a place for that.

There is—*literally*—no place for products of this kind.

A small amount of research into American history illuminates how just about every "right" and "freedom" people of color and white women achieved was the result of economics. The Civil War was not about compassion and decency, it was about real estate. The alleged "rights" of "land settlements bestowed" upon Native tribes are also real estate. Granting white women and people of color the "right" to vote was about creating a class of peon workers who were less able to grumble over the poor pay and working conditions when they had such a glorious "right" as casting ballots that placed a variety of white men in office.

Hoop dee-doo.

In our society's time-tested economic model, men make and women consume. Our fingernail polishes, snowboards, vacuum cleaners, computers, clothes—pretty much most of our stuff—was manufactured by male-dominated and -owned companies. Utilities and credit card companies claim yet another portion of our income for the male producers that make stuff for us ladies.

Accordingly, one of our most promising stakes of power is our undisputed role as consumers.

As consumers, we exist.

This is a resource that is presently part of our reality.

Exploit the fuck out of it.

Cuntlovin' Consumerism

Time and money are power.

Conscious decision making about the expenditure of both nourishes a market that is somehow considered "fledgling," although it represents 51 percent of the population.

Many phallocentric religious organizations, from the Promise Keepers to the Church of Jesus Christ of Latter-Day Saints, heartily extol the benefits of keeping money in the community of the brethren.

Patriarchal society never has to bother preaching the benefits of keeping the money with the men because, at present, there's no place else for it to go.

In the marketplace of the patriarchy, the "competition" tends to be people living in Mexican, Latin American, South

African, and Southeast Asian communities (often referred to as "guerrilla terrorists"), fighting for the right to live on the planet with an identity other than that of expendable factory worker–slaves.

It sounds *terribly* ideological to say women's power as consumers is a major economic stronghold, but it seems the most promising strategy that does not involve retreat.

Cuntlovin' Consumerism is a matter of research and potential inconvenience.

It requires no thought to amble to the Mega-Food-O-Rama and buy a name-brand loaf of bread. Finding a bakery in your community that is owned by a woman struggling to bring up three children by herself may take a bit of phone work. Because this baker does not produce and distribute on the massive scale of Wonder Bread, her product will be of higher quality and nutritional value, but it may also be more expensive.

Cuntlovin' Consumerism is a matter of common sense.

When it becomes the custom to visit only women gynecologists, naturopaths, and midwives, the clientele of male doctors will fluctuate precariously, and cuntcare will eventually become the sole women-dominated field in the medical industry outside nursing.

Cuntlovin' Consumerism is a matter of commitment.

The only women-owned bookstore you know of is twenty-five miles away from your house. Once a month, you and your friends make a special trip to this store instead of bopping into the local Mega-Book-O-Rama whenever you happen upon disposable income.

Try this experimental test.

You will need a sheet of gold stars to conduct it properly.

Stand in the middle of your kitchen. Scan every single appliance, work of art, food product, fixture, and piece of furniture in the room. Place everything in one of three categories:

1. Definitely/probably produced by women or a woman-run corporation.
2. You aren't sure.
3. Definitely/probably produced by men or a male-run corporation.

Every time your vision rests upon something that falls into category 1, put a gold star on it. After you have perused the contents of every cupboard and drawer, count up the number of gold stars.

Unless you have already researched the matter and actively sought out products made by women, your kitchen will not be very golden starry.

Conduct this experiment in every room of your house.

Now, live your life from this day forward with the objective of filling your home with as many gold stars as possible.

The day you got gold stars on most all of your stuff will be the last day of the patriarchal age as far as you, the consumer, are concerned.

Cuntlovin' Investment Portfolio

An investment is a portion of capital (money or time) that is spent now for bigger, better results later.

There are a number of different kinds of investments.

One is the personal investment. This is where you buy a coffee maker that you set before you go to bed so that in the morning you will have time to do yoga, which in turn centers you for the day ahead and subsequently helps you make optimal decisions that improve the quality of your life day by day.

Another investment is the pain-in-the-ass-job investment. This is where you sacrifice X amount of time each and every week Whoring yourself at some meaningless job in order to finance your life so you can, say, finish your book.

Yet another kind of investment, the kind we're concerned with here, is a group investment. This involves getting your women friends or family members together and figuring out how much capital you have, collectively, to invest.

First you determine how much time you have to invest in your investment group.

Then you figure out money and resources.

If each of you has five dollars, and there are ten of you, that is fifty dollars. *The amount of money you have is not important.* What *is* important is how you answer the following question:

How can we make this fifty dollars into one hundred dollars?

This is the beginning of a Cuntlovin' Investment Portfolio.

The best way to have a productive investment group is to exploit the resources you already have available to you rather than expending energy looking for the resources you imagine are necessary. I'm gonna say this again in a few moments because it's a fundamental rule here.

Perhaps two women in your group are seamstresses, one has an industrial sewing machine in her closet, another inherited a garage full of fabric from her great-grandmother, you happen to be a genius at computer design, and the remaining three are very talented songwriters and musicians.

Hmmmm.

Seems like the eight of you should be able to bring all those things together in a lucrative manner.

How?

I haven't the faintest clue.

That is where the brilliance of your investment group comes in.

An investment group meets on a regular basis and focuses energy on the process of making collective capital experience gains.

Your group may decide to start a business, play the women-owned companies that have gone public on the stock market, present an investment proposal to your local woman-run record company, have bake sales, or throw huge, elaborately themed parties where you charge people to get in.

Once again, I underscore the following: the challenge for an investment group is exploiting the resources you have readily available. This yields *much better results* than agonizing over how to make something out of a good, but presently inaccessible idea.

When an investment group gets enough capital, it pays dividends to the group's members, which helps improve the quality of life; it reinvests or loans money to woman-run businesses or production companies; it starts a scholarship fund or buys an entire city block to provide housing to young women athletes, scholars, and artists who are fighting like the devil to survive and fulfill dreams at the same time.

Time and money are power.

When women proactively seize both, we take power.

Every iota of power women claim and use to the advantage of our sisters brings the destructive patriarchal age that much closer to its timely, timely, timely end.

It has been a long time, but the Goddess is waking up from her nap.

She's yawning, stretching her muscles, and scratching her big beautiful butt. Rest assured, the Goddess has a thing or two to say about man as the maker. When the Goddess gets the

sleep out of her eyes, I daresay my face won't have many op-
portunities to get all ugly about cultural atrocities like Kevin
Costner movies.

But my sister will probably always remind me I'm a lucky
hooker.

P.S.

You're a Big Cunt now.

You find out who Mammon is.

A Wee Train Ride

Once upon a time, there were thousands, if not millions, of trains running in the world. Every culture had its own tracks, schedule, and system.

The Lummi Train never imagined crossing paths with the Narragansett Train.

Africa, Asia, Europe, and India positively *teemed* with trains.

Then the Romans came along and decided to build a really big train system that swallowed up all the other little trains in the way. Later, the Ottomans did the same thing, though they were nicer about it than the Romans.

Along came the Anglo-Saxon Train, causing ancient Roman and Ottoman rulers to writhe in their tombs with envy. The Anglo-Saxon Train took around five hundred years to encompass the entire globe, introducing very specific brands of white supremacist racism, slavery, sexual violence, and capitalism to everyone in the whole wide world. These realities also provide an endless source of energy for the train to run.

This is called symbiosis.

I conjured this fun rendition of world history one recent summer afternoon at the inspiration of a friend. He was bumming about the state of the world and letting it ruin his day—which happened to be taking place in the sun, at the river, with a cooler full of yummy snacks and refreshing drinks, not to mention the effervescently delightful company of me.

I said, "Just because you don't want to know, think about, or see horrible things going on in the world does nothing to negate the fact that you are riding on the Anglo-Saxon Train. You were born on it and you will probably die on it. If it makes you feel sad, guilty, or ashamed, then those are your choices, but they have absolutely no impact because you're still not getting off of the Anglo-Saxon Train. So come swim in this gloriously incandescent river with me."

Point being, if you are gonna sit around and think about how shit realities make *you feel,* you're *probably* doing a crap job of engaging with the world around you.

Let's say you're a white person and let's say you don't think white supremacist racism is a very big problem. Let's say all of your friends and family members are majority white/white-identified and, although all of you agree there might be isolated pockets of racism in the world, in the main, people of color are really just overreacting and trying to cash in on how bad it makes us feel to be told we're racists all the time.

That makes a lot of sense, right?

That makes a lot more sense than entertaining the possibility that you were born on the Anglo-Saxon Train, fueled by white supremacist racism, slavery, sexual violence, and capitalism, and it's *much* easier than looking out the window and realizing that you're riding full bore into a very murky future that's being destroyed by the train we're all riding together.

The Women's March in January 2017 was amazing. The Transgender, Queer, and Gay marches that followed were strobe-light-blindingly brilliant. The Standing Rock movement brought power and consciousness shifting. The March for Science was inspiring. The Black Lives Matter movement is breathtakingly important. The immigration march was glorious.

It's wonderful when folks goes a-marchin', but no one ever marches *together*.

Just imagine:

Everyone marching in mutual respect and admiration for the positive things we all bring to the table, the unions holding hands with the drag queens, the Taiko drummers backing up the Prancing Elites who've choreographed a ditty with disabled vets and Star Trek nerds, while the Puerto Ricans, Ethiopian Coptic Christians, and feminists chant in unison, creating a rhythmic, pulsating aisle for Black Lives Matter to dance through, all because someone threw a shitbag at a mosque, 2,440 miles away.

Just imagine this fantasy population's response if a corporation wanted to build a pipeline that threatened the water supply of millions of people, including those who live on a remote reservation.

This is, of course, the inverse of how these things actually go down. The people of Standing Rock fought against a corporation to defend the water supply for millions. Many people stood with the Water Protectors, but the white/white-identified folks who joined had crash-course lessons on white supremacist racism to process on the fly, and, though their presence was appreciated, it also wasn't entirely helpful. People living through this trauma and threat were put in the position of teaching folks how to be respectful and helpful without letting nasty infringements like entitlement, fragility, and superiority get in the way. It is a leap forward to have so many people standing in support. It is three hops back expending resources to make sure these supporters don't actually cause further and/or unforeseen damage because they didn't bother to educate or de-indoctrinate themselves before they showed up.

Half-Ass versus Whole-Ass

Here's the deal: you cannot be a feminist and perpetuate white supremacy at the same time.

Or, at least, you can, *physiologically,* but you are a half-assed feminist, at which point you gotta hark back to *Parks and Recreation*'s Ron Swanson, who says, "Never half-ass two things. Whole-ass one thing."

Whole-assing feminism involves delving deeply and uncomfortably into white supremacist racism. If you haven't felt uncomfortable, then you haven't gone deep enough.

Humans do amazing things once we set our minds to do amazing things. We make use of our opposable thumbs and gigantic brains, to greater or lesser degree, and neither of those evolutionary game-changers are determined by gender or race, no matter what fascists and eugenicists have to say on the subject.

Most white feminists I meet readily inform me they're not racist, thus sustaining this chasm in ideals. Anyone who seriously entertains the necessity of not perpetuating white supremacist racism will never, ever say, think, or act upon the supposition "I'm not racist."

You *know* you're racist because you've seized upon the absolute mathematical impossibility that you are not.

Once you open yourself up to the horror show people of color live with in white supremacist cultures, you cannot help but notice how deeply white supremacist racism pervades *everything.* Slowly, over time, like training yourself to savor a high-quality, properly barrel-aged bourbon, you learn to revel in the clarity engendered by *morphing your perspective* rather than clinging to it like a shitty lite beer you just can't bring yourself to accept is familiar corporate spittle whose ubiquitous presence no one ever thinks to question.

Maybe it makes you uncomfortable—to be wrong, to apologize for your behavior, to take responsibility for your actions—and maybe it serves you to save yourself from dis-comfort. The social graces of accountability are not readily available to us while learning all the lessons of survival on the Anglo-Saxon Train. Learning them, however, brings such sat-isfaction and edification, it's difficult to remember how de-fensiveness or guilt ever made sense in the first place.

When someone tells me I did or said something ignorant and/or insulting, I'll say, "Oh, fucking hell. I'ma think on that one. I apologize and beg your pardon. Thanks for pointing that out. I appreciate the opportunity."

This manner of response often opens up a conversation in which *the victim of my ignorance feels the inclination to give me valuable insights* so I don't make a similar blunder in the future.

This is a gift.

Let's look at this situation: I have just insulted you. I apologize.

Instead of trouncing off *as is your right,* you elucidate and *as-sist me* in not making the same mistake again. You know full well I will probably make other mistakes, as may you. But for now, you lend me your time and knowledge after I said or did some dumb-assed shit.

You took time out of your sacred and glorious life and I appreciate it.

Thank you, everyone who has set me straight.

You are the salt of the earth.

This kind of interaction has come to pass on numerous occasions—as a result of my ignorance around various religious, ethnic, cultural, transgender, or racial issues—because, like everyone, I make mistakes. An open, apologetic response often garners kindness instead of (the incredibly rational) wrath, silent disgust, and/or general disappointment in humanity inspired by defensiveness, fragility, denial, and/or guilt. If my intentions serve well, my insultee feels listened to, validated, and, best-case Ontario, no longer an insultee at all.

My fuck-up has the potential to become a winning situation.

Not always.

There's been plenty of times the person doesn't feel like taking the time to explain and I'm left to figure it out for myself.

My stupid game, my stupid prize.

No one has any responsibility to educate anyone else about anything.

Which is why it's a gift when someone takes the time.

By arguing, debating, or reframing things to suit your perception of yourself, you look a gift horse in the mouth.

Take the gift.

Unwrap it in the peace and quiet of your home.

Look at it from all angles and sit with it in quiet contemplation.

After stripping away my white supremacist indoctrination over the course of many years, it became apparent that in situations where someone informs me I fucked up, unaccountability *of any kind* undermines the viability of what this person is *taking time out of their life* to communicate.

Perhaps it will come to pass that I decide I did/said nothing wrong and the person was, in fact, being overly sensitive, paranoid, unfair.

Though this has yet to occur, certainly, statistically, at some point, perhaps it might.

I won't come to *any* conclusion before serious reflection, which involves painstakingly looking at the situation from the other person's point of view, for I am well acquainted with my own.

And I don't know what your process is, but this caliber of thinkin' takes me a sleep or two.

Therefore, regardless of anything else going on in the whole wide world outside of an earthquake in which I miraculously save everyone's life by shoving them under a sturdy piece of furniture, righteous vindication (if, in fact, that is what I am seeking) will never, *ever* happen when someone calls me out on my stupid white/cis person shit.

Subsequently, I see few plausible storylines where I'd defend my position any time prior to the ensuing forty-eight-odd hours.

By the time I got my thinkin' done, I've generally absorbed this new perspective into my frame of reference and, like I say, feel thankful and have since moved on to other days and experiences, of which life doles out a seemingly infinite supply.

This is *exactly like* how it's

just

fucken

best

for men to sit back and engage the idea they may be wrong rather than clutching at the tenuous, illusion-of-masculinity-based reality that they're right, mansplaining their way into a pit of disdain from which they will never, in your estimation, arise.

This has happened to you.

You know how shitty it feels to watch someone be gross like this.

Don't be gross like this.

Apple trees grow apples.

Racist cultures grow racist individuals.

There is simply no math that adds up to the possibility I'm not racist.

Because of my race and the culture I was born into, I am a work in progress, and that is *the best I can achieve* throughout the course of my life.

This is not a bad place to be, and I am happy, doing my best, screwing up and rectifying as I go, but this shit goes deep. I'm *trying* over here and clearly see the mathematic insurmount-ability of achieving a personal racist-less status. There are too many contexts in which racism can rear its head and no way on earth I can conceive of and/or anticipate them all, for I am and always will be a white person living in a society designed for my white ass. So long as I stick to the dominant white culture, I am *never* in the position of being a perceived racial antagonist.

That is an incredibly luxurious way to live life, whether or not I have access to health care, clean water, food on the table, or a roof over my head. I experience a daily freedom that people of color can only conceive of.

This is the definition of luxury and privilege.

People of color living in white supremacy always have to be *on*. The only times that afford relaxation and absolute safety are those when white folks are largely absent, and even then, you got your general catty behavior, family-projected dysfunction, cis-centricism, homophobia, gossip, and overall shitty behavior everyone finds everywhere.

No wonder black folks (statistically) have high blood pressure.

White persons who grow up in white-dominant societies *automatically inherit and unconsciously enact our role* in white supremacist racism. Only by tearing down our indoctrination can we stop ourselves from perpetuating this murderous, soul-crushing legacy.

Which is why you can only be a half-assed feminist if you are unwilling to see how racism—and not some general, faraway KKK racism, *but your personal racism*—oppresses others. Further, you're in an incredibly weak moral position to call out anybody about oppressing anybody or anything else. Much moreover, you are doing your part to keep everything nice and divisive in our society, so you pose no real threat in bothering anyone's racist, sexually violent, corrupt, environmentally destructive train that runs on racism, sexual violence, corruption, and environmental destruction.

Chugging along the rails of normalized everyday racism won't kill you, and, equally, it won't make you stronger, but it will assassinate any mutation of feminist unity you may be toying with in your (otherwise glorious) imagination.

Be brave.

Find empathy inside yourself and then sow an empathy farm.

Go no-contact with your limited perspective like the abusive family member it is.

Persist, resist.

Listen closely to women surviving in white supremacy. Listen to stories, listen to songs, watch films, go to art and music shows. Spend time doing this. *Then* you can figure out what job best suits your skill set. White feminists are incredibly useful the instant we can sit at the table with women of color, everybody looking into each other's eyes, communicating from a place of authenticity rather than fear, projection, and insecurity.

In the meantime, just listen.

Listen and read.

At the back of the book, you'll find an extensive reading and listening list of books and music by women of color and indigenous women.

May I suggest absorbing these myriad perspectives solely for one year.

Bear explicit and constant witness to women who live each day tangling with white supremacy. This doesn't mean white women's feelings do not matter. It means we allow room in our hearts for feelings we may not readily perceive.

It may feel like a lonely position sometimes, but think of it this way:

Everyone on earth who grew up representing the dominant race in any white supremacist society is racist. That means every white person in Canada, England, Scotland, Ireland, France, Germany, Finland, Greenland, Iceland, Spain, Italy, the Netherlands, Denmark, Sweden, Switzerland, Israel, and South Africa. *It takes courage* to face off with denial and horror at the realization of the enormity of all of this racism.

Further, white supremacy—specifically the nefarious lessons and pernicious legacy of colonialization—informs cultural and social norms throughout India, Mexico, Central and South America, the Middle East, Asia, and Africa, where, for example, the lighter your skin or wider your eyes, the better off you are—particularly if you're a woman. Exploitative "beauty" industries thrive off these white-is-best standards, hawking skin-bleaching products and cheap eyelid surgery like Susie selling seashells by the seashore.

We're just offering what people want, the beauty executives say.

This is a negative loophole.

Comprehending the negative loopholes readily instilled by our society and why we resort to them is crucial to feminism.

Keep a watch out for the loopholers in our world. They insult people by making small-minded demands for strains of equality that are only imagined in a fantasy of unchecked white and/or male superiority.

A loophole loopholers love to argue about is "Why can *they* use the N word but we can't?"

Maturity level of a four-year-old and the fact that life isn't fair notwithstanding, you can't use the N word for the same reason you can't use *faggot* unless you're queer, you can't use *chink* unless you're Asian, you can't use *kike dyke* unless you're a Jewish lesbian, and you can't use *poor white trash* unless you're white and do, in fact, suffer from generational economic disenfranchisement.

Help yourself to *cracker, honky, jiveass turkey, ofay, tech twat,* and *Bitchy Useless Snit from Pettytown,* because if you think about it for a second, why the fuck are you fighting for the right to use a word that's just plain shitty?

What's the point?

If black people want to use this word, that's black folks' business, and a short Internet foray into the black community informs us that black folks are quite divided over usage of this word. Some folks love it and find power in reclaiming it. Some folks have normalized it to the point of a pronoun, sloughing off its hateful sting. Some folks think it's just shitty and want everyone to stop. Some folks think everybody has a point.

It's really no one else's business.

A classic loophole found in rape culture is the manufactured stereotype that women lie about being sexually assaulted. This narrative serves patriarchal society very well, and when someone *does* lie about being raped, it's played hell for leather in the media, garnering more attention than any actual rape has, ever.

Conversely, white supremacy assumes that a white woman would never lie about rape so long as it was a black man doing the raping. History is rife with this phenomenon.

Two possibilities to keep track of here:

If a (white/successful) man raped you, loopholers will accuse you of lying on the basis of the fact that women have lied about being raped in the past.

If you are a white woman who did a shitty thing, you can create a loophole for yourself by throwing a black man under the bus. These days, you may or may not get away with it, but history is certainly in your favor.

Remember: lying about being raped in general and lying about being raped by a black man—any man of color will do, depending on your geographical locale; in Texas, for instance, he should definitely be Mexican or Chicano—are processed as *two entirely different and unrelated issues* in this society we normalize and call home sweet home. That is, by changing the race of the perpetrator, you can change the crime itself.

This is objectively batshit crazy, you gotta admit.

Unpopular and Popular Crimes

Treason is an unpopular crime.

It's unpatriotic and disloyal to spy on your people and report about it to their enemies.

Nobody likes you when you do shit like that. Your fellow citizens consider you weak, which you are. Your family is totally shamed. Your spouse and children have to change their names and slip off the radar somehow if they want to have nice-ish lives.

Moreover, history has shown us time and again that treason is harshly punished. We're talking "pull out the guillotine we haven't used in decades" harshness.

Unless you got some stellar information up your sleeve, treason is death.

Rape is an incredibly popular crime, involving short prison stints if you're miraculously prosecuted and as long as you didn't kill anyone. Rapists get a second, third, fourth, fifth, and, hell, why not a sixth chance to redeem themselves.

Some fraternities, sports teams, street gangs, militaries, and militant groups, in fact, won't *really* let you in unless you rape someone in front of your probationary brothers.

Ensures your loyalty.

We live in a world where judges ask women why we didn't keep our legs together and insist (generally, but not always, white) college boys-will-be-boys gang rapists receive probation and suspended sentences.

If rape was an unpopular crime like treason, none of this would go down.

If rapists' hands were cut off after serving a minimum three decades in prison and red R's were tattooed on their hand stumps, sexual assaults would decline and rapists would have a difficult time living the rest of their lives, just like the person they assaulted.

Still not justice, though.

Justice is a federal therapy fund for sexual assault victims, reparations until the flashbacks allow for meaningful employment, lifelong health care, and a plaque from society at large apologizing for creating an environment in which sexual predators thrive, with a sealed promise that we are actively working to do better.

That approaches justice, but I probably forgot a few things.

Sexual predators are the penultimate bullies and as such are, by definition, cowards. Sexual predators are people who enjoy having power and control over others, and patriarchal society breeds like bunnies people who want power and control.

If harsh punishments awaited them, they'd take the responsibility for their actions we all so desire. Facing brutality, isolation, lifelong shame, or death, they'd bury their urges until they couldn't handle the pressure anymore and either sought help or killed themselves.

There exist no justifications for the lackluster rape laws found in patriarchal societies.

You live in a society that preys on the powerless.

Bullies surround us every day, in school, in the workplace, in government, in traffic, at home.

Being a bully is *precisely how* to get ahead in our society. Sexual predators are, therefore, an organic by-product of a society that exalts and worships bullies. We stand aside as the CEOs who rape entire communities make their way to the boarding gate. We laud trillionaires, who could give a million dollars to every man, woman, and child on the planet and still be trillionaires. Developers tear down our neighborhoods and are given free rein to do so by corrupt city officials we vote into office.

The devil is in the details and the details always end up being a bully.

We do not have harsh rape laws because, like most people living in patriarchal societies, we think rape isn't really all that bad, and if it is bad, it's not that common, and if it is common, it's the victim's fault, and if it's not the victim's fault, then men can't help themselves, and if men can't help themselves, then they shouldn't be punished too harshly.

Not like treason.

Let's, for the moment, take the whole spectrum of sexual violence—the emotional abuse, exploitation, and sexual abuse of children; family molestation; stranger and date rape; the paltry sentencing laws; the acute vulnerability of indigenous women, women of color, and transgender communities; rape culture; the degrading humiliations war brings; and the ongoing dangers and indignities refugees suffer—let's take it all and lump it together under one encompassing term: rapism.

Racism and rapism could be eviscerated by a historian/cartographer/time traveler who invents experiential laser surgery and has an infinite amount of patience for bearing witness, but it'd be a mess.

Barring this development, racism and rapism will continue to enjoy a synergistic relationship in which one functions most effectively when the other thrives.

Both flourish on denial, lies, bureaucratic unaccountability, defensiveness, guilt, unmitigated power trips, and shifting shame and blame—all great tactics for getting ahead in life on the Anglo-Saxon Train.

When someone is raped, and that person is eligible for the possibility of justice, a litany of further insults and injuries awaits.

There is a rape kit in a sterile hospital room and the collection of other evidence, which means you need to have someone bring you fresh clothing, which also means further humiliation if you don't have someone you can trust with this task.

You answer questions.

You relive the violence again and again and again, for attorneys, depositions, in the court room.

This can take years and, meanwhile, you work to rebuild your life.

Each time you're compelled to go over the violence visited upon your sacred person, everything you've built up comes crashing down.

You take one leap forward and three hops back.

Your friends and family might or might not know, might or might not have your back.

You are just like a soldier returning from war. You learn who you can count on, and it's not most people.

You have a difficult time connecting.

In this manner, you lose people who were once close to you.

Your whole life is affected by this single act of violence, and any attempts to deny or bury it result in sketchy behavior and/or suicidal thoughts.

Then comes the trial.

You've risked it all for this, and it turns out his lawyer is better than yours, and you go home and start rebuilding your life yet again, only this time, you know he's out there, free.

Do you make it?

Only if you have a kickass support system and a strong constitution.

Employing your imagination to enact vengeance can be helpful too.

In a white supremacist racist society, indigenous women who have been sexually assaulted rarely pass through the anemically luxurious doorway where people, however grudgingly, *acknowledge* a crime has been committed.

Justice is a completely alien term on reservations, unless it's served up by friends and family or tribal court, where nontribal members cannot be tried.

Justice, the kind with lawyers, courts, and jail sentences, is *never* served on reservations.

Indeed, that kind of justice is against the law.

Civic, state, and federal governments in North America have no jurisdiction on reservation land. Likewise, tribal police have no power anywhere but on the reservation. Sexual predators have found the Grand Canyon escape valve here, and I'll explain it in case you can't think like a sexual predator:

You are the son of the mayor of a small city near a reservation. You're an entitled, violent piece of shit and you want to rape someone. You drive to the reservation and find someone to rape. Then you go back home and watch the game. The tribal police cannot arrest you because you do not live on the reservation. What they can do is appeal to the local police, which means allowing them onto Native land to conduct their investigation. Rarely, if ever, is either party willing to cooperate here. For cooperation to happen, communities surrounding reservations would have to refrain from largely comprising racist white folks who garner less than grave distrust.

The person who was raped doesn't even *think* about justice and—*this is important*—neither does the sexual predator, who is free to rape again.

And again, and again, and again, until motor skills fail and you can't get any of your grandkids to drive your creepy, loathsome ass out to the reservation anymore.

This shit is fucked up.

More fucked up, however, is that there's *no* place for this reality, which affects hundreds of thousands of *our sisters,* in mainstream feminist discourse, our one-stop shop for buying in to the fight against rape culture.

With only *marginally* more risk, sexual predators operate similarly in ghettos, barrios, favelas, refugee camps, Oxy-infested ghost towns in middle America, and truck stops throughout the world.

That is, if they're not police officers. In the aforementioned locales the police are known to be just another street gang. The reservation rapist will be sentenced to death before the cop rapist is even questioned.

We're talkin' diplomatic impunity levels of inconsequence.

Your Jagged Tile Piece

I distinctly recall one of the events that brought victim blaming and slut shaming to the fore on a massive scale. In 2011, a Toronto police officer offered alleged safety tips to a group of students at York University, one of which was to refrain from dressing like "sluts."

Criminal-level unhelpfulness aside, this incident led to the first of many SlutWalks throughout the world, where women demanded *everyone* share in the onus of sexual violence. It was a breathtaking moment and has indeed inspired men to start having difficult discussions with their peers.

Most of these actions and discussions are taking place in the relative safety of college campuses, and make no mistake, sexual violence on college campuses is a huge problem. There's a lot of sense in men holding themselves accountable. In college, young men often live in close quarters and it's not terribly difficult for them to bear witness, make a stand, take action, or otherwise influence each other in healthy and productive ways.

However—and this is a goddamn mammoth *however* right now—sexual violence on college campuses is one jagged tile on the *Guernica*-style mosaic we're looking at.

How can you possibly see the whole picture if you are only interested in painstakingly examining your jagged tile piece?

You know what your piece looks like.

Look at other pieces.

That is how we end up with a nice, satisfying, all-encompassing image that brings the expanse of our illusory, perception-deluded divisions together.

It's also how humanity might commandeer the Anglo-Saxon Train, but that's another story for another time.

For now, how do you think mainstream feminism appears to a seventeen-year-old woman living on the Rosebud Reservation in South Dakota?

Let's spin the globe and find some clues.

Haiti.

Imagine one of Haiti's refugee camps, where sexual predators prowl at night and safety is dangerously, expensively purchased; where UN Peacekeepers have streamlined a black market for pedophiles to adopt children; where food is a luxury, clean water a dream come true. Imagine you are the oldest sister, ordained to protect your siblings, because both of your parents work when they are not asleep.

Now imagine a US or Canadian feminist having an earnest sit-down with you. She points out that the onus for sexual violence should no longer rest on women's shoulders, which amounts to victim blaming.

Men are responsible for stopping sexual violence.

If anyone tells you wearing dresses is dangerous, they're not, in fact, pointing out that wearing pants is a time-consuming pain in the ass for a sexual predator to deal with; they're slut shaming you.

Standing there in your refugee camp, how would you process this information from a white feminist?

From my limited vantage point, at best, it looks like someone serving their own myopic self-interests at the expense of someone else.

At worst, it looks like someone expending resources, which could otherwise be put to great, practical use, traveling to Haiti for the express purpose of pouring insult onto someone's grave, ongoing injury.

Colleges and universities refer sex crimes to their campus police, whereas the local judicial system should deal with any criminal allegation against a student, same as for other crimes. This is a soft spot ripe for feminist examination.

Another squishy point is the obscene amount of funding athletic teams generate that universities (and in some cases, high schools) rely on. This economic reality exacerbates the boys-will-be-boys mentality pervading society—how can a school rein in the above-the-law behavior of the very money-making system it depends on for its survival? The highest-paid state employees in the United States are athletic coaches at universities because winning the championship puts you at the top of the heap, and I think we all know how important it is to be at the top of the heap.

Chess, debate, cooking, engineering, music, and film

are all activities that could, given the same level of academic/
community attention, support, and focus, bring in an equal
amount of funding as male-centered athletics.

Beyond these important issues is an entire universe of hurt
and pain, and in *that* universe, the onus for fighting sexual violence rests solely in the realm of the perceived powerless.

Jagged mosaic tile piece.

You know what yours looks like.

White and/or entitled folks are by no means the entire problem here. There's a dismal, ghostly abyss of room for improvement in the Chicano, Mexican, Central American, black,
Jewish, Hindu, Christian, and Muslim communities here in
the United States, Mexico, and Canada. Y'all treat gays and
transgender folks like shit, which sometimes involves brutal
rape and murder without any kind of criminal investigation.

Meanwhile, white cis-gendered gays are some of the most
racist people I've ever had the disquieting displeasure of being
around, and you menfolks can be unsettlingly virulent misog-
ynists. The first person in line to agree with me on this is every
white gay man who can't deal with the racism and sexism of his
peers (Jerry Knight, I'm lookin' at your rainbow unicorn ass),
so don't even think of *attempting* to bust my balls on that one,
Mister. Asian American and Southeast Asian communities
got yer bags of racist worms to contend with and, again, y'all
have a penchant for shunning your gay family members on the
regular. Indigenous people get shit from so many different

vantage points, it's difficult to stand where I stand and criticize. In my limited experience, you've (in some instances, grudgingly) welcomed your homo and trans sons and daughters who I number among my friends, but there's nonetheless some serious wiggle room for stepping up how y'all respond to sexual violence.

And there again, everybody has wiggle room on their response to sexual violence, most likely starting with our families.

If a young man has made it to college, he should be smart enough to comprehend the boundaries around sexual consent and violence. I know my sister and brother-in-law are busy beavers having these discussions with their teenage son and daughter. These are labyrinthine talks, filled with endless questions and potential scenarios.

I extend my gratitude to these two for doing their part.

Young men in higher education who have parents like my nephew's are also expected to invest in teaching others about those boundaries, and my sister and I expect nothing less from my nephew.

Checking your friends is what kind-hearted, intelligent men *do,* and though it should just be normal behavior, I thank y'all for your efforts. It's thorny and difficult, which is a fuckton of fun compared to being raped.

Be brave.

I count six men in my biological nuclear family. Statistically, 1.5 of them will commit—again, *statistically*—multiple acts of sexual violence at some point in their lives.

This is a painful consideration.

And though it would break my heart to learn that anyone in my family sexually assaulted someone, I'd also spend the rest of my life having some roof-raising family conversations and holding Mr. So-and-So to explicit account after he served his (statistically) paltry prison sentence. I would never "forget" about it. There is no amount of Happy Family Lacquer that'd put a shine on that shitshow. Long after his probation officer was a murky figure in an ill-fitting, sweat-stained tracksuit, I'd be there, requiring regular reports, until one of us no longer sailed upon this planet's hull.

So, yes, up to a very certain point, the onus is on men and the families they call home.

I accept that, 100 percent.

One fly in this ointment is the fact that rapists *want* to rape. They seek out situations where rape is a good possibility.

Sexual predators are not woefully uninformed, non-feminist-ideal-raised individuals who just need a good talking to from their friends about how to behave when they've been drinking.

They are *sexual predators* with deep-seated mental issues they have no interest in resolving if, indeed, any resolution is possible.

How might a peer-based conversation go?

"Excuse me, sexual predator, but I was wondering if we could talk about boundaries and consent?"

"Oh, yeah? Sure. Let's talk about that."

*"Well, you're responsible for your actions, you see? You mustn't act
violently or aggressively toward those you view as powerless."*

"Really? Okay. Wow. Interesting. Interesting as fuck. I'm enthralled here."

*"Oh, good news! So, no more raping, okay? It's damaging, and really,
you should just stop."*

*"Will do! Great talk! Thanks for taking the time. Absolutely. No more rape.
You can count on me."*

Does anyone really think yer garden-variety, invested sexual predator is going to change their mind after any such conversation?

How many times have you stopped doing something that brings you deep satisfaction because someone told you to stop?

People are famous for not doing this.

I fail to feature how sexual predators might enjoy an evolutionary edge that exists as a void for the rest of humanity.

Fight Pitch

My father was an asshole chauvinist pig who decided his daughters would be victimized by men like himself over his dead body.

That is part of what I am: a projection of my father's fear, progeny of an asshole.

When I came home crying because a boy at school picked on me, he queried, "Is he bigger than your brother?" to which

I, sniffling, replied, "No." And my father said, "Well, kick his ass. You can almost kick your brother's ass."

And so I did.

Boys did not pick on me.

I do view this parenting strategy with circumspection.

It's not a good idea to teach a kid that physical violence will solve their problems.

On the other hand, physical violence has solved many of my problems.

Men do not expect me to physically react, and I physically react.

When a man in a crowded nightclub grabbed my pussy, it was pure instinct for me to grab his wrist, follow that arm through a sea of people, and smash my beer into his face.

Was this a healthy reaction?

I'm sure many would say it wasn't.

Be that as it may, that particular man definitely thought twice the next time he figured it was a good time to grab someone's pussy.

And, no, I'm not riffing off unfortunate political history; this is something that happened and happens whenever cowardly bullies gather in crowded places the world over.

Please know, a cunt, like balls, is really sensitive. Many aspects of our lives revolve around our cunts. If you want to grab one, and you haven't been invited to partake in responsibility for everything that comes with it—blood, orgasms, babies, debilitating cramps, and piss—you might get a beer smashed in your drunk shitface.

All's fair in sexism and war.

To this day, I'm satisfied with my response.

I was raised in this tradition and nurtured it throughout my life.

I am not bragging, nor am I judging.

Rather, I'm trying to sell you on the idea of teaching yourself how to fight.

For fight though I may know how, safe passage through this little life of mine is nowhere near ensured.

When I talk about self-defense to folks who adhere to the victim-blaming view of sexual violence, it gets translated into, "Women who don't learn how to protect themselves are to blame for any violence that visits their person."

First of all, let me segue into clearing up one major point here: cis-women and transfolks are perfectly capable of being sexual predators, and cis-men are perfectly capable of being sexually assaulted.

I was reminded of this just a few years ago while dancing at one of the safest clubs I know of—one I've been dancing at for over twenty-five years. There I was, having a fun time, grooving. And then I felt the hand. It swooped quite professionally between my butt cheeks and was sliding down. (*What is it* with pussy grabbers at night clubs?) I twisted, grabbed the wrist, and followed it up the arm, yanking at a fleeing lesbian, but the pause of my shock allowed her to wrench herself out of my grasp. She disappeared into the crowd. If she were a man, she would not have gotten away. I wouldn't have been stunned with icicle stabs of betrayal. It's a lesson I've had to learn a few times now. Although cis-gendered men certainly have the corner on this market, sexual predators come from every walk of life.

Back now to our larger topic.

Let's say 100 percent of the female-identified population learned self-defense.

This involves everything from being physically, psychologically, and emotionally assertive, aggressively using our voices, knowing how to deescalate a salvageable situation, learning to recognize the difference between salvageable and unsalvageable situations, fighting to get away, fighting to maim, and, finally, fighting to kill.

Let's say we know how to do all this stuff.

One thing that will happen: sexual predators will go through a period of Social Darwinism. Those wimpier predators who manage to survive will have their highly inconvenient predilections mercilessly beaten out of them.

Next up, those sexual predators fit enough to survive will have to make sure they get one of us alone, ensuring there is no chance we might stumble upon them doing their nefarious deed, because we *will* put a stop to it.

We are all trained to do so.

It would be difficult to rape and sexually assault us; we would not be relying on the judicial system to come to its senses.

This represents the maximum potential of risk minimization.

It still would not stop sexual violence, but it would put a fuck of a dent in it.

Twenty-five percent of the adult cis-female population is reported to have been sexually assaulted, and even though we all know this statistic is low-balled so hard it slips through the grating and into the sewer, stinking up the underworld, even though that never-changing stat does not count anyone who doesn't feel entitled or doesn't have the evidence or doesn't have the support system to report, still, let's go with it.

One-fourth of the cis-female population.

Hmm.

If one-fourth of the kids in your child's class came down with measles, would you consider that action-worthy, or would you wait until half of the kids had measles?

If 25 percent of the people at your job were fired every year, would that concern you? Would you look into it and wonder what you might do to maintain your job security? Would you consider looking for another place to work? Or would you do absolutely nothing?

Let's say a quarter of the cars on the freeway in front of you get into independent accidents, blocking most of the lanes. Would you wiggle your way through the wreckage, or would you pull over to help?

These are the kinds of questions I ask myself when I see women insist on their safety on the Anglo-Saxon Train. Sexual violence is one of the things that makes it go.

Remember, Mia Zapata was strong.

People didn't mess with Mia Zapata.

She knew how to fight, knew how to carry herself, and was in the habit of walking around alone at night because she felt safe in her body. None of her friends could figure out how she was overpowered. Mia was solid muscle, trained on the stage, living the rigorous life of a budding punk rock star.

Those questions were all answered when, in 2003, they finally caught the monster. He was six-foot-four and weighed over two hundred pounds.

A Mack truck of a man.

No one blamed Mia, the warrior woman, for her horrible death. It's beyond the capacity of thought.

It makes the exact same no sense to blame someone because they do not know how—or have physical impairments that prevent them from learning—to fight. Mia's skills did not hold up against this man, so, in the end, her training comes into play just as if she'd never trained at all.

Let's take a look at safe bicycling practices.

It's a good idea to have lights, reflectors, a helmet, and well-maintained tires and brakes. A lot of bicycle safety involves eye contact with drivers, while simultaneously knowing full well that eye contact does not equate to cognitive recognition. Various arm signals give cars a chance to know your intentions, and no safe bicycle is complete without some kind of loud warning device. Other accoutrements, such as a tire pump, tube-patching kit, snacks, water, and first-aid kit, are readily available to further trick out your bike for safety.

Bicyclists know there are a lot of dangers for them in the world, which they work hard to minimize whenever possible.

If a bicyclist dies because they weren't wearing a helmet, there's sorrow and wishful thinking, but no one blames the bicyclist for their death. In general, the driver who plowed into them lives in that spotlight.

Imagine the hue and cry there would be for more bike lanes if one out of every four bicyclists was guaranteed to get hit by a car each and every year.

Imagine how dangerous the world might appear.

And if this were the case, if 25 percent of bicyclists got nailed by cars each year, would you couch yourself in denial about the prevalence?

Would you simply refrain from bike riding?

Nowhere near that many bikers get nailed by cars each year, and yet it makes perfect, unquestioning sense for bicyclists to take safety precautions. We take these precautions even though we're aware of the possibility that we could be mowed down by a bus or semi-truck, like Mia Zapata was.

Illusions of Safety among the Aphids

The sexual predator crouches by the tomatoes, well hidden from the street but within easy launching distance from the curb, when a car pulls up.

A woman.

Alone.

The sexual predator thinks, "Wow, how just insanely convenient," as the woman swings open her car door, sets one foot on the curb, and starts to apply lipstick. Is she wearing a dress? Kinda. Mid-length skirt, thin cotton leggings, boots. A breezy late spring day. She decides to text someone once her lipstick has been blotted and air-kissed in the rearview mirror. The sexual predator sees emotions cross the woman's face as she corresponds. A fond smile, a troubled crinkle in the corner of her mouth, a slight eyebrow raise.

"How much information do I have on this woman?" the sexual predator wonders. Alone, fairly easy-access clothing, completely oblivious to my presence, absorbed in communication with someone who matters to her, invested in her appearance to the detriment of awareness of her surroundings, has a decent job—or at least is able to keep her head above credit card debt because her car hasn't been repossessed, as is evidenced by its presence. So, robbery possibilities as well.

It's been slightly over three minutes since she put her transmission in park.

Just as the sexual predator is about to spring, sending the woman sprawling across the car seats, I notice an infestation of aphids.

There is no sexual fuckwad predator.

Just me, pruning my tomatoes, registering profound frustration over a total stranger's complete devotion to the illusion of safety.

Before the frustration rose up, I found myself in a weird spot, where if I moved, I'd startle her, and I didn't want to do that.

Seriously, I was whisper-close to this woman and she had *no idea* I was there.

After I thought about it for a minute is when I got frustrated.

What if I wasn't me?

What if I wasn't even someone who cared about scaring people when they're vulnerable and stood up right when she was applying her lipstick?

She would've been startled and unnerved.

I didn't want to be responsible for that.

I made a choice to protect her in her absolute insistence that the world is a safe place and I later kicked myself for that, but the alternative was to scare her and I didn't want to do that *more* than I wanted to present her with a teachable moment while I was dealing with the asshole aphids.

I counted her lucky stars that I *wasn't* a sexual predator as she finished up her various self-absorbed businesses and left, whereupon I uncamouflaged myself and moved along to the next shitstorm of aphids, without her knowing of my existence on the planet.

Warriors

A recent social-media emotional manipulation gave me pause. A dear friend posted a video about young women jujitsu experts in which he lamented any hope his daughters—one of whom is very "girly"—would take an interest in learning to defend themselves.

It must be noted that a "girly" person isn't always a girl, doesn't necessarily identify as a girl in any way, or may be someone who experiences gender fluidity; *all children*, no matter their gender(s), can find themselves in a risk-filled situation. In this instance, though, we're dealing with a girl who was born a girl and is girly as girldom can conjure and who doesn't have any interest in things such as fighting.

Regardless of race or gender, those devoid of an experiential understanding of humanity's depravity are at extreme risk in this world. Children are 100 percent at risk until they're old enough to understand the bad things bad people who seem like they're good might do. High percentages of this same void of understanding can also be found in some populations of elderly folk and those with mental challenges.

I felt for my friend and wrote his daughter a letter:

> *Dear Girly One,*
> *I want you to live in a happy world, filled with unicorn wishes, glitter cupcakes, rainbow pops, and sparkling happiness, but who am I? We haven't even met and the world doesn't care what I want for you.*
> *This world, Girly One, it was not made for you.*
> *You have to make it for yourself.*
> *You can dream about royalty sweeping you off your feet, you can dream about castles where you are safe and loved, you can dream about anything.*
> *You're free to do that and dreaming is nice.*

The castles in this world are built on the backs and at the expense of poor folk, Girly One. Living in such a castle will make you complicit and that opens up a can of worms you will then have to contend with, consciously or not, for all your days.

*If, by some glitch in reality, royalty sweeps you away, you will experience considerably less freedom than you do at present. Your closet, for instance, will be filled with clothes you are expected to wear and your calendar will be filled with social engagements that may or may not interest you. You better hope they **do** interest you, royal Girly One, because you'll seriously die of boredom if they don't.*

We are, after all, talking about the calendar for the rest of your life.

That is no life for anyone, really.

Well, royalty, I s'pose.

Instead, you have the option of being a Girly Warrior Girl.

You do this by making yourself of strong mind and body and then when you grow up, you pull the world in around you and make it what you want it to be. Maybe you want to make a big world like Queen Rania of Jordan or maybe you want to make a small world, with a nice quiet cottage by the river, a beautiful garden, five goats, and eighteen chickens, like me.

There are millions of worlds to be made inside this rather ugly one, but you will never know this if you do not feed your mind and work your body.

Look at Michelle Obama's law degrees and biceps.

Michelle Obama's mind gets fed and her body gets worked.

This applies not less, in fact more, if you are a Girly One in a wheelchair or have other physical challenges. You must work harder than able-bodied people. I wish, too, this was not the case, but it is, for there are people in the world more vulnerable than a Girly One in a wheelchair and you must be strong because one day you may need to protect someone more vulnerable than you.

Why must you be strong for them?

Because I was not lying when I said this world was not made for you, and for you to make a world of your choosing, you must train. And when you train, you become a Warrior and Warriors just naturally offer their assistance. You aren't a Warrior if you don't offer assistance. Only greedy mercenaries and crappy cops don't offer their assistance, though they have the training to do so.

This means reading, writing, and arithmetic, and it also means learning how to use your voice, which is one of a human being's most powerful weapons. Training is learning war strategy, playing chess, and spending many hours of your time teaching your body how to respond to threats, in thousands of different contexts.

There won't always be someone to protect you, so you must be strong and learn how to protect yourself, Girly One.

If you have loving caregivers, you are already ahead of the game. You are precious to them. Make a mark on your heart, because some Girly Ones don't have loving caregivers. Some Girly Ones live in homes where people might not care as much as they should.

No matter what, though, whether you have loving family or not, you must train to make a world for yourself. Having a loving family makes **everything** easier, and if you have that, hold onto it and keep it somewhere safe.

If you let the world make itself for you, you won't end up being happy with the result.

*So you make the world for yourself, sweet Girly One. Make it as big as you can imagine or make it as small as your heart desires, and no, it probably won't be easy, but nothing worthwhile is easy and the important thing is that **you** make it.*

Love,

Inga

For good measure:

Dear Boys Will Be Boys,

Really, your letter isn't much different than the one to Girly Ones. It is likewise one of your jobs to know how to protect yourself and others more vulnerable than you.

Other than that, don't rape people. Learn about boundaries before you start involving someone else in your sexual expressions.

Love,

Inga

The End: Who the Old Woman with Black Eyeballs That Swallow You in Love Is

The end of this book came to me in a message from an old woman in a dream. What follows is a verbatim account of this dream that I wrote in my journal directly after waking up:

In Dream that woke me up.

I am a thirteen-or-so-year-old Latino boy. I am freaking out in some room that feels like a place where the community gathers, but it's not a church. I—the young boy—am angry beyond orange, beyond red, beyond white. People are futilely trying to physically restrain me. Some white men have served an unnamed injustice to my people. *Mi familia.* I want to kill. I want their blood to stain my hands. I want to pull their hearts from their chests. No one can control me.

An old woman walks into the room. All attention falls upon her. I feel her black eyes bore into my being, but still, I thrash and fight to get to the white men, outside the place where I am.

The old woman walks directly up to me. She takes my wrists

in her hands, and my strength—which has defied every woman, child, and man in the room—is useless against her.

Holding my wrists, she gently brings my arms down to my sides and begins to cry, oh, she cries from the depths of every soul that has ever graced this planet.

Through her tears, she calmly, soothingly whispers, "Don't you know, don't you know, only our stories can fight against these men. Only our words. You must say, 'Excuse me, sir, but I would like to tell you this story about my grandmother.' And the man will listen, our words will enter his heart, and kill his power from the inside."

She stares into me.

"Only our stories. Only our words."

She continues crying as she says all this; she is crying for ancestors, for grandchildren, for all the civilizations who have been decimated.

Her crying is in my body.

My sleeping, dreaming body.

Her crying storms through the core of my heart. Her crying, *the feeling,* not the sound, her crying wakes me up.

There are no tears on my face.

Her crying is inside me.

This is the message from the old woman with black eyeballs that swallow you in love and make you understand there is nothing to fear.

Blessed Be.

Grandmother.

Cunt.

The Work: Reading and Listening Lists

My best learning is done alone.

I'll leisurely spend a few months reading someone's memoir, fantasizing about the author's perspective or reaction to things that come up during my days. It doesn't matter whether or not I "agree" with the author's perspective. Barbara Bush's memoir took me *years* to actually finish reading, for I found her position on many issues reprehensible. Still, her book enriched my life.

I'm not sure if it was the advent of social media, with its insta-celebrity culture and everlasting gobstopper comment section, bored trolls professing opinions they do not adhere to for the sake of arguments, and constant insinuation that what you "like" actually matters in the grand scheme of things, but at some point in the early 2000s, I started getting emails and comments from people not only assuring me they "agree" with many of the points I make in my books—a concept I could seriously give two fucks about—but also demanding that I clarify my position on those points they *do not* agree with.

So let's clear something up.

Writers write books to put interesting thoughts into the world.

Sometimes it's stories; sometimes it's theories. If the writer says something erroneous, such as "sea sponges are little plant bodies that live in the ocean," and readers chime in, letting the writer know that sea sponges are, in fact, animals, that's a helpful contribution.

The writer might thank these readers for helping to make their work more factual.

However, if Tammy from Nebraska emails the writer a three-page diatribe expounding on why the writer is wrong about leaving the safety of her home to buy soymilk at three a.m., we're dealing with a different ball of wax. Tammy is trying to change the actual story, on the basis of her ideas of how it should have gone, and Tammy therefore should write her own fricken book.

For the love of sweet allah lawd jezus gawd.

I mention this because it's dawned on me that people have perhaps forgotten how and why to read. If that statement comes off as condescending, I apologize, for I am being totally sincere here.

Reading is a highly intimate and sacred exchange between two people.

More can be involved, but generally, writers are crafting their words for you, the reader: one person.

If they've done their job well, the writer has written something worth reading. They've put an enormous amount of thought into each and every word, sentence, paragraph. It's taken years of concentration and focus.

And here is where the intimacy and sacredness come in.

The reader chooses this book.

In doing so, the reader is making a proclamation, "I am putting my trust in this writer."

You may be trusting the writer to be a corporate-ladder-climbing sociopath in an effort to teach yourself better job skills, but once you open that book and start taking in the words laid down for you, you have engaged in a trust relationship.

That is a done deal.

Don't try to make it something more or less.

It's sacred and important that you hold up your end of the deal.

Do you despise football? Do you think it's a huge waste of time and money? If so, then *QB: My Life Behind the Spiral* by Steve Young is the hallowed tome for you! To be clear, one doesn't read *QB* in an effort to learn to love American football. *The entire reason* you'd read this book rests on the fact that you have no interest. What does Steve Young go through? What does he think about? What's important to him? What is he not saying? What does his memoir teach you about hyper-masculinity, *whether or not* Mr. Young ever discusses hyper-masculinity?

I learn scads more by going into the heart of the beast than by sticking to academics who've already proven that we do/do not share similar outlooks on a given subject. (Not to knock academics, who are indisputably important thought designers.)

Slavery was a very bad idea, but that's not gonna keep me from reading the biography of a slave holder. I want to know what he thought, how he rationalized his choices, and then I go and find out that so many of his rationalizations are alive and well today.

Fascinating, horrifying.

White supremacist racism, today, makes a lot more sense to me because I learned from the pen of someone who held slaves how slavery was substantiated while it was going down. Such connections wouldn't be made if I decided it was best to limit my reading to slave narratives I empathize with.

Everyone has something to teach you.

What they're teaching and what you *learn*, well, that's up to you.

My high school geography teacher did not teach me geography. He taught me there exist teachers who go to the beach in the summer and stand by the seawall ogling their barely post-pubescent female students. He taught me my inexperienced friends and I were fodder for sexual fantasy. I learned to recognize that look in a man's eye and steered clear as crystal glacial lakes.

Not geography, but valuable lessons I kept close, nevertheless.

You are in full control of what you learn.

You have no control over the manner in which others teach.

When you open the cover of a new book to read (yes, I'm resistant to ebooks), consciously enter that trust relationship. Honor the work the writer has done and honor your work as a reader to digest and process that writing.

Take away whatever you will, but *you* take responsibility for what you learn.

That, my love, is not the writer's job.

Keeping in mind that our world is fast, furious, sleepless, clear, and present, I've opted to create an olde-fashioned reading list for The Work. This list is designed for you to turn to in quiet times, preferably with a nice pot of tea and a stack of vinyl records, and it oughta keep even the most avid reader busy.

Books

Chimamanda Ngozi Adichie
Americanah
Dear Ijeawele, or a Feminist Manifesto in Fifteen Suggestions
Half of a Yellow Sun
Purple Hibiscus
The Thing Around Your Neck
We Should All Be Feminists

Gloria Anzaldúa
Borderlands/La Frontera: The New Mestiza

Ryka Aoki
He Mele a Hilo
Seasonal Velocities
Why Dust Shall Never Settle Upon This Soul

Toni Cade Bambara

Gorilla, My Love

The Salt Eaters

Those Bones Are Not My Child

War of the Walls 1976, My Love

Mary Brave Bird (a.k.a. Mary Crow Dog)

Lakota Woman

Ohitika Woman

Gwendolyn Brooks

The Bean Eaters

Black Steel: Joe Frazier and Muhammad Ali

Maud Martha

In Montgomery

The Near-Johannesburg Boy and Other Poems

Octavia Butler

Bloodchild and Other Stories

Clay's Ark

Kindred

Mind of My Mind

Parable of the Sower

Parable of the Talents

Patternmaster

Wild Seed

Anne Cameron

Child of Her People

Daughters of Copper Woman

Dreamspeaker

Dzelarhons: Mythology of the Northwest Coast

Family Resemblances

Orca's Song

Selkie

Ana Castillo

Give It to Me

The Mixquiahuala Letters

Peel My Love Like an Onion

So Far from God

Staceyann Chin

The Other Side of Paradise: A Memoir

Margaret Cho

Drive-By Comedy

Drunk with Power

I Hate Boys

I Have Chosen to Stay and Fight

Sandra Cisneros

Caramelo

The House on Mango Street

A House of My Own: Stories
   from My Life

Woman Hollering Creek and
   Other Stories

Maryse Condé

The Children of Segu

I, Tituba: Black Witch of
   Salem

A Season in Rihata

Segu

Tree of Life

Victoire: My Mother's Mother

Who Slashed Celanire's Throat?
   A Fantastical Tale

Anna Julia Cooper

A Voice from the South

J. California Cooper

Age Ain't Nothing but a Number:
   Black Women Explore Midlife
   (contributor), edited by Carleen
   Brice

The Future Has a Past

Homemade Love

Life Is Short but Wide

A Piece of Mine

In Search of Satisfaction

Some Love, Some Pain,
   Sometime: Stories

Some People, Some Other
   Place

Some Soul to Keep

The Wake of the Wind

Kimberlé Williams Crenshaw

Black Girls Matter: Pushed
   Out, Overpoliced and
   Underprotected

Critical Race Theory: The Key
   Writings that Formed the
   Movement

The Race Track: Understanding
   and Challenging Structural
   Racism

Reaffirming Racism: The Faulty
   Logic of Colorblindness,
   Remedy, and Diversity

Words That Wound: Critical Race
   Theory, Assaultive Speech,
   and the First Amendment

Edwidge Danticat

Behind the Mountains
Breath, Eyes, Memory
Create Dangerously: The
    Immigrant Artist at Work
The Dew Breaker
The Farming of Bones
Krik? Krak!

Louise Erdrich

The Bingo Palace
LaRose
Love Medicine
The Plague of Doves
The Round House
Tracks

Clarissa Pinkola Estés

The Faithful Gardener: A Wise
    Tale About That Which Can
    Never Die
The Gift of Story: A Wise Tale
    About What Is Enough
Untie the Strong Woman: Blessed
    Mother's Immaculate Love for
    the Wild Soul
Women Who Run with the
    Wolves

Alicia Gaspar de Alba

Desert Blood: The Juarez Murders

Joy Harjo

Conflict Resolution for Holy
    Beings: Poems
Crazy Brave: A Memoir
A Map to the Next World
She Had Some Horses
Soul Talk, Song Language:
    Conversations with Joy Harjo
What Moon Drove Me to This?

Daisy Hernandez

Colonize This! Young Women
    of Color on Today's Feminism
    (ed.)
A Cup of Water Under My Bed:
    A Memoir

Ayaan Hirsi Ali

The Caged Virgin
Heretic: Why Islam Needs a
    Reformation Now
Infidel
Nomad: From Islam to America

Pauline Hopkins

Contending Forces: A Romance Illustrative of Negro Life North and South

Of One Blood: Or, The Hidden Self

Slaves' Escape; Or, The Underground Railroad

Zora Neale Hurston

Tell My Horse

Their Eyes Were Watching God

Gayl Jones

Corregidora

Eva's Man

The Healing

The Hermit-Woman

Mosquito

Song for Anninho

White Rat

Xarque and Other Poems

June Jordan

Haruko: Love Poems

His Own Where

I Was Looking at the Ceiling and Then I Saw the Sky

June Jordan's Poetry for the People: A Revolutionary Blueprint

Soldier: A Poet's Childhood

Some of Us Did Not Die

Adrienne Kennedy

Funnyhouse of a Negro

The Ohio State Murders

The Owl Answers

Sleep Deprivation Chamber

Nia King, Jessica Glennon-Zukoff, and Terra Mikalson (eds.)

Queer and Trans Artists of Color: The Story of Some of Our Lives

Nella Larsen

Passing

Quicksand

Audre Lorde

The Cancer Journals

I Am Your Sister: The Collected and Unpublished Writings of Audre Lorde

Audre Lorde *(continued)*

*The Marvelous Arithmetics of
    Distance*
Sister Outsider
*Uses of the Erotic: The Erotic as
    Power*
*Zami: A New Spelling of My
    Name*

Janet Mock

*Firsts: A Memoir of the Twenties
    Experience*
*Redefining Realness: My Path to
    Womanhood, Identity, Love &
    So Much More*

Cherríe Moraga and Gloria Anzaldúa (eds.)

This Bridge Called My Back

Toni Morrison

Beloved
The Bluest Eye
*Playing in the Dark: Whiteness
    and the Literary Imagination*
Song of Solomon
Sula

Gloria Naylor

Bailey's Cafe
Mama Day
The Men of Brewster Place
*The Women of Brewster
    Place*

Malika Oufkir

*Stolen Lives: Twenty Years in a
    Desert Jail*

Ann Petry

*Harriet Tubman: Conductor on
    the Underground Railroad*
*Miss Muriel and Other
    Stories*
The Street
Tituba of Salem Village

Claudia Rankine

Citizen: An American Lyric
*Don't Let Me Be Lonely: An
    American Lyric*
The End of the Alphabet
*Nothing in Nature Is
    Private*
Plot

Jewell Parker Rhodes

Bayou Magic
Douglass' Women
Ghost Boys
Hurricane
Magic City
Ninth Ward
Voodoo Dreams

Gabby Rivera

Juliet Takes a Breath
America

Arundhati Roy

The God of Small Things
Power Politics

Sapphire

The Kid
Push

Marjane Satrapi

Persepolis
Persepolis 2

Assata Shakur

Assata: An Autobiography

Ntozake Shange

Betsey Brown
*For Colored Girls Who Have
    Considered Suicide When the
    Rainbow Is Enuf*
Liliane
Sassafrass, Cypress & Indigo
Some Sung, Some Cry

Warsan Shire

*Teaching My Mother How to Give
    Birth*

Vandana Shiva

Biopolitics
India Divided
Making Peace with the Earth
*Stolen Harvest: The Hijacking of
    the Global Food Supply*

Leslie Marmon Silko

Almanac of the Dead
Ceremony
Garden in the Dunes
Oceanstory
Storyteller
The Turquoise Ledge

Sister Souljah

The Coldest Winter Ever

A Deeper Love Inside: The Porsche Santiaga Story

Midnight and the Meaning of Love

Midnight: A Gangster Love Story

A Moment of Silence: Midnight III

No Disrespect

Alice Walker

The Way Forward Is with a Broken Heart

Jacqueline Woodson

After Tupac and D Foster

Another Brooklyn

Autobiography of a Family Photo

Brown Girl Dreaming

If You Come Softly

Locomotion

Music

Before creating a playlist on your device or relaxing with a shiny black vinyl record, sit down and read the lyrics of the songs. Make it a practice to take this time. Absorb what our songwriters are saying before allowing your body and senses to be swept away by the rhythm and song.

I mention this because of phenomena where people pay absolutely no attention to what an artist is communicating, beyond that which might be of immediate service to them, resulting in folks deciding it's appropriate to get prideful and xenophobic over "Born in the USA," an antiwar protest song, highly critical of the US government's involvement in Vietnam as well as its treatment of returning vets.

We're not gonna do this.

We're lyrics readers who pay attention to the world around us.

We also buy vinyl and spend evenings listening to records, taking the time to flip and change them between chapters, instead of watching cat videos on the Internet.

I'm hoping with critical listening skills and a few home-choreographed dance routines I'll be watching on the Internet at some point, these artists will serve your music needs for a year.

Susan Aglukark

Big Feeling

This Child

Dreams for You

Unsung Heroes

White Sahara

Apryl Allen

Morningstar

Shape Shifter

Joana Amendoeira

Amor Mais Perfeito

Magia do Fado

Sétimo Fado

Maya Angelou

Caged Bird Songs (Tribute Album)

The Poetry of Maya Angelou

India.Arie

Acoustic Soul

Songversation

Testimony: Vol. 1, Life & Relationship

Testimony: Vol. 2, Love and Politics

Joan Armatrading

Back into the Night

Hearts and Flowers

Joan Armatrading

The Key

Lovers Speak

Starlight

Steppin' Out

Aterciopelados

Caribe Atómico
Gozo Poderoso
La Pipa de la Paz
Rio

Erykah Badu

Baduizm
Mama's Gun
New Amerykah Part One
New Amerykah Part Two
Worldwide Underground

Joan Baez

Come From The Shadows
Dark Chords on a Big Guitar
Diamonds & Rust
Joan
Speaking of Dreams

Beyoncé

B'Day
Beyoncé
Dangerously in Love
4
I Am . . . Sasha Fierce
Lemonade

Björk

Debut
Post
Volta

Tracy Chapman

Crossroads
Let It Rain
New Beginning
Tracy Chapman

Neneh Cherry

Blank Project
Homebrew
Man
Raw Like Sushi

Radmilla Cody

Precious Friends
Seed of Life
Spirit of a Woman
Within the Four Directions

Alice Coltrane

Transcendence
Transfiguration

Samantha Crain

Kid Face

Songs in the Night

You (Understood)

You Had Me at Goodbye

Missy Elliott

The Cookbook

Da Real World

Supa Dupa Fly

Under Construction

Cesária Évora

Cabo Verde

Cesaria

Mar Azul

Miss Perfumado

Voz d'Amor

Roberta Flack

Blue Lights in the Basement

Born to Love

First Take

I'm the One

Oasis

Quiet Fire

Roberta Flack & Donny Hathaway

Set the Night to Music

Jean Grae

Attack of the Attacking Things

Cake or Death

The Orchestral Files

This Week

Hard Kaur

P.L.A.Y.—Party Loud All Year

Supawoman

Helly Luv

"Revolution" (Single)

"Risk It All" (Single)

Nona Hendryx

The Art of Defense

Female Trouble

Mutatis Mutandis

You Have to Cry Sometime

Lauryn Hill

The Miseducation of Lauryn Hill

Billie Holiday

All of Nothing at All

An Evening with Billie Holiday

Lady in Satin

Lady Sings the Blues

Music for Torching

Stay with Me

Grace Jones

Hurricane

Nightclubbing

Slave to the Rhythm

Warm Leatherette

Sharon Jones and the Dap-Kings

Dap-Dippin' with Sharon Jones and the Dap-Kings

Give the People What They Want

I Learned the Hard Way

Soul Time!

Diana Karazon

Diana 2010

El Omr Mashi

Super Star El Arab

Kelis

Food

Kaleidoscope

Kelis Was Here

Tasty

Chaka Khan

Chaka Khan

ClassiKhan

Funk This

I Feel for You

Naughty

The Woman I Am

Eartha Kitt

Bad But Beautiful

Sings in Spanish/Canta en Español

I Love Men

I'm Still Here

Sentimental Eartha

Thinking Jazz

Solange Knowles

A Seat at the Table

Solo Star

True

Queen Latifah

All Hail the Queen

Black Reign

Nature of a Sista

Order to the Court

Persona

Bettye LaVette

Change Is Gonna Come

Interpretations: The British
*   Rock Songbook*

I've Got My Own Hell to Raise

Tell Me a Lie

Light Asylum

A Certain Person

Heart of Dust

Light Asylum

Shallow Tears

Audra McDonald

Build a Bridge

Go Back Home

How Glory Goes

M.I.A.

AIM

Arular

Kala

Matangi

Maya

Piracy Funds Terrorism

Nicki Minaj

Pink Friday

Janelle Monáe

The ArchAndroid

The Electric Lady

Me'Shell Ndegeocello

Comfort Woman

Peace Beyond Passion

Plantation Lullabies

Pour une Âme Souveraine: A
*   Dedication to Nina Simone*

Ventriloquism

The World Has Made Me the
*   Man of My Dreams*

Jessye Norman

Amazing Grace

I Was Born in Love with You

Lucky to Be Me

Odetta

Lookin for a Home
Movin' It On
Odetta Sings Ballads and
    Blues
One Grain of Sand

Poly Styrene

Flower Aeroplane
Generation Indigo
Translucence

Pura Fé

Caution to the Wind
Follow Your Heart's Desire
Full Moon Rising
Hold the Rain
Sacred Seed

Gertrude "Ma" Rainey

Ma Rainey's Black Bottom
The Very Best of Ma Rainey

Toshi Reagon

Have You Heard
I Be Your Water
Justice
The Rejected Stone

There and Back Again
Until We're Done

J. R. Rhodes

Afriqueen Stare
Elixir
I Am
Songs of Angels

Minnie Riperton

Come to My Garden
Perfect Angel
Stay in Love

Albita Rodríguez

Albita Llegó
Cantare
Hecho a Mano
Son

Sade

Diamond Life
Promise
Soldier of Love
Stronger Than Pride

Buffy Sainte-Marie

Buffy
Changing Woman
Running for the Drum
Up Where We Belong

Jill Scott

Beautifully Human: Words and
  Sounds, Vol. 2
The Light of the Sun
The Real Thing: Words and
  Sounds, Vol. 3
Who Is Jill Scott? Words and
  Sounds, Vol. 1
Woman

Shonen Knife

Burning Farm
Minna Tanoshiku
Pretty Little Baka Guy
712
Yama-no Attchan

Si*Sé

Gold
More Shine
*Si*Sé*

Shakira

Dónde Están los Ladrones?
El Dorado
Laundry Service
Sale el Sol
She Wolf

Joanne Shenandoah

All Spirits Sing
Covenant
Matriarch: Iroquois Women's
  Songs

Nina Simone

The Amazing Nina Simone
Baltimore
Black Gold
Forbidden Fruit
Here Comes the Sun
High Priestess of Soul
I Put a Spell on You
Little Girl Blue
To Love Somebody
Nina's Back
Nina Simone and Piano!
Nina Simone Sings the Blues
Pastel Blues
Silk & Soul

Nina Simone *(continued)*

A Single Woman
A Very Rare Evening
Wild Is the Wind

Mariee Sioux

Bonnie and Mariee
A Bundled Bundle of Bundles
Gift for the End
Pray Me a Shadow

Sister Souljah

360 Degrees of Power

Mavis Staples

Time Waits for No One
The Voice
You Are Not Alone

Angie Stone

Black Diamond
Mahogany Soul

Yma Sumac

Earthquake in the High Andes
Legends of the Sun Virgin
Malambo!
Voice of the Xtabay

Sweet Honey in the Rock

All for Freedom
In This Land
Sweet Honey in the Rock
The Women Gather

Tanya Tagaq

Animism
Auk/Blood
Retribution
Sinaa

Sister Rosetta Tharpe

Live in Paris
The Lonesome Road
Precious Memories
Singing in My Soul
Sister on Tour

THEESatisfaction

awE NaturalE
EarthEE

Ana Tijoux

Elefant Mixtape
Kaos
La Bala

Martina Topley-Bird

Anything

The Blue God

Quixotic

Some Place Simple

Tina Turner

Break Every Rule

Foreign Affair

Private Dancer

Twenty Four Seven

Wildest Dreams

umami

Conquer the Night

Ephemeral

I Come to Hanertano

theme for travel

Umami

Sarah Vaughan

Dreamy

Feelin' Good

It's a Man's World

The New Scene

Sarah Vaughan in Hi-Fi

d'bi Young

#CivilRightsMixtape (W/ THE 333)

333 2012

when sisters speak, live

wombanifesto

Selected Bibliography

Acker, Kathy. *Blood and Guts in High School*. New York: Grover Weidenfeld, 1989.

———. *In Memoriam to Identity*. New York: Pantheon, 1992.

Allen, Paula Gunn. *Spider Woman's Granddaughters*. Boston: Beacon, 1989.

Allison, Dorothy. *Bastard Out of Carolina*. New York: Dutton, 1992.

———. *Two or Three Things I Know for Sure*. New York: Dutton, 1995.

Angelou, Maya. *I Know Why the Caged Bird Sings*. New York: Random House, 1970.

———. *Just Give Me a Cool Drink of Water 'fore I Die: The Poetry of Maya Angelou*. New York: Random House, 1971.

Atwood, Margaret. *The Handmaid's Tale*. Boston: G. K. Hall, 1987.

Block, Francesca Lia. *Girl Goddess #9*. New York: HarperCollins, 1996.

———. *Weetzie Bat*. New York: Harper & Row, 1989.

Bloss, Roberta, Joseph Corneli, Chris Moon, and Lucas Tomsich. "The Dalkon Shield." *History of Science* 3333 (December 8, 1997). http://www1.umn.edu/scitech/dalkfina.htm. (This resource is no longer available online.)

Brown, Judith C. *Immodest Acts: The Life of a Lesbian Nun in Renaissance Italy.* New York: Oxford University Press, 1986.

Brownmiller, Susan. *Against Our Will: Men, Women and Rape.* New York: Simon & Schuster, 1975.

Bufwack, Mary A. *Finding Her Voice: The Saga of Women in Country Music.* New York: Crown, 1993.

Burgos-Debray, Elisabeth, ed. *I, Rigoberta Menchú: An Indian Woman in Guatemala.* London: Verso, 1984.

Cameron, Anne. *Daughters of Copper Woman.* Vancouver: Press Gang, 1981.

Caprio, Frank S. *Female Homosexuality: A Psychodynamic Study of Lesbianism.* New York: Citadel, 1954.

Carter, Angela. *The Bloody Chamber and Other Stories.* New York: Harper & Row, 1979.

———. *The Old Wives' Fairy Tale Book.* New York: Pantheon, 1995.

Castillo, Ana. *The Mixquiahuala Letters.* Binghamton, NY: Bilingual Press, 1986.

Ceronetti, Guido. *The Silence of the Body: Materials for the Study of Medicine.* New York: Farrar, Straus & Giroux, 1993.

Chadbourne, Eugene. *MAXIMUMROCKNROLL* (March 1990).

Chicago, Judy. *Beyond the Flower: The Autobiography of a Feminist Artist.* New York: Viking, 1996.

Cohen, David, ed. *The Circle of Life: Rituals from the Human Family Album.* New York: Harper, 1991.

Crawford, Joan. *My Way of Life.* New York: Pocket Books, 1972.

Dunn, Katherine. *Attic.* New York: Warner, 1990.

———. *Geek Love.* New York: Warner, 1983.

Eisler, Riane T. *The Chalice and the Blade: Our History, Our Future.* Cambridge, MA: Harper & Row, 1987.

———. *Sacred Pleasure: Sex, Myth, and the Politics of the Body.* San Francisco: Harper San Francisco, 1995.

Ellison, Katherine W. *Imelda: Steel Butterfly of the Philippines.* New York: McGraw-Hill, 1988.

El Saadawi, Nawal. *Woman at Point Zero.* London: Zed Books, 1984.

Erdrich, Louise. *Love Medicine.* New York: Holt, Reinhart & Winston, 1984.

———. *Tracks.* Boston: G. K. Hall, 1989.

Findlen, Barbara, ed. *Listen Up: Voices from the Next Feminist Generation.* Seattle: Seal Press, 1995.

French, Marilyn. *Beyond Power: On Women, Men, and Morals.* New York: Summit, 1985.

———. *The War against Women.* New York: Summit, 1992.

Galeano, Eduardo. *Century of the Wind.* Memory of Fire Trilogy. New York: Nation Books, 2010.

———. *Faces and Masks.* Memory of Fire Trilogy. New York: Nation Books, 2010.

———. *Genesis.* Memory of Fire Trilogy. New York: Pantheon, 1987.

Gilbert, Olive. *Narrative of Sojourner Truth.* Mineola, NY: Dover, 1997.

Golub, Sharon. *Periods: From Menarche to Menopause.* Newbury Park, CA: Sage, 1992.

Graves, Robert. *Mammon and the Black Goddess.* Garden City, NY: Doubleday, 1965.

———. *The White Goddess.* New York: Farrar, Straus & Giroux, 1966.

Green, Karen, and Tristan Taormino, eds. *A Girl's Guide to Taking Over the World*. New York: St. Martin's, 1997.

Griffin, Susan. *A Chorus of Stones: The Private Life of War*. New York: Doubleday, 1992.

Guerrilla Girls. *Confessions of the Guerrilla Girls*. New York: Harper Perennial, 1995.

Harding, M. Esther. *Woman's Mysteries, Ancient and Modern*. New York: Harper & Row, 1976.

Haver, Ronald. *David O. Selznick's Hollywood*. New York: Knopf, 1980.

Hine, Darlene Clark, Wilma King, and Linda Reed, eds. *We Specialize in the Wholly Impossible: A Reader in Black Women's History*. Brooklyn, NY: Carlson, 1995.

Hite, Shere. *Women as Revolutionary Agents of Change: The Hite Reports and Beyond*. Madison: University of Wisconsin Press, 1994.

Holiday, Billie, with William Dufty. *Lady Sings the Blues*. Garden City, NY: Doubleday, 1956.

hooks, bell. *Ain't I a Woman: Black Women and Feminism*. Boston: South End, 1984.

———. *A Woman's Mourning Song*. New York: Harlem River, 1993.

———. *Wounds of Passion: A Writing Life*. New York: Holt, 1997.

Hulme, Keri. *The Bone People*. Baton Rouge: Louisiana State University Press, 1985.

Hurston, Zora Neale. *I Love Myself When I'm Laughing . . . and Then Again When I'm Looking Mean and Impressive*. Old Westbury, NY: Feminist Press, 1979.

———. *Their Eyes Were Watching God*. Urbana: University of Illinois Press, 1978.

Jackson, La Toya. *Growing Up in the Jackson Family.* New York: Dutton, 1991.

Kaplan, Janet. *Unexpected Journeys: The Art and Life of Remedios Varo.* New York: Abbeville, 1988.

Khashoggi, Soheir. *Mirage.* New York: Forge, 1996.

Leamer, Laurence. *The Kennedy Women: The Saga of an American Family.* New York: Villard, 1994.

Lerner, Gerda. *Black Women in White America: A Documentary History.* New York: Vintage, 1972.

Lindgren, Astrid. *Pippi Goes on Board.* New York: Puffin, 1977.

———. *Pippi Longstocking.* New York: Viking, 1950.

———. *Pippi Sails the South Seas.* New York: Viking, 1959.

Lord, M. G. *Forever Barbie: The Unauthorized Biography of a Real Doll.* New York: Avon, 1994.

Lorde, Audre. *I Am Your Sister: Black Women Organizing Across Sexualities.* New York: Kitchen Table, Women of Color Press, 1985.

———. "Uses of the Erotic: The Erotic as Power." In *Sister Outsider: Essays and Speeches.* Trumansburg, NY: Crossing Press, 1984.

Lunardini, Christine. *What Every American Should Know About Women's History.* Holbrook, MA: Bob Adams, 1994.

Lynn, Loretta, with George Vecsey. *Coal Miner's Daughter.* Chicago: Regnery, 1976.

Mankiller, Wilma, with Michael Wallis. *A Chief and Her People.* New York: St. Martin's, 1993.

Marx, Karl. *The Woman Question: Selections from the Writing of Fredrick Engels, V. I. Lenin, Joseph Stalin, and Karl Marx.* New York: International Publishers, 1951.

Maus, Cynthia Pearl. *The World's Great Madonnas*. New York: Harper, 1947.

Mitchell, Margaret. *Gone with the Wind*. New York: Macmillan, 1939.

Morgan, Marlo. *Mutant Message Down Under*. Lees Summit, MO: MM Co., 1991.

Morrison, Toni. *Beloved*. New York: Knopf, 1987.

———. *The Bluest Eye*. New York: Knopf, 1993.

———. *Sula*. New York: Knopf, 1974.

———. *Tar Baby*. New York: Knopf, 1981.

Nagel, Jill, ed. *Whores and Other Feminists*. New York: Routledge, 1997.

O'Connor, Flannery. *Everything That Rises Must Converge*. New York: Farrar, Straus & Giroux, 1965.

———. *Wise Blood*. New York: Farrar, Straus & Cudahy, 1952.

Orenstein, Peggy. *SchoolGirls: Young Women, Self-Esteem, and the Confidence Gap*. New York: Doubleday, 1994.

Palmer, Rachel Lynn, and Sarah K. Greensburg. *Facts and Frauds in Woman's Hygiene*. New York: Vanguard, 1936.

Piercy, Marge. *Woman on the Edge of Time*. New York: Knopf, 1976.

Presley, Priscilla, with Sandra Harmon. *Elvis and Me*. New York: Putnam, 1985.

"*The Progressive* Interview: Desmond Tutu, February 1998." *Utne Reader*, May/June 1998.

Queen, Carol. *Real Live Nude Girl*. San Francisco: Cleis, 1997.

Raymond, Janice G. *Women as Wombs: Reproductive Technologies and the Battle over Women's Freedom*. San Francisco: HarperSanFrancisco, 1993.

Redding, Judith M., and Victoria A. Brownworth. *Film Fatales: Independent Women Directors*. Seattle: Seal Press, 1997.

Roseanne. *Roseanne: My Life as a Woman*. New York: HarperCollins, 1989.

Rothblatt, Martine. *The Apartheid of Sex: A Manifesto on the Freedom of Gender*. New York: Crown, 1995.

Sasson, Jean. *Princess Sultana*. New York: Morrow, 1992.

———. *Princess Sultana's Daughters*. New York: Doubleday, 1994.

Scholz, Suzette, Stephanie Scholz, and Sheri Scholz, with John Tullius. *Deep in the Heart of Texas: Reflections of Former Dallas Cowboy Cheerleaders*. New York: St. Martin's, 1991.

Sen, Mala. *The Bandit Queen*. New York: HarperCollins, 1995.

Sharp, Saundra. *Black Women for Beginners*. New York: Writers & Readers, 1993.

Silko, Leslie Marmon. *Almanac of the Dead and Ceremony*. New York: Simon & Schuster, 1991.

———. *Ceremony*. New York: Penguin, 1986.

Smith, John M. *Women and Doctors: A Physician's Explosive Account of Women's Medical Treatment and Mistreatment in America Today and What You Can Do About It*. New York: Dell, 1993.

Solanas, Valerie. *S.C.U.M. Manifesto*. London: Phoenix Press, 1991.

Tan, Amy. *The Joy Luck Club*. New York: Putnam, 1989.

———. *The Kitchen God's Wife*. New York: Putnam, 1991.

Taormino, Tristan. *The Ultimate Guide to Anal Sex for Women*. San Francisco: Cleis, 1997.

Tea, Michelle. *The Passionate Mistakes and Intimate Corruptions of One Girl in America*. New York: Semiotexte, 1998.

Walker, Alice. *The Color Purple*. New York: Harcourt, Brace, Jovanovich, 1982.

Walker, Alice, and Pratibha Parmar. *Warrior Marks: Female Genital Mutilation and the Sexual Blinding of Women*. New York: Harcourt, Brace, Jovanovich, 1993.

Walker, Barbara G. *The Crone: Woman of Age, Wisdom, and Power*. San Francisco: Harper & Row, 1985.

——. *The Women's Encyclopedia of Myths and Secrets*. San Francisco: Harper & Row, 1983.

Winterson, Jeanette. *Art and Lies*. New York: Knopf, 1995.

——. *The Passion*. New York: Atlantic Monthly Press, 1988.

——. *Sexing the Cherry*. New York: Atlantic Monthly Press, 1990.

Woods, Beatrice. *I Shock Myself*. San Francisco: Chronicle Books, 1988.

Woods, Donald. *Biko*. New York: Vintage, 1979.

Woodson, Jacqueline. *Autobiography of a Family Photo: A Novel*. New York: Dutton, 1995.

——. *I Hadn't Meant to Tell You This*. New York: Delacorte, 1994.

X, Malcolm, and Alex Haley. *The Autobiography of Malcolm X*. New York: Grove, 1965.

Yoshimoto, Banana. *Kitchen*. New York: Grove, 1993.

Zahavi, Helen. *The Weekend*. New York: Donald I. Fine, 1991.

Zinn, Howard. *A People's History of the United States, 1492–Present*. New York: HarperPerennial, 1995.

Credits

Gracious Thanks

Writers tend to put acknowledgment pages in their books because—unless authored by the very vain or very hermetic—books do not come to fruition without the support and love of many, many individuals.

In college, I learned the value of unqualified support from a single human being. Dr. Leo Daugherty read my stories, poems, essays, and interviews with a sensitivity and insight I hadn't experienced since elementary school, when Mrs. Lingle and Mrs. House—my second- and third-grade teachers, respectively—prodded my imagination with a gusto I was wholly unappreciative of at the time. I extend my deepest regards to these three educators.

From the outset of this book, Holly Marie Morris was the single human being who believed in me so much my heart *positively swells.* Trust and respect are huge gifts. I do not take lightly Holly's inspiration for bringing these gifts into my life. *Cunt* would never, ever, ever have been written if I hadn't seen her that day in New York, gliding 'cross the room in her cream linen suit like *grace* was a word made 'specially with her in mind. Holly, I love you dearly.

This new edition required the focus and dare I say love of Laura Mazer, Christina Palaia, and Michael Clark, for which I am grateful. Leah Jenkins and many other staff at Seal/ Hachette also went above and beyond for me and this book. Thank you kindly.

Nobody knew it was going to end up being an author photo, but Bob Jordan, your unerring eye for light and color saved the day when I needed it. Thanks so much.

My mother was the first person to read an early draft of *Cunt*. Because her experiences are so integral to my writing, I hoped to procure her blessing before venturing on to a rewrite. Not only is my mother from a different culture but many of my beliefs are difficult for someone of her generation to understand. Regardless, she never paused in support of my words. She did not ask me to edit out a single iota of her life experiences. Her courage overwhelms me. I am honored to be her daughter.

I gave the final draft of *Cunt* to my brother, Joe B., and my sister, Elizabeth, for Christmas 1997. A man of few words, my brother left a concise message on my voice mail two weeks later."It's killer," he said. "Goddamn, this is just killer." My sister, a person I have aptly nicknamed "Hard Customer," called me at least twice a week for a month, gushing with excitement and love.

Jennie Goode and Faith Conlon. Goode and Faith, need I say more? Their Goode Faith in *Cunt* deserves accolades of candy and champagne forever. I know it is considered a "risk" to publish this book, and they, along with the entire staff of Seal Press—Lee Damsky, Ingrid Emerick, Laura Gronewold, Kate Loeb, Lisa Okey, and Lynn Siniscalchi—rose to the occasion like prima ballerinas aloft. And don't even get me started on Jennie Goode's paranormal levels of comprehension. Lordisa.

Loraine Harkin, naturopathic physician, kindly read the manuscript and shared her knowledge. Her input and support for *Cunt* were greatly appreciated.

When it was time to get jacket and press photos taken, I went with a gut feeling and called Rebecca McBride. The resulting photographs freaked me out. It was as if she prowled around in my dreamworld and somehow duplicated the precise images I could conjure only nebulous words to describe. Rebecca is a genius.

Sybil, Paul, Memphis, Erin, and Christopher were so kind to me during a very difficult time. Ditto Peri Heydari Pakroo, Oh My!, Turtle, Parisha, and Jason Speewhoreski.

Whenever I feel like maybe there's no magic in the world, maybe I've been wrong this whole time, I just think of Ashley and Mr. Quintron, and I know there are always spells to cast and pussycats to cavort with.

Elizabeth Faye spoils her women with laughter and massages. Gasperini sends her women skateboards in the mail, which makes them have total spontaneous orgasms of joy.

Dawn Kiss, the beautiful, passionate snowboarding punk rock valkyrie ablaze.

Bridget Irish, 100 percent Irish, born on St. Patrick's Day. Bridget tells me I can do anything I want. When voices in my head say stuff like, "Inga, you *can't* call him 'Keith "Piece of Shit" Richards,'" Bridget's face floats into my frontal lobe, and I *know* I can call him "Keith 'Piece of Feral Dogshit Smeared on the Washington Monument' Richards," if I want.

If home is where the heart is, my heart is where Bambi, Shug, Sini, and Alisun are. All four of my housemates listened to me wrestle with various chapters, put up with my freakish hours, and respected the importance of bunny ears. My week *sucks* if Bambi and I don't have our Sunday morning coffee 'n smokes session. Shug's bright, blazing smile is a pillar of our community. I could listen to Sini's hilarious stories for hours on end. Alisun's logical mind has improved the quality of my life hundreds of times. She never misses a *follicle* of inconsistency.

I love you all so very much.

Thanks to Dr. Steven "the Ballerina" Flusty for filling my head with history and other fun stories.

And the genius filmmaker Harperetta Carter. My heart *grieves* for those who underestimate her scathing perspective on life and society, which she cleverly hides in her sweet, sweet smile and grandmother-spiced tenderness.

At three o'clock in the morning, when I *hafta* share something, to cry or hear a beautiful story, I call Riz, my sunshine in the dead of night. He never gets mad at me even if I wake him up. He is groggy for a few minutes and then swings right into a tirade about love, Oprah, his grandmother. If I was stuck on my book, I always knew somehow or other Riz would unstick me.

Kinnie Starr, Toni Childs, Diamanda Galás, Me'Shell Ndegeocello, Sinéad O'Connor, Tracy Chapman, the Immortal Caruso, and Chet Baker: I wore out their CDs working on my book. I wore out the repeat button on my CD player. I disgusted neighbors who wondered what kind of freckin' fruitcake would listen to the same goddamn CD for six hours straight, night after night. I thank them for making music in the world. Diamanda, especially, helped me with the chapter on rape. It was the most painful one for me to write and without Diamanda's presence in my kitchen, I don't know how I could have managed.

I extend my deepest gratitude to Dr. Daniel Schiff, but ask his forgiveness for not including him in the acknowledgments last time around.

Many thanks to Zabrina for setting me straight.

Jon Milazzo, Felipe Perez, Rob Leander, Jessica Orr, Laura Louise, "El Tea" Taylor, the folks at Seattle Fitness, and again, Riz, Esther, and Eddie, thank you for pulling me out of the darkness when the darkness came around.

I am filled with thanks to all of the people who've read *Cunt.* I've received many emails and letters from folks and I am very grateful that people have taken time out of their lives to let me know my book has had an impact.

Locally owned independent bookstores, newspapers, websites, zines, and magazines have been very kind to *Cunt,* and I thank them with all my heart.

Support your local bookstore.

Lastly, I would like to thank all librarians, everywhere. My worship of librarians dates back to the age of four. Since I have become a published author, my reverence for librarians knows no bounds. Librarians are unheralded revolutionaries, and without them, all semblances of "civilization" that this country still manages to muster from time to time would be shot to shit.

Long live librarians!!!

About the Author

Inga Muscio is a writer and public speaker who addresses the issues of sexism, racism, sexual violence, and feminism. She teaches writing and appears frequently on college campuses. She lives in Seattle, Washington.